£ 12

The Wind in My Hair

Brigitte Muir was born in Belgium, and spent many of her teenage years caving and rock-climbing in central Europe. Her thirst for adventure soon developed into a passion for climbing, taking her to mountains around the world. After completing a degree in archaeology she moved to Australia to be with her husband, Jon Muir. Together they live in Natimuk, Victoria, running their international climbing and instructing business, Adventure Plus.

Brigitte Muir is the first Australian to climb the highest mountain on each continent, and the first Australian woman to climb Everest.

BRIGITTE MUIR

the Wind in My Hair

VIKING

All photographs that appear in this book
are from Brigitte Muir's private collection.

Viking
Penguin Books Australia Ltd
487 Maroondah Highway, PO Box 257
Ringwood, Victoria 3134, Australia
Penguin Books Ltd
Harmondsworth, Middlesex, England
Penguin Putnam Inc.
375 Hudson Street, New York, New York 10014, USA
Penguin Books Canada Limited
10 Alcorn Avenue, Toronto, Ontario, Canada M4V 3B2
Penguin Books (NZ) Ltd
Cnr Rosedale and Airborne Roads, Albany, Auckland, New Zealand
Penguin Books (South Africa) (Pty) Ltd
4 Pallinghurst Road, Parktown 2193, South Africa

First published by Penguin Books Australia Ltd 1998

1 3 5 7 9 10 8 6 4 2

Copyright © Brigitte Muir, 1998

Designed by Cathy Larsen, Penguin Design Studio
Typeset in 12/15 pt Weiss by Post Pre-press Group, Brisbane
Printed and bound in Australia by Australian Print Group, Maryborough, Victoria

National Library of Australia
Cataloguing-in-Publication data

Muir, Brigitte.
The wind in my hair.

Includes index.
ISBN 0 670 87955 X.

1. Muir, Brigitte. 2. Women mountaineers – Biography.
3. Mountaineering. I. Title.

796.522092

To Jon

Contents

Acknowledgements

Many expeditions over twenty years, including the Seven Summits, happened not only because I was stubborn enough to see my projects to completion, but also, and most importantly, because a lot of good people helped me and inspired me along the way.

First of all I want to thank my darling husband, Jon Muir, for putting up with my obsession for nine years, and for his moral support all the way through my Seven Summits quest and during the writing of this book. What would I have done without his extraordinary memory for names and places? Thank you also to our families – Mary, Bob, Jim, Pat and Brianna Muir, Jeanine Durwael-Koch and Jacques Koch, Veronique Hill and Pascal Koch – for accepting us and loving us the way we are.

There are a few people I have met through my quest or my work, a few players without whom I might have given up a long time ago. I am privileged to now have them as close friends: Anne Tindall, Ian and Min Darling, Roddo O'Connor. Thank you.

A number of companies have supported me through thick and thin, and have given Jon and me the chance to meet and appreciate an incredible number of good people. My thanks to Martin Richmond and Sony; Wayne and Anne Tindall and Big Time Media; Ian Sheppard, Chris Bell and Fairydown; John Clarke and Ray Williams from HIH Winterthur Insurance; Garry Farrar and Foxtel; Jon Tinker and Out There Trekking; Henry Todd and Himalayan Guides; Nick Costos and all the staff at World Expeditions; Howard Whelan and Australian Geographic; James Hoadley and the International Wool Secretariat; Ian Dalton and

Acknowledgements

Ted's Camera Stores; Jeff Shea from the Duct Company in the United States; John Willett & Associates; and lastly, Martin Bride and Greg Pritchard from Adventure Plus.

Many thanks also to the following sponsors: Roger Gibbons, Travis Atkins, Shannah van Eerden and Bollé; Peter West and Mars; Marcus Tarrant from Me Advertising and Mike Bollen; Catherine Birkin and Horsham Institute of TAFE; Rob Woolley and Deloitte Touche Tohmatsu; Michael Morrison and Woodside; Blackmores; Thai Airways International; the Bank of Melbourne; Kym Lewis and Beaurepaires; Margaret Prieme and Duracell.

To the many people who have helped along the years, thank you so much for believing it could happen: Win Lockwood; Kim McKeogh; Keith and Sally Lockwood; Rudy Panozzo; Dave Mudie; Jean-Marie Bolly; Kerry and Rod Holt, from Holts' Business Equipment; cameraman Tom Gelay; photographer Leslie Fratkin; Mark Buchanan and Eastern Mountain Centre; Michael Morrison at Chiat & Mojo; Maree Taberner at the Wimmera Base Hospital; Barry Ross; Glen Singleman; Jonathan Chester; Kirsty Melville; Sherie Stumm; Anna Gregory from Channel Nine; Mal Duff; Rob Hall and Adventure Consultants; Icom; Mark Williams and Horsham Traveland; Chia Moan; Marion and Cec Delaney and the Willows Milk Bar; and Rose Firkin, who had faith in me.

Thank you lastly to Selwa Anthony, my literary agent, for thinking my adventures might inspire others; to Bob Sessions and Penguin for publishing my scribbles; and to Rachel Scully, my editor, for wading through years of rambling, and words which were not always in the dictionary (pardon my French, Rachel!).

Prologue -
Slave to a Dream

I woke up coughing. *Damn! Here we go again.* My scarf was full of mucus, expelled from my lungs each time I tried lying down. This was rather tedious, but I was too tired and cold to care. Next to me, Dorje settled under the sleeping bag he shared with Kipa. I don't think he'd planned to spend a second night at Camp Four, but, here we were, anyway. We all helped ourselves to the oxygen bottles; nobody would need them now, we were the last team up. Most people had already left Base Camp and were homeward bound, and the three Sherpas I shared a tent with were certainly keen to get down to Base Camp as soon as possible and return home too.

Mindu, Dorje and Kipa packed quickly when the first light came, and after a couple of brews, slowly I did the same, feeling exhausted and weakened by the unforeseen bronchitis. Kipa forced some more gear into his already huge pack. 'You're okay?' A worried look on his face.

'Yeah, I'll be right, I'll just take my time.'

'Sorry I can't take more gear, pack very heavy.'

'That's fine, Kipa, you go for it.'

Yes. I'd be all right. If only I could drink ten litres of something hot, and sleep for two days. Well, I could not. Lakpa, who was working for Thomas and Tina, who were in the process of summiting a rise on the South-east Ridge, pushed me into their kitchen tent and gave me a stove and some ice. I was quite spaced-out, but I managed to get it all in order: matches, gas, ice in the pot, tepid water in a cup. Lakpa was outside packing. Everybody was packing these days. The great migration to the lower lands was imminent. 'Lakpa!' I whispered, my voice a memory, 'Want some tea?' He didn't. I gulped down two or three cups, and contemplated moving. I shuddered. *Ugh. Has to be done though. Can't stay here forever. Don't want to stay here forever.*

I extracted myself from the tent and sat on my pack to muster the energy to get it on my back. The wind had picked up. It was really quite cold now. *Right. Let's do it. Oh God. This is going to be fun.* I took ten measured steps, using my ice-axe as a walking stick. *Shit. This is going to be hard.* Another ten steps, then twenty. I sat on a rock outcrop. All in the right direction, had to keep patting myself on the shoulder. Except my neck was too stiff to do it. Metaphorically would do. I continued down, and down and down, sitting at the end of each of my twenty-step sessions. My pack was too heavy for me in my condition. Thomas, Tina, Lakpa and their other two Sherpas were coming down briskly. Thomas and Tina were still on oxygen. 'Do you want a bottle, Brigitte? Look, you can have one, no problem.'

My mask and regulator were buried somewhere in the middle of my pack. Couldn't be bothered to get them out. 'I'll be all right, Thomas, thanks all the same.'

'You're sure?'

'Yep. I'll see you at Camp Two.'

'Okay. Come over for a drink.' They all ran down. I was the last one on the mountain.

I kept staggering, down, down, down. My rest sessions were getting more frequent. Longer. Second thoughts about the oxygen bottle. *Oh well, too late now.* At the Yellow Band, I had to take my pack off and leave some gear behind if I was to make it back to the next camp, Camp Three. I had given up on the

2

Camp Two idea by now. It was too far, and I was too buggered. The last 300 vertical metres. I could hardly stand up any more. Breathing was hard with all that muck in my lungs. I sat, pushed myself down along the fixed rope, lay on my back, looked at the sky, looked down at the little port in my storm of fatigue. Camp Three. I had never liked the place, but at that point it was where I wanted to be, inside the orange tent with the floor looking like a roller-coaster ride, with the overwhelming heat of the middle of the day making the atmosphere tropical. A beach. I remember thinking, *I could do with a beach.* Maybe Jon and I could go to Discovery Bay when I finally got back to Australia. Maybe . . .

An eternity of suffering had passed. I was at Camp Three, in front of the tent, contemplating the zipped door. *Let's get inside, girl, and get a brew on. You certainly could do with a drink.* Done. Somehow, I had opened the door, taken my pack off, found the flattest spot, a sleeping bag, a stove and a half-empty cartridge. The place was a mess, rubbish everywhere. *I'll tidy up tomorrow, promise.* There was even a radio, with batteries that needed a boost. I stuck them in my undies. Some spots stay warmer than others. While the snow melted in the pot, I tried calling Kipa, to let him know that I'd spend the night there. I managed a few words before the batteries tired out again. I could relate to that.

I didn't feel like eating, but knew that I should have something. A few leftover chocolate bits, another drink, time to sleep if I could. I couldn't. Not lying down, anyway. Three breaths, and I started choking. I'd have to spend the night sitting up. Lovely. I needed sleep, desperately, and it looked like I'd have to do without. I must have had about four hours of sleep in the previous sixty hours. Could I go another twenty-four till my tent at Base Camp? One more day of holding onto concentration, a few more hours of cheating death, placing feet carefully on steep slopes, keeping sleepy eyes open for hidden crevasses. Then the last trip through the dangers of the Khumbu Icefall, rushing in the slow motion of fatigue under the tottering ice towers, across the ladders spanning the gap between hell and my heaven: Base Camp. Where I could finally sit, stunned, in the kitchen tent, and smile incredulously, eyes focused on the past few days' reality, and celebrate with the Sherpas, and tell myself, *wow, I can't believe this, I've done it, I've climbed Everest, completed my Seven Summits quest.* I was free.

———

I live in Natimuk, in a sweet cream house, with a big red husband. If you are a climber, you will think, ahhh, yes, Natimuk, that sleepy town at the foot of Mount Arapiles, the Mecca of Australian rock climbing. If you are not a climber, your first thought could be, where the **** is Natimuk?! Glen Bancell and I painted some T-shirts once sporting that bold comment, for the Tractor Pull Festival, a few years back. We sold a grand total of two T-shirts in eight hours. Most people who were there knew where Natimuk was. Since then, and since I became the first Australian woman to have stood on top of Everest, I have been told that I've put Natimuk on the map. But that's what they said when my husband, Jon, climbed Everest in '88. Somehow Natimuk got lost in between. And if I have to be precise, I did not actually stand on top of Everest. I sat on it. Never stand if you can sit – my mountaineering motto.

Climbing the highest mountain in the world was an accident, really. I only singled Everest out because it is the highest mountain in Asia. See, the great plan was to climb the Seven Summits, meaning the highest peak on each of the seven continents.

It all started . . . No. I can't pinpoint a minute in time when I decided to climb my seven mountains. No Big Bang Theory of the Seven Summits. What I do know is that, about the time Jon was on his way to Everest for the third time, I crossed my arms, pouted, furrowed my brow, and declared that I was going to climb the Seven Summits, so there.

The impromptu decision – which ended up shaping my life for the next nine years – was strengthened by a wish to assert myself, by a need for new horizons (not the Himalaya again!), and by a desire for a new lease on life. It had been time to re-assess my values, to deconstruct the 'Bri' I had become when I moved from Belgium to Australia, and to re-build her into a 'Brigitte' in harmony with my new life resolutions.

Nineteen eighty-eight turned out to be the year a new me was born, against all odds and against my deeper self (I had always been someone damn good at starting things, but never good at completing them) when I took the plunge and made an oath, crossed my heart but certainly not hoped to die, that I would not give up until I had climbed the 'Seven Bloody Mountains', as Jon later came to call them.

Natimuk. Five hundred souls, nineteen 'climbing' households, and growing. Natimuk, which means 'Little Creek' in the local Koori language. Not to be missed when in Natimuk, the Natimuk Creek (Little Creek Creek), and the Little Natimuk Creek (Little Little Creek Creek!). Glen and I also had a T-shirt reading 'Stuck in the 'Muk'.

Natimuk. I used to hate the place, plonked in the middle of the Wimmera, Victoria's wheat land. Treeless as far as I was concerned, and flat, oh so flat. How could my soul ever feast in a land without curves, and mist drifting along the crests, and blue-tinged ridges fading on the horizon? I came from a Belgian land of factories, belching chimneys and hooting trains, but that had been home, you know, there is no place like home?

It took years. One day, I woke up at peace with that Australian country of space and light. I noticed the beauty of a winter day, green and scented by the intoxicating aroma of the wattle. I opened to the warmth of the people, locals and immigrant climbers alike. Home, home, home. In the mountains of the world, and in the new country which had taken my soul.

A World Out There

My entry into the outside world was a reluctant one. After spending nine months and ten days inside a cosy womb, I was not interested in exploring what lay beyond. The decision was taken from me though, and at the maternity ward in Ougree, a dull town spreading its sooted buildings and factories on the side of the industrial Meuse Valley in Belgium, the doctor in charge extracted me like a bad tooth. The forceps shaped my head funny, and must have had some influence on my behaviour because I have never been late for anything since. I was baptised a few days later in the hospital chapel, blessed with the name of a star. It was the late fifties, and Brigitte Bardot was the ultimate smouldering French screen deity. I shared with the actress a first name and blond hair. I missed out on the pout and the big boobs.

My young parents had just completed the building of what was going to be my home for twenty-odd years – a square block of red bricks bordered at the front and back by railway lines. In his rush to escape in-law hospitality, Dad decided to move in before the stairs were completed. Going from kitchen to bedroom involved some tricky climbing and a juggling act with the bundle of joy, and so it came that I was introduced to the joys of climbing at a tender age.

Being first born, I was of course the centre of attention for my mother, Janine. She was the child of a Flemish mother and a Yugoslavian father, although to me he was only *parrain*, meaning godfather, because at the time of my mother's conception he happened to be her mother's lover, and my *bobonne* (grandmother) never admitted his paternity. In 1929, Sali Mehic, my real grandfather, had migrated to Belgium. He had been seventeen, and with his older brother's passport, had left the white mountains of his ancestors to find work in the sooty factories of the Meuse Valley. Parrain had found love as well when he met my grandmother, and he became her live-in lover after her husband died of peritonitis at the start of World War Two. Bobonne never acknowledged Parrain as our grandfather, or talked to my mother about him being her father, so the story of their meeting, of my mother's birth, or even the happenings surrounding her husband's death, are all vague and based on uncertain memories.

My relationship with 'Papa' was something else. I was a goddess to him and my every wish was granted. The house he had built was in front of his father's house in a drab street sandwiched between factories and slagheaps. The fifth child in a family of seven, he missed out on tertiary education; his family could only afford to send the eldest son to university and the others had to make do with a technical education. Dad studied to become a carpenter, but the profession was deemed an unreliable source of income by Janine's mother, who declared that my mother would only be his if he got himself a stable job – at the great steel factories, for example. Dad surrendered and took his lunchbox every day to the dark and screaming corridors of the factory down the road.

By the time I was four I was a curious little girl although, despite the adoration towards me, I was shy. The world out there fascinated me, but I found it hard to leave the folds of my mother's skirt. Reading became my path to discovery, and broadened my horizon and my mind: I was a steel worker's daughter, living in a street of anonymous houses in the back-yard of The Factory, and my adventure books, from Tintin to Jules Verne, took me to places I couldn't even picture in those days without television. Mind you, children can find the world in dross. Adventure was to be had, but by proxy: my dolls became adventurers, while I directed the action. The poor things, skimpily clad in handkerchiefs, were forever trampling jungles and swimming mysterious oceans!

When I was seven, my parents bought a shiny red Opel and started planning a family expedition to Yugoslavia. The team was to include my three-year-old sister, Veronique, a scared-looking little thing I was not sure what to think of, my parents, my grandparents and myself. We were to visit the native land of my Parrain. In the black-and-white pictures of our holiday he wore a tie-less suit, a hat cocked on his ear and a cigarette at the corner of his mouth. I remember him best leaving my grandmother's house on Sundays, with a green wooden box swinging on his side, rooster's red tail feathers poking from the hole at the back. He took his rooster to singing competitions every Sunday, and, pride of prides, he won a pair of sheets once, thanks to the red-feathered champion. He delighted in introducing his brood to the large family he had not seen for forty years. We could not talk with them as we spoke different languages, but blood is blood, and we entered the whirl of Podhum – a small, happy, mainly Muslim farming community in the south-east of Croatia. I remember trotting through the village dust on little legs, eyes full of wonder, and asking about the white crosses painted on the doors of some houses. These homes belonged to Christians.

Our cousins took us for walks in the nearby fields and on visits to faraway places. Everybody piled into the dusty Opel and Dad chauffeured us around the countryside, to enchanted places along potholed dirt roads – Dubrovnik, Mostar and many other towns whose names I probably never knew. Adventure, at last, was mine. What stayed with me from that first trip beyond my familiar environment was a sense of wonder at the immensity of the world (we slept twice before we got to Podhum), and at how much dust my dad made with his car on Yugoslavian dirt roads. Maybe that's why I still associate dust with adventure!

Upon returning home to our life in Belgium, the world of 'outside' opened itself to me. Behind the railway line in front of our house, the slagheaps rose to the sky, legacy of decades of coal mining. Adventure was upwards, out of the grey that anchored our house, and over the silver birch slopes leading to summits of burning ash. Occasionally Veronique and I, accompanied by older cousins, would venture into the tame wilderness. I stayed on the treed slopes then, and gazed at the summits' fumes of smouldering coal waste with awe, curiosity and a newly born unconsciousness of sensuality. (It would take me many years to recognise it for what it was). Mum did not want us to go to the summits, where parts of the barren, hot slopes would sometimes collapse. Children had been swallowed by the unstable ground, but the thrill of danger and the unknown – as well as the attraction of the forbidden – made the summits even more of a temptation.

Most of the time, though, I was far from rebellious thoughts, quite content to do my best to please to receive the rewards of subordination, that confidence in the self directly linked to the degree of acceptance among others. My years of primary school were heaven on earth, in the grounds of a girls' school built on the perimeter of a convent. Some of us, in a fit of irrepressible dare, did once steal consecrated wafers from the chapel, but I was mostly a well-behaved little Catholic girl, who enjoyed studying because she loved learning, and who dreamt of the Prince Charming she had read about in fairytales, and of the wild adventures to be shared from riding on the back of his white horse. That was until we acquired a black-and-white television and I saw a series called *Maya*, with a little boy and his elephant in India. For a while at least, I abandoned the prince, and set myself centre stage. But I had an elephant of course, and in real life I did not.

What I had was a new family in the nuns and secular teachers of my new kingdom, and some school bullies I soon learned to bow to, because I really did not have it in me to pull hair as a way to gain leadership and respect. That was in the concrete courtyard. The school also had a garden, with majestic trees and unruly lawns. Here, among the high grass, the games of hide-and-seek and the bouts of running, I found again the wild streak in me, and my heart would burst with the delight and illusion of being free. My ever-present thirst for the unknown led me to be a wild child during recesses, and top of my class at the end of each year.

In 1969 I was introduced to the male factor through a little boy born to us, Pascal, and through a recession. Finances were thin and pupils too few, and the inevitable happened. We were gathered and sent across the road to hell, up until then a boys-only primary school we had always looked upon with awe. There were four of us girls in year six, added to a class of twenty-six boys. Shyness forgotten, I made the most out of the new situation. During recess, my three girlfriends would all be standing in a corner of the courtyard, prissy, demure and talking about boys, while I was in the thick of the action, running around, playing all the games boys played. I was a tomboy, in my element. Of course, the seed of romance and romantic notions had been implanted in that head of mine a long time ago, but it was missing a crucial ingredient for its growth: puberty.

After a couple of years of uncomplicated soccer games and challenging classes, the embarrassment and exhilaration of adolescence hit me at high school. Pimples and budding breasts appeared, and I fell desperately in love. I had had a couple of innocent puppy loves in previous years – idolising from a distance, whispering to girlfriends, exchanging silly notes. But Stephane was the real thing. A dark, handsome Italian boy, he was seduced by my practised and very best girlfriend, Danielle. She had a waist and did not have to wear unsightly glasses to see the blackboard. Danielle and I still spent a lot of our time together, but I was torn between love for her, a feeling of being deserted, and blind passion for the now impossible love. The world seemed to have lost its colours then.

By the time I had turned seventeen, I was prepared to try anything to get myself out of the sentimental quagmire. I found escape in subterranean mud. Until then, the favourite pastime of Danielle and me had been talking about boys, going to folk music concerts and cycling races, and seeing how many movies we could watch during a weekend. But one day I happened to go with another girlfriend, Carine, to the local Commercial Fair in Jemeppe. There happened to be a caving club advertising their activities, and we happened to be feeling bold and free. We enrolled. As soon as Carine returned home, her mother crushed her daughter's dream in the egg, forbidding her to go caving. My mother was not exactly enthusiastic about the idea either. Talk about mother hen seeing a fox in the distance! She screamed, she cried, she brooded. I resisted the assaults with my own loud arguments, and eventually won the support of my dad. I really, really wanted to go. The unknown was calling, and this time I would answer, regardless of the cost.

I went to the first meeting not wearing my glasses, and absorbed the new faces – always looking more everything than me – while making myself inconspicuous in a corner. New recruits were given a thorough slide lecture, with pictures showing determined cavers in bright yellow overalls on a background of dark rock walls shining through black water (I had sneaked my glasses on in the dark). This was followed by a brief abseiling and ladder lesson in the local school gym, and we were then declared fit for the real thing and told to be ready for a day out, meeting on Saturday at six a.m.

Of course, I didn't sleep on Friday night. I was too scared I wouldn't hear the alarm. At four-thirty a.m. I was in the cold kitchen, butterflies fluttering in my stomach, and I had forgotten the screams of horror my mother had regaled us with the night before. I gulped down a few heart-warming bowls of *café au lait*, packed my overalls and lunch in a satchel and entered the empty streets of the early morning. I must have looked at my watch a hundred times that morning as I skirted the factories, their orange lights, black smoke and unexpected screams. I was the first one at the meeting point, by a long shot.

As people started to arrive, my heart started beating faster. I was quiet, listening to every word proffered by those guys who had done it all before: crawls in muddy, body-hugging underground passages, abseils into unknown wells, epics in buried chambers. It made me feel the way I usually felt before an exam at school. Excited and scared, and looking forward to throwing myself into the unknown, in a perverse kind of way.

We piled into the cars and drove off into the mist, through sleepy grey factory suburbs, up the road onto the plateau, away, away into the Belgian countryside. Our cave, le Trou Wynant, was nestled in an evergreen forest dripping with the last rain. Jokes about what was about to happen to us were filling the air with laughter and nervous giggles. I followed the leaders up a narrow, slippery trail, heading straight to the cave's entrance: a rock window opening onto the darkness of a permanent night.

The cave was only about sixty metres deep, but it may as well have been the deepest on earth. Past the entrance, a tunnel led to the top of a forty-metre well, and I could hear voices echoing spookily underground. There were ten of us queuing to get to the rope, which doubled as a safety line for the wire ladder we were to use on the way out. My turn came, I swallowed hard and the cave engulfed me. With eyes bulging in the semi-darkness, I managed to tie on my abseiling device, and started the descent on wobbly legs. I could see pinpoints of light at the bottom, and hear voices reverberating on the walls of the well, coming to me in mixed-up words. Whoo-ee, this was fun! I reached the end of the rope far too fast for my taste, and strolled over to the group squatting in a corner.

On my side, the cave ended in a stagnant pond of black water which was the centre of the ongoing conversation. I squatted too, and listened, trying to look cool.

'Shit man, it was only last week, you know.'

'What was only last week?' I asked.

'A guy went scuba diving in that lake there . . .'

'Yeah?'

'. . . and he got stuck in the mud at the bottom. Couldn't make it back up.'

I swallowed hard. 'You mean . . . he died?'

'You bet!'

Gone the cockiness. Marie-France was scared. She was the only other girl in the group. Long after she had stopped joining us on weekend expeditions, she went home on Sunday nights covered in mud. It turned out that she was still rolling in the dirt, but on romantic outings with members of the opposite sex!

When Marie-France left it was just me and the boys, and some serious caving fun. I developed a taste for leadership and satisfying my desires, often sharing the head of the mob with my friend Thierry Dufour, who was like a big brother to me.

We used to practice abseiling and jumaring in an ancient mine shaft located in the citadel of the Liège enclosure. The citadel had been built earlier in the century to fight the Germans, and most of it was accessible, if one did not mind darkness, spiders and suspicious smells. We were forever roaming the underground bunkers looking for spent cartridges and bodies, never finding anything but never losing the hope that we would. The well was one-hundred metres deep and had been used to mine coal as early as the fifteenth century. Abseiling to the centre of the earth was great. The weight of the rope was so much that we had to push it through our descender when we first started on it, and we still wouldn't get anywhere.

My appetite for adventure grew with every outing. I was caving every Saturday and Sunday, and if I could find someone to accompany me during the week I'd be off on my bicycle, my gear tied on the back, exploring all the caves in a thirty-kilometre radius from home. Mum would shake her head each time, but did not try to stop me any more. My passion was a tidal wave.

The summer holidays were approaching and with them the temptation to join my friends on a caving camp in the north-east of France, in the Jura Mountains. After the usual battle of wills my parents agreed to let me go, on the condition that they would pick me up at the end and that I would join the family on the annual beach sprawl in Italy. So it came that I spent a blissful fortnight with Thierry and a few others from the caving club, staying in a deserted schoolhouse in Ornans, and raiding the country's caves in methodical and passionate fashion. We were just as dedicated to having fun while on our trips, so dancing at local balls and drinking countless beers in numerous cafes were also part of the game, just as they had been during our Belgian weekend outings. 'On ne vit qu'une fois!' ('One only lives once!') was always Thierry's motto. I made it mine as well.

A few days into our stay, we met a small group of experienced Belgian cavers. Alain Grignard, their leader, was dark and handsome, seven years older than me. I fell in love again. Romance was impeded drastically by the fact that six other people were sharing our room, but the countryside around Ornans was welcoming, and heated by a perfect summer sun. When we were not abseiling down bottomless abysses we could not be found, strolling as we were the rolling fields, and hugging in the flowery meadows. My friends laughed at me, but listened to Alain's stories as intently as I did.

I was to spend some time with Alain – it was Alain who introduced me to the life which became mine for keeps. He took me to see interesting films, encouraged me to listen to beautiful music, talked to me about expeditions and faraway

14

places. He poured his knowledge of the outside world into my avid ears, mind and heart. Alain was a rock climber and a mountaineer as well as an avid book collector, and I devoured all his books on the golden years of climbing. He had also been a paracommando during his military service and he loved talking about it. I used to return home carrying huge piles of books on the Algerian and Vietnam wars, and spent hours devouring them. Alain took me to Marche les Dames, a military camp at the foot of a limestone crag, and the place where Albert, King of Belgium, had died in a solo climbing accident. I gazed in awe at the rock faces and strangely dressed people struggling on them, and I followed him clumsily on the obstacle courses where volunteers for the Korean War had trained in secret.

Among other things, Alain attempted to introduce me to the art of loving, one Christmas night in a hay shed in the south of France, as we were on our way to a caving trip in the Basque country. It was not a success. Our fellow caver was snoring three metres away from us and, in this particular field, Alain's methodical approach left me rather cold. My libido had not found itself yet but I was willing to explore a little, even if I still did not understand what it was all about. I enjoyed his company though, and revelled in meeting the people he knew.

Alain had been a member of the 1977 Belgian Alpine Club expedition to the Logan Mountains in Canada, and listening to his stories had made me salivate. *When would I be part of one of those incredible adventures?* Only the gods and goddesses of the Alpine Club qualified for the fun, it seemed, and Alain obviously did not see me as one of them, as I was never considered for more than European adventures.

———

Finally Alain invited me to climb with him at Dave, a small cliff skirted by the Liège–Namur railway line, where I met Jacques Collaer, the Zeus of Belgian climbing, and his retinue. The gods were wearing the latest in French design. Their socks were cream in colour, thick, woolly and piled on their ankles enhancing the bulging lines of their powerful calves. Dark blue was the chic of the day for bodyhugging stretch overalls, and they were all squinting. Hard not to when you do everything with a cigarette at the corner of your mouth.

The nectar they drank tasted of hops. I choked on it, too shy to talk, and drank their words of wisdom, hiding my feet under my chair as my first pair of climbing shoes were security boots my dad had nicked from the factory for me. (Nicking things from factories used to be a national sport in those days, with adulated heroes. Now all the factories have closed down, and the great steelworks are being dismantled and sold to China.) My boots made me feel like a debutante who had a few dances to learn from rubber-soled deities.

I had a vision the day I met the gods: Dave, the small limestone crag on the bank of the River Meuse, was echoing with guttural Dutch lingo, *'Trekke Jan!'* ('Keep the rope tight, John!') was the rally cry of the invaders from the north. The real climbers were sitting at a small cafe under the rocks drinking nectar and reminiscing about past glorious feats, raising their deep voices to overcome incredulity and the roar of the trains zooming by. Images of fairytale peaks and distant wonderlands formed behind my wide eyes. Logan Mountains, Yukon, Klondike, Cirque of the Unclimbables, Canada. New World. I was dying to go, anywhere.

Of the Jacques Collaer pantheon, Camille Piraprez was the most approachable, having fallen to earth with the disgrace of climbing failure. He had been left with a bitter aftertaste of the 1977 Belgian Logan Expedition, remembering starvation through bad planning, petty conflicts and heavy arguments. My unwavering enthusiasm to get 'there' convinced him to go back to Canada and 'show 'em all'.

Our goal would be the Lotus Flower Tower, a beautiful-looking mountain that Camille had fallen in lust with in 1977. We started training — in secret, as Camille wanted it to be a surprise to the others. Dawn would see us on misty winter days, bouldering beside a shrouded river, and gulping cold air as we jogged the sweet earth-smelling woods. Camille is the only one, to this day, who has managed to inspire me enough to consider training – a torture at the best of times – at that unspeakable hour. After our training Camille would go about his business of being a physio, working on his forearm muscles as he pummelled clients, and I would catch the bus to uni, where I had enrolled in an archaeology course, and sit through the history of Greek art, my mind floating above Mount Olympus, home of the gods. I secured a job working behind the cash register in a local supermarket, and happily spent my days slaving on saving for the great adventure.

———

One grey morning in May, Mum and Dad drove us to Brussels airport, not really knowing what it was all about and having completely given up trying to restrain me. Just to be on the safe side, Mum took up burning candles at the church. I had never caught a plane in my life and I was *très* excited. Seven take-offs and landings later, I was just tired. I owned hardly any mountaineering gear so I had had to discreetly borrow essential items from considerate friends. Bibiche had kindly loaned me his spare sleeping bag on the eve of the departure 'for a weekend climbing in the French Alps'.

Watson Lake, Yukon, was a thrilling place compared to my usual surroundings of factories and slagheaps – a main and only street, a line of motels, a supermarket, two souvenir shops, surrounded by zillions of acres of dark green forest. Camille rang his wife to tell her he missed her. I sat in the motel room, eating pizza (carefully extracting the pieces of pineapple), and wrote to my boyfriend, Pierre Bochmer, the first of a series of penciled letters that he later confessed he never read, because of the hieroglyphic quality of my handwriting.

I don't remember much of the bus trip to Tungsten, the little mining town which was to be the starting point of our adventure. Only the lunch stop at a cabin in the middle of the expanse of the green pines stuck in my mind. The insides of the cabin walls were plastered with one-dollar notes, dedicated to the lady behind the bar.

The middle of the night became the end of the road. I sat on the dirt curb, surrounded by our luggage, my eyes heavy with sleep. Blank lights shone on the dust of the road, and were reflected on the surface of a muddy dam gradually fading into the unknown. We dragged our gear to a flat spot nearby and thankfully collapsed for the night.

In the morning, Camille decided that we would pack the tent, hide the bags full of gear in the shrubbery, and head for town. Tungsten was a conglomerate of dusty streets and small prefab bungalows, dull and devoid of humanity. Pictures of sizzling bacon and eggs had been slowly forming in our heads, and instinct took us straight to the local canteen.

The lady behind the counter held her ribs, tears of laughter pouring down her cheeks. We had just told her in our broken English how we of urbane Belgium were scared of bears, and where we were camped. It happened to be the rubbish tip, a favourite night spot for scavenging grizzlies.

We had no gun and no radio, which puzzled the helicopter pilot who was to take us from Tungsten to the Cirque of the Unclimbables, and made me wonder if I would ever see my beloved factories again. We took off as soon as all the gear and the three of us were wedged inside the plastic bubble of the cockpit, and only then did I grasp the enormity of the situation. Wow! I was actually on my way to enter those photos Camille had shown me of his previous trip here! Still, it did not look real at all, with the den of the engine and the unfamiliar perspective. It was like flying above a huge television broadcasting visions of the Last Frontier.

As the Lotus Flower Tower materialised, Camille pointed out the features of our future adventure ground. We were headed for the Cirque of the Unclimbables proper, a horseshoe area enclosed by incredibly sharp and steep towers of granite.

He referred to it as the Lower Cirque. The 'Flower', as it was already affectionately known to us, was in fact part of the back wall of a smaller cirque above it, the Upper Meadow. The highest mountain in the area, a nondescript Sir James McBrien, peaked at 9049 feet on its northern border. We landed on the side of the Lower Cirque, and ran under the blades with our loads of equipment. The pilot shook hands with us and was off, leaving the two of us completely alone in the wilderness for twenty days.

Camille led me through deep snow to the shelter he had used for his last expedition. Our home for the next two weeks would be a cave. Traces of previous occupation were visible. I put on my archaeologist hat and inspected the man-made paving. 'We built that when we were here two years ago,' said Camille, 'and the pier at the lake as well. Oh, and a cabin at the foot of the scree . . . It rained a lot,' he added. A justification for energy spent on things other than climbing, I guessed.

It rained a lot, yes. Well, something familiar, after all. We had a wealth of experience in *not* climbing because of rain in Belgium. I stood in front of the cave, looking at a cardboard cutout of unimaginable peaks curving their steep granite faces in the shape of a horseshoe, forming the Lower Cirque of the Unclimbables. It was too real to be manageable, so I busied myself with making our shelter more homelike, arranging our gear on rocky shelves, and cooking pancakes on our small kerosene stove – anything to distract me from the thought of hanging from one of those horrendously huge rock faces. I was petrified.

One rainy morning, we started the hike to the Upper Meadow, home of the Flower. Out of necessity, Camille developed a new 'moving through deep snow technique', which I gratefully added to my still rather slim 'mountain and related situations' handbook. It consisted of throwing your pack as far as you could in the direction you were following, then wading through the mushy snow towards it, and then doing it all again.

Apparently, this was easier work than carrying the pack and sinking deeper in the snow because of the extra weight. But it didn't make for rapid progress and, looking back on it, we would have been better off sticking to the side slopes of the basin where snow cover was visibly thinner. But it wasn't the shortest line between us and the mountain, and I was merely an apprentice, too inexperienced to have the confidence to voice an opinion.

It was late by the time we made it back to the cave. In the greyness of the sub-Arctic night, Camille's silhouette startled me with a frenetic twist. 'A beast! There is a beast at the cave!' I never found out what he had seen. As soon as we arrived (the beast had by then decided to put some distance between itself and the gesticulating creature approaching), Camille made for the fuel jerry can and gingerly poured kerosene around our abode. He took a lighter out of his pocket and frenetically set fire to the line. It looked quite nice, that crescent of fire, I thought happily to myself. 'There, that will scare the shit out of it.' 'It' had certainly scared the shit out of *him*!

The next day we decided to stretch our minds and muscles on a tempting crack nearby. On the way to the small crag overlooking our camp we met with a set of tracks in the snow. Footprints – or should I say paw prints – meandered through the boulders surrounding us. I looked around suspiciously. The prints were those of a clawed creature. I wasn't happy at all as I belayed Camille climbing out of reach of the 'thing'. It didn't take much to convince Camille to head back to our cave.

———

The Lotus Flower Tower was a dream of stone in the distance. Harrisson Smith, on the Lower Cirque, had exuded maleness, and the Flower in the Upper Meadow complemented it by offering us a sublimated image of femininity. Everything about it was feminine. The Tower's delicate slenderness uncurled itself against a blue-sky background of eternity. I fell in love with her.

20

Immediately, I hated her too. I was scared of touching her. She looked too much like an impregnable virgin in spite of all the people that had climbed her before. I hadn't.

I did not know much about her, not even her height. Just that she had been first climbed by a couple (or was it three?) of American climbers in the sixties, and that the upper half of her face was overhanging, which meant we would be dangling from our harnesses for a whole day on the way to her summit. We would then traverse north from the top to abseil down an easier ridge back to the ground. That was enough information for me. I had seen her picture, and I knew I wanted to climb her. That was all that mattered. A dance with a mesmerising partner.

That night we camped at her feet. We had settled on a line of attack. It had been easy; there was only one climbing line, a huge corner losing itself in the trunk of the mountain. Instead of spending a sleepless night hanging in our harnesses at the highest point reached, we would climb up, haul some gear and, leaving our ropes in place, abseil down to the ground to sleep in the tent.

Early the next morning, Camille led off to the start of the climb. I had done most of my previous climbing in the lead, but Camille had made it clear that he would never climb with a woman in the lead again since one of his female friends had taken a nasty fall, scaring the shit out of him. To discover the world I was willing to agree to anything. I followed, and jumared with the two packs if it looked like the second pack were going to get stuck under overhangs. The blasted thing often did, making my jumaring sessions very hard work. We fixed our ropes and descended to camp for a light supper, in a thick cloud which enveloped our tent and the rest of the world. We retreated sheepishly to the cave.

Rain, rain, rain. If there had been any wood in the Cirque, we would have built an ark. Instead, the next morning we put on our raincoats and went down to the lake for a change of scene. Between us and the lake was an enormous scree and a dark forest. I expected bears to appear behind every boulder and tree, erect in their horrifying splendour, ready to tear me to pieces. It wasn't a relaxing change. I couldn't sleep for fear of waking up dead in a bear's stomach. I breathed relief only when we were back to the secure familiarity of our cave.

———

The day had started with an argument. Whatever it had been about made me put on my pack and head towards the mountain. Camille followed. As he caught up with me close enough to the Flower, it went without saying that we were on our way to climb it. It was a strange feeling to be on a rock wall *that* big, after having climbed only on Belgian crags. I was there, but I wasn't there at all. That's it, I was dreaming, therefore nothing could happen to me.

From the top of the fixed lines, Camille hoped to make it to the terrace halfway up. The slabs spreading past the initial corner fitted in my dream all right: small yellow flowers grew in patches at the bottom of granite wrinkles, the sky was blue and birds were singing in my head. The climbing was a delight; I didn't even have to carry the second pack, which enjoyed a stroll up the vertical garden, behaving itself very nicely at the end of the haul rope. I could almost see the terrace where we hoped to spend the night, a couple of pitches up the chimney. It was then that clouds started to creep up from the valley, gradually filling the Upper Meadow. Snowflakes plummeted gracefully from the sky. Lots of them. My only experience of mountaineering before I embarked on this adventure had been a promenade up a friendly, rounded 4000-metre peak in Italy, in perfect conditions, but to me, it looked like we might get into trouble. Camille seemed to be thinking along the same lines. Our time in the mountains was running short; we had an appointment with a float plane on the lake only a few days from now. Camille decided to abseil back to the camp to wait and see.

Snow was by now falling heavily, the cloud trapped

against the Flower doing its best to lighten its load in its impatience to cross over to the other side. Visibility was greatly reduced and it was just as well: I was a veteran of the abseil practice, but I had graduated underground, where what you cannot see cannot get you. A lot easier to deal with than mountainous abysses.

My budding climbing career almost ended there and then, when the piton I was hooked on slid out of its crack. Camille hammered in another one in a flash and I was safe again, if a little shaky. At the foot of the last abseil, I wobbled to the tent and lay down on darling, sweet, ground-level earth.

The weather was setting in, and the cloud was clearly going to hang around this side a little longer. This saved us from a difficult session of decision-making. From then on, it was down and out. Back to the boulders, back to the dark forest, back to the bears. By the time we reached the lake, the prospect of being a bear's meal was almost attractive. I was too tired to care. The plane arrived on time and I collapsed on the back seat. So long, bears.

The float plane landed on Watson Lake in a flurry of spray. Camille dashed to the nearest phone to call his wife, and I sat in the motel lounge, sipping coffee and writing the last of the hieroglyphic letters that would never get read. I smiled to myself over the piece of paper. I had learned a lot during this first escapade in the outside world: that it doesn't take a summit to make for an interesting time, that I needed to go somewhere else, soon, and that I would always need to have somewhere to go, somebody to meet. A mountain to court.

Land of Space and Light

Grey silhouettes fighting umbrellas and rain gusts ran on a background of old stone buildings and lit-up shop fronts. Liège in winter is not an inspiring place. I'd been visiting Marcelle Casarotto, my travel agent, between courses at uni, desperate to find another country, another landscape, another mountain to explore in this big world of ours. As much as I tried, I could only get vaguely enthused about life's prospects in Belgium: a diploma, a career in archaeology? Not after the taste of freedom that had been mine in Canada.

'Uh. Did you know that the fare to Australia is the same as the one to Kenya?' Marcelle raised her piercing blue eyes to meet mine.

'Really? Well, why not? Forget about Kenya, I'll try Australia instead!'

Africa had first taken my fancy, but Australia? What was I getting myself into? I hardly knew a thing about the place; Australia was a big country a long, long way from Belgium and there were kangaroos hopping all over it . . . that would have to do!

I convinced some friends, all caving accomplices, to come along: Pierre, receiver of the letters never read, Michel and Jean-Paul. After a few more months of university and after-hours

24

supermarket work, I went back to see Marcelle and bought a ticket to Australia. I still did not know much about the continent at the bottom of the world, but its mystery only added to our adventure. We would find out for ourselves when we were there!

We landed in Sydney on a crisp spring morning, hired a campervan and headed up north, promising the agent to stick to bitumen roads. So we did for a while. There was no need to venture off the beaten track or leave Australian civilisation to realise that this was a very different place to us over-urbanised citizens of Ye Olde Europe. There were pelicans on the beaches and people ate shark with their chips instead of mussels. Businessmen in Sydney wore shorts, and thongs seemed part of the national dress. Bizarre.

Our grand tour took us to some rock-climbing areas, but we weren't particularly interested in climbing anything: climbing was more an excuse and a way to discover the world than a reason for travel itself. There was so much more to climbing than climbing. It was always a total adventure, the drive to a crowded cliff in Belgium as much as the walk to the foot of a great mountain in some other far corner of the world. Our journey in Australia turned into an exploration game, which took us from capital cities to a deserted island off the Townsville coast, to the outer reaches of the continent and to Uluru at its centre. We lost ourselves in the Olgas, marvelled at underground homes and opals in Coober Pedy, bought spears and boomerangs, drank Australian beer. We had a hell of a holiday.

Prior to leaving Belgium I had tracked down some information on a cliff called Arapiles, located halfway between Adelaide and Melbourne. So, after a thorough study of the Barossa Valley wineries, we found ourselves peering through the windows of our campervan at a row of orange crumbling cliffs, because really, our friends back home would question the seriousness of our enterprise if we did not at least touch a rock. The old feeling of butterflies in the stomach returned. Did we really want to do this? After all, we were on holiday. We drove to the camp site and parked our home under a pine tree. Kangaroos grazed in a paddock by the cliff, kookaburras cackled in the gum trees and a gaggle of dishevelled climbers clustered around a small camp fire. The boys around the fire raised their eyebrows at our intrusion. One of them, a tall, blond bushy-haired youth with a smile on his face, ambled towards us. 'You are from overseas!' he announced.

'How do you know?' I was amazed.

'Easy,' he smiled, 'your clothes are clean!' He wore a pair of baggy shorts falling beneath a healthy-looking tummy button and a torn T-shirt. Roddy Mackenzie introduced us to his companions and the landscape, and invited us to visit 'Hillside', his parents' place – a true blue Aussie sheep farm.

After a few days spent demonstrating to the local climbers that one can come from halfway around the world to fail on easy climbs and still have fun, we made our way to Ararat and the sheep country. Roddy did the honours, driving us through sheep-dotted paddocks in the old beaten-up farm truck. I was starting to find Roddy rather attractive, despite the fact that he was not dark and handsome. He was fair and gorgeous. There was an energy about him, an exuberant joy in being alive, and I wanted to share with him my own intensity. I invited him to the Blue Mountains, our next port of call. 'What a great idea,' he said, 'We can go and pick up Jon on the way.'

Jon Muir was the antithesis of Roddy Mackenzie. He lived in Wollongong, a big industrial town; he was short and stocky with Popeye forearms, sported a permanent grin under a red moustache and hardly ever talked. We all piled into the campervan and headed to the 'Bluies'. At Mount Victoria, I followed Roddy up a beautiful climb called Eternity. It was hard work, and I felt quite pleased when I finally reached the top and collapsed beside him. He had shifted into talking gear as soon as my nose had appeared above the edge of the cliff, and I tried to make sense out of the words reaching me through my gasps for air. Roddy was telling me how he and a few other friends, including Jon, were planning a world climbing tour for 1982, starting with scaling a mountain called Changabang, in Northern India. My eyes lit up.

'Would you like to come along?'

I almost choked on the answer. 'Yes! Oh yes, yes!'

'Good,' said Roddy, and he sealed the deal with a kiss on my lips. Now, had I been Australian, that would have been the end of it. But being of Belgian blood, I thought he was kissing me seriously, and I kissed him back wildly. Thus started my life in Australia.

Being on a tourist visa meant that I now had to go back to Belgium, supermarkets and studying old bones, but I was hooked. I spent the following two years shifting between Europe and Down Under, bringing back books, photos and knick-knacks each time I returned to Australia. My heart was still in Belgium, but I was most definitely making a slow mental shift to the other side of the planet. A shift which became even harder as in Belgium, I had met a man made of fairytale stuff. He was so charismatic that I found myself, so used to being in control, a babbling mess in front of him. Which did not stop me from chasing him, relentlessly. He had a child and a lover, I had a love in Australia, and I could not live without my ever-longer visits there. However, I loved Europe as fiercely, and my love for Michel Kozuch had the intensity, desperation and boundless happiness of life on a deadline. He painted mountains and feelings. I flew to open spaces and isolation. Then I would return home again, and dive with great relief into the tumult of friends and family. Despite the kindness of Roddy's family to the Belgian girl who was not quite fluent in the tongue of Robbie Burns and Shakespeare, I felt uncomfortable and stifled at gatherings which appeared too formal for my working-class background.

Michel and I had made friends with Jean-Michel Stembert, a young climber with a burning passion for life and soloing. The three of us became inseparable, in having fun if not climbing. We listened to jazz in smoky bars, swapped trousers under tables in pubs, and shared our dreams until the light of dawn woke us from our reveries. Michel was a talented painter and musician, I was a traveller at heart. He had a family responsibility, but I thrived on my freedom and the wind in my hair. Our common love for Jean-Michel kept us close at a time when my approaching departure made things difficult. Jean-Michel became the incarnation of the life and the child we would never have together.

Jean-Michel went climbing in the south of France once, and did not come back. A root he was tied to became dislodged from the white rock shroud, and he fell, tragically, to his death, yelling in anger all the way down. (Later on, at Arapiles, I talked to a guy who had been nearby when Jean-Michel fell.) The loss of Jean-Michel sealed my fate. I had to go away, leave Europe and the love which was tying me down. Michel was sad, very sad indeed, but he loved me too much not to let me go.

In August 1982, still suffering and confused from the losses of both Jean-Michel and Michel, I flew from Belgium to India where I was to meet Roddy and the rest of the Changabang team. Travelling in India was a complete assault on the senses and it soon distracted me from the dramas I had left behind. People were *everywhere*. A pervasive smell of smoke, street food, excrement and decaying life lingered in the cities. The country-side was wild and hilly, the clamour of life overpowering. We westerners were flabbergasted by the permanent show India imposed on its visitors; it was like being part of an interactive vaudeville. Mark Moorhead, Jon's best friend, was making up amusing little stories on whatever was happening to him, and sharing giggles with Jon. Craig Nottle was a medical student and a Gary Glitter fan, forever humming his songs, and his beautiful girlfriend, Elke Rudolph, was a physio student, as inexperienced in mountaineering as I was. Elke and I planned to pool our skills together on 'small' 6000-metre peaks, while the boys concentrated on conquering Changabang, a 6800-metre sharp granite blade of a mountain, hoping to do the second ascent of a steep-looking route. A Japanese expedition had been the first to successfully climb Changabang, in 1976. Six climbers took thirty-three days to reach the summit and come back down. Jon, Roddy, Mark and Craig ended up climbing it in one continuous push, taking only six days!

We were forced to undertake our expedition on a shoe-string, which was not exactly to the taste of our liaison officer, Anil, a middle-aged squadron leader who had been sent to accompany us by the Indian Mountaineering Foundation. Every mountaineering expedition to the Himalayas is obliged to support a liaison officer, who comes along to help with communications with local porters, and to ensure the expedition does not stray onto mountains which have not been booked and paid for in advance. Anil was a serious man, but he soon loosened up. Elke, Anil and I climbed easy snow peaks in the company of a dog which had been hanging around our camp since we arrived and had been baptised Shiteater, for obvious reasons.

Meanwhile, Mark, Jon, Roddy and Craig were having an interesting time on Changabang. Poor weather had forced them down from reasonably high up on the mountain, but they now planned a second attempt. During Take Two, Elke, Anil and I had been asked to go down to Lata Karak, our porter's village, and send some of them up to Base Camp to wait for the boys to return. Autumn offered a colourful display in the fragrant forests leading back to the India we had forgotten about. In Joshimath, the service town near Lata Karak, we made friends with a local woman and she organised some saris for us to wear as a surprise for the boys, who were making their descent after successfully climbing Changabang. Elke and I strolled up the track towards them, happy with our new outfits, giggling in anticipation. Jon was the first one to appear. 'Wow! You two look great!' he said, followed by Roddy, looking tired, wincing, 'Brigitte, you look ridiculous!' So much for the nice surprise.

I felt ice invading my heart. My relationship with Roddy was not what I had hoped for. He loved arguing for the sake of it and my English was simply not up to it. Boredom must have crept into his feelings while a longing for affection and simple conversation had invaded mine. But I could not live in Europe any more. I had discovered space, and become addicted to it. I had also been exposed to Jon's kindness during the expedition, and his uncomplicated gentleness was comforting after Roddy's tormented affection.

Back in Australia, the attraction between Jon and me blossomed, and we embarked on a secret affair which could not last, our feelings for each other becoming too urgent and overpowering to be restricted to occasional gratification. I returned to Belgium and Jon was left with the task of talking to Roddy. Friendship won over and Roddy accepted the inevitable gracefully. A few months later, Jon travelled to Belgium to meet my parents as a prospective son-in-law. They were not impressed. Who was that Kangaroo who dyed his crewcut bright red and wore torn 'The Jam' T-shirts, graffitied karate pants and thongs? Their dreams of a respectable marriage vanished, but they soon warmed to Jon's irresistible personality and accepted his idiosyncracies as exoticism. 'He is from Australia,' Mum would knowingly whisper to the neighbours, who would open their mouths and shake their heads blankly.

Jon and I were so engrossed in loving each other that acceptance from the rest of the world was not even marginally of interest to us. I had left behind the uncertainties of my past life and loves. Jon was the person I wanted to grow old with. Our fairytale continued with our marriage in Jemeppe, my home town near Liège. Jon had had a few drinks before the ceremony to give himself heart and I had to nudge him in the ribs when the time came for him to say: '*Oui,*' his well-rehearsed one line in a play that was not subtitled. A major party followed the wedding a couple of days later, with all my wild caving and climbing friends doing their best to ensure I left the country with memories of drunken fun and love, and a seriously damaged liver.

We settled at the foot of Mount Arapiles, which had become Jon's home following a fortnight climbing from which he had never returned. His parents very generously bought us our first home – a family tent with a separate bedroom. I wrote to my parents to describe our happiness and living arrangements, and my sister reported later that Dad had erupted on reading the letter: 'I put her through five years at university, she graduates with distinction, and all that for what? To live in a tent with a Skip on the other side of the world!'

And so I had. If there ever were intentions of pursuing a career in archaeology, they soon turned into puffs and clouds in the sky over the 'island of Arapiles'. Jon and I lived in a eucalyptus fringe, with a tribe obsessed by a twofold religion: climbing rocks, and having fun away from society. If necessary, one was allowed to seek sponsorship from the dole to pursue one's calling.

Everyone was earnest, intent on enjoying life day by day: the getting up with the cackle of the kookaburra, the slow shuffling of thonged feet around the camp site to re-awaken fire, the smell of coffee and pine needles as one listened to storytellers or discussed vague plans for the day ahead in the shade of Centenary Park. Out would come the 'Bible', the *Arapiles Climbing Guide Book*, a mouth-watering two-thousand-plus climbs menu complete with degree of difficulty and route description. The tinkle and clang of metal and rope climbing paraphernalia accompanied the after-breakfast walks, guide in hand. Treasure seekers, following the map to where no X marked the start of the climb.

Jon and I took it in turns to lead routes at our respective levels, and with him I rediscovered the rewards of being the one in front, a pleasure I had given up to climb with Camille. The early days of our life together at Arapiles was a time of

31

wonder – wonder at a new world, a new way of life, and a partner in his element, relaxed and happy to share. It was a sensual experience, excitingly refreshing in its simplicity. I loved – what am I saying – I adulated Jon, and on the wings of his love I flew up climbs I would not even contemplate seconding these days. I was Alice in Wonderland, in more than one way. There were diamonds in the sky.

Arapiles in the early eighties was a place where loosely organised chaos could still reign, where individuals could express themselves in more or less any way they chose, where the dreaming was the living. Those were the days before rock climbing became hyper-trendy and too popular, before sheer numbers brought an end to the right of freedom on a too-small island of orange rock and whispering gums, no longer lost in the ocean of the Wimmera wheat fields. Those were the days before us eighties castaways were rescued by society rules and the time to move on.

———

Jon was gasping for air, sweat beading his forehead. I looked up from the book I was reading in the shade of the gum trees and smiled. 'How did you go?'

'Good, I am getting very fit, you know. I ran up the road to the lookout and back. I reckon a few more of these and I'll be ready for Everest. Do you want to go climbing this afternoon? Your turn to lead.'

I managed to smile, while mentally chewing my fingernails at the thought of my next climb. 'Sounds good. I wouldn't mind giving New Image a go.'

My arms were getting tired, my forearms heavy and as hard as stone. 'Watch me, Jon!' I yelped, as I made the last moves to the top. Despite wobbly legs, I scrambled safely to a seated stance and joyfully declared myself done with it. Jon was in a cheeky mood, and he roped up, tying the climbing rope around his neck. He followed easily, retrieving the bits of equipment I had placed in small crevices to protect myself from a possible plummet. 'Well my love, I don't think you'll find Everest too technical, will you?'

Jon had been asked by Peter Hillary to join a team consisting of himself, Roddy Mackenzie and Craig Nottle of Changabang fame, Kim Logan, a Queenstown guide, and Fred From, a Brisbane climber. Mark Moorhead would have been there too, had he not been killed on Makalu a year earlier. Jon had had a very hard time coping with his best friend's death and his face still showed dismal shock whenever memories of happy times with his beloved Mark surfaced.

When Peter had mentioned to Mark on Makalu, the idea of a six-man team for the Everest climb, Mark had wanted Jon to come along. It was a logical choice, as Jon was his usual climbing partner, and a very talented one at that. Not only that, but Everest was always foremost on his mind – Jon had left school when he was sixteen, after seeing a documentary on the first ascent of Everest's South-west Face, and had been obsessed by climbing the mountain ever since, directing every one of his life's moves towards reaching his goal: from working at the BHP factory in Wollongong to be able to afford spending months learning to understand the mountains in New Zealand, from opening new rock routes at Mount Arapiles to scaling increasingly difficult routes on summits around the world.

I knew that being invited to Everest was very important to Jon, but I was not too happy about him taking on the highest mountain on earth.

9 March 1984, Mount Arapiles

> All that Everest business makes me feel far from my love. Beginning of the climb, first of September. That's the date of our wedding! The first anniversary is going to be a lonely one . . . And I am getting a little nervous too. I would be better off thinking that Jon will come back from Everest, that we will be happy together for the next fifty years, that I will always weigh an ideal fifty-four kilograms, and climb like a champion. I just can't wait

to be in November, with the expedition over and my fears gone, one way or the other.

Of course I was proud that Jon had been considered for the team, but I was also concerned about the route and style of ascent: they were going to climb along the West Ridge Route, not exactly the easiest way up Everest, and without supplementary oxygen or the help of Sherpas. Fortunately, I would not be eating my fingernails at home as I was to come along to Base Camp and go trekking in the Khumbu area with my sister, Veronique, and a friend of Craig's, James Langley. Murray Nicholl, a radio journalist covering the expedition for the Macquarie network, was to complete our team. It was all very impressive for a reformed gang leader, casanovette, newly born demure young wife who at the time only lived through her husband. I followed Jon like a shadow, dreading the time where he would leave me to climb above Base Camp, up the Khumbu Icefall, and out of sight into the jaws of the ice dragon.

Everest '84 turned out to be the longest expedition I have ever been on. Not because it spanned two months of hardship in the mountains, but because fear inhabited me, from the time I woke up in the morning to the time I collapsed at nightfall after a day of trekking . I had never been so scared, for so long. I hated Everest. I hated climbing, which was taking my love away and throwing him in potentially dangerous situations. I even thought of the ways I could kill myself, should Jon's lover, the mountain, decide to keep him for herself. Love and fear were constantly blanking my mind, erasing the beauty of my surroundings and the kindness of the Sherpa people.

14 September 1984, Gokyo

And time does not pass. Went up Kala Pattar today, 5483 metres! And saw fuck all. Back at eleven a.m., been in bed ever since. Waiting for lunch. Boiled potatoes. I've seen too many of these in the last few days. What I saw of Everest, up there, scared the shit out of me. Sometimes I get that horrible impression that the nightmare will never end. I live a life between brackets, a life of waiting, of impatience, fear, love. I live to live again. I want Jon back.

I had no reason to be so terrified, really; Jon was an excellent mountaineer, one who never hesitated to turn back when his intuition told him that going ahead would breed insurmountable danger. So why was I plagued by fears of doom and gloom? The boys were making steady progress on the very long and committed West Ridge and nothing was forecasting tragedy. We left them as they rested before their summit attempt, Camp Three having been established as a snow cave on the Western Shoulder. Murray would cover the ascent from Base Camp. Veronique, James and I were scheduled to climb Island Peak, and to make it back in time to celebrate the return of the Everest climbers. Island Peak was an easy climb, and for the first time on that trip I really enjoyed myself, introducing my sister to the hardships and rewards of Himalayan climbing. Fond memories are captured forever in our summit shots of smiles and laughter. It was with the satisfaction of a climb well done and the joyous anticipation of seeing our friends again that we walked back to Everest Base Camp.

There was no one around as I approached the mess tent, having rushed ahead of the others in my eagerness to hear from Jon. Sherpas were usually busy as bees, cooking, collecting water, talking and laughing under the fluttering prayer flags stretched between the tents. This time the heavy silence of a ghost town greeted me as I skirted the kitchen towards Murray's tent. He had settled on a high rise for better radio contact with the climbers on the mountain. Our liaison officer, Shilandra, was slowly walking down the tumble of rocks leading to his little radio station. He looked forlorn, and held a handkerchief to his face. His hand on my shoulder, his eyes sad, his head nodding, his voice sobbing, 'I am so sorry.'

35

My heart exploded in my chest, my knees gave way under me. *O God, O God, O God.* Legless, I somehow managed the climb to Murray's tent. Headphones on, talking on the radio, frown on his usually smiling face. Out of breath, destroyed, collapsing beside his tent. His eyes catching mine. 'Jon is all right!' he yelled. A wave of relief engulfed me. Jon was alive. My body shook uncontrollably with delayed shock. My love was all right. Life could go on.

Murray then told me the story. The boys had started early from a high camp to climb the Hornbein Couloir towards the summit. Roddy, not feeling well, had stayed in camp. Soon the wind had picked up, making cramponing on the very hard snow hazardous. Jon had told Peter and Craig that he was going to turn back, and both had agreed that it was a reasonable idea. Craig had been tired and feeling the effects of altitude, and he must have been relieved that someone else had made the decision to go down. Fred and Kim were higher up and signalled that they wished to keep going for a while. Slowly, carefully, Jon and Peter started downclimbing, when the horrid noise of someone falling caught up with them. At the same time a body cartwheeling down the slope almost swept them from their tracks. Craig's lifeless body stopped falling a couple of hundred metres below them, and lay motionless in the snow.

Peter volunteered to go down to him. Kim and Fred, although much higher up, noticed that something was wrong and started retracing their steps down the couloir. Fred – impulsive, impatient, caring Fred – hurried down to help his climbing companions, did not notice a patch of deep snow and lost his balance as he stepped in it. Fred fell all the way to the bottom of Everest's North Face, making an illegal and permanent foray into Tibet. He would have had a giggle about that one.

Broken by grief, the boys returned to Base Camp, abandoning the climb. It was a sorry group that descended the icefall, tragedy imprinted on their faces and never to be forgotten. Craig and Fred. We would never see them again. I could not help but remember that I had been the last one to kiss them. 'Shall we shake hands?' Fred had said, and I had shrugged my shoulders, smiled, and kissed and hugged him goodbye.

We were to fly out of Luckla, and the walk down to the airport turned into a drunken stumble, every stop at tea shops an excuse for more *chang*, *rakshi* and oblivion. I was over-whelmed by mixed emotions – vast relief at still having my husband alive, and guilt for harbouring such selfish sentiments. Elke and Judy, Craig and Fred's partners, had not been as lucky as I had been. Reality was a nightmare they would take a long time to wake up from.

———

Was it all worth it? I had acquired a taste for high places in Nepal, and back in Australia I soon played down the potential perils and pains of climbing. It was the high price of the free-dom that bloomed on high summits, and one did not even think about it when dreaming of other faraway peaks clouded in mys-tery. When Terry Tremble and Ed Neve invited Jon and me to join them the next year on a beautiful mountain called Shivling, I realised that I was becoming addicted to going high. Moun-taineering was replacing travelling as a way of asserting myself and establishing my shaky self-worth in the eyes of others. I would be climbing with Jon, a vastly different proposition from that of just waiting around for something to happen.

My feelings for Jon were gradually changing, too; the Everest tragedy brought home the fact that I could not live through and for him any more. Once again, death close to my relationship coloured my way of thinking and made me realise that I had to carve my own dreams, my own challenges, if I was to survive what destiny served me. My English and ability to communicate in my Australian environment had improved dras-tically as well, and I would be able to make friends of my own.

On beautiful Shivling, we did not climb the new route we had had our eyes on; thunderstorms of a premature monsoon caught us a long way from the summit, and we decided to postpone our climb until the following year, 1986. This time, it would be Jon and me travelling to India, with Graeme Hill, an old friend of Jon's and the person who had taught him to climb in New Zealand. I had met Graeme at his home in Wollongong and, playing matchmaker, had thought that he might be just the man for my sister, who had returned to Belgium to complete her studies. Jon and I booked Shivling for September '86 and went grape picking to raise money for the climb. My sister wrote that, yes, she would come along for the walk. A few friends from Australia announced their intention to join us for the highest party in the world. It promised to be be some expedition.

Touching the Sky

Finally, the date that marked the beginning of our trip arrived. We all met in Delhi, in a sweltering August at the end of monsoon. I was feeling uncomfortable, not able to convey to Jon my increasing need for a radical change of roles in our relationship. He was as happy as ever, not realising that there was something wrong, and I felt uneasy darkening his serenity with my own feelings of inadequacy difficult to put into words. I could not be a shadow and a surrogate mother any more; I needed to be again my own master, to have my own goals, my own self-worth. I felt worthless without Jon, and worthless living through him. I built a cage around our relationship, to have an excuse to run away from it.

13 April 1986, Pahar Ganj, Delhi

> First *bedee* (Indian cigarette). I simply could not sleep. Jet lag, I thought, fooling myself. I slipped out of the room and meandered the streets of the early morning. Dogs were wandering about, sniffing refuse. One of them was crawling in the gutter, hind legs paralysed, the front of its body clinging to life. Was that a better life than the two dogs, fed every day but tied on a terrace, left to doze all day, never getting the exhilaration of a run

in the wind, and barking, barking always at the skinny motleys gambolling free in the street below the balcony?

At the Indian Mountaineering Foundation, we met Doctor Mohmed Vahanvati, eye surgeon and liaison officer. He had some climbing experience himself, so he told us, having led an expedition to Kamet reaching 7000 metres on the Normal Route. We agreed to him joining us on our acclimatisation climb of the Normal Route on Shivling, which Veronique would also climb. Shivling is a fishtail mountain with two summits; the main summit, 6545 metres high, which most routes lead to, and the West Summit, 6505 metres, which at that time had only been climbed once before by its South-east Ridge, by British climbers Chris Bonington and Jim Fotheringham. After acclimatising on the Normal Route, Graeme, Jon and I planned to tackle the impressive unclimbed South-west Ridge on West Shivling.

This time we travelled to the mountains by truck, a decision we all favoured. Travelling in the back was a lot of fun, nose in the wind, bouncing on top of a huge pile of equipment. Driving through towns was entertaining, with the locals gawking and laughing at the funny white people bopping along to the rhythm of the shock absorbers.

Man Bahadur was waiting for us in Uttarkashi, the town in the foothills where we would buy supplies and organise porters. 'Ganga Baby', as Graeme nicknamed him, completely bypassing the fact that he was straight as an arrow (*ganga* refers to marijuana in India). Man Bahadur came from Nepal and worked as a cook on mountaineering expeditions around the Gangotri area. The previous year he had accompanied us on our unsuccessful but happy attempt to climb Shivling's virgin South-west Ridge, and we were delighted to have him again as a chef (of sorts) in Base Camp.

We visited the principal at the Nehru Institute of Mountaineering to discuss our plans and the conditions. Nestled on a forested slope overlooking Uttarkashi, the Institute had been established to train Indians in the art of mountaineering. Over a cup of tea the principal, ill at ease with the fact that I had been introduced as the expedition leader, explained that a lot of snow had fallen recently. He had been at Tapovan, the Base Camp for Shivling, and a few other peaks nearby, only a week ago; it was still covered by two metres of snow. Tapovan is a holy place where *babas* (holy men) live in hobbit holes and smoke *ganga* all day to be on a plane where they can communicate with the gods. In our memories Tapovan was a flowery meadow, not a cold snowfield.

The principal had not exaggerated. Not only was the meadow covered by a thick mantle of snow, but there was also plenty more falling from the sky. A total eclipse of the moon was expected that night. We could only assume that it was happening on the other side of the snow curtain.

Our kitchen under the big boulder of last year was not the welcoming place we had hoped it would be. Despite the big tarpaulin covering the boulder and sheltering the only communal space of our camp, the ground was slippery, wet in the afternoon, icy in the morning. This did not make for a relaxing meeting ground. We had been joined in our travels by the 'party' team, a group of friends set on having the highest party in the world. Greg Pritchard, a colourful character on the Australian rock climbing scene, was the leader of the newly founded party party Party, and the brain behind its conception: a political entity dedicated to having parties anywhere in the world, for whatever reason. But the weather would definitely have to improve to ensure the party's success – the weather and the mood. I was still feeling out of place and could only think of running away to sort myself out. Furthermore, I was plagued by altitude headaches.

The headaches worsened, and the only cure was to leave Tapovan and spend another night at Bujbasa, lower down. As soon as I arrived there my frustration subsided to curiosity and astonishment. I elected to stay at the ashram, where pilgrims spent the night before venturing to Gaumukh, the ice mouth spitting the newborn Ganges on the glacier below Shivling. The novelty of this experience freed my mind from the troubled thoughts of the last few months.

24 April 1986, Bujbasa

In the misty twilight, prayers, voices, songs, smoky fires and flickering candles led me to a peaceful abandon. Welcome, welcome. A cup of sweet milky tea in hand, I sat on the floor, my eyes growing wide. Lots of pilgrims here tonight. Some fresh from the valley, others back from their trip up to the source of the Ganges, that most holy of rivers, and filling the newcomers with the excitement of what lay ahead. Shrilling voices, bobbing heads. Bells ringing. People had come from all over India. As night fell, the cold grew more intense and we were invited to move inside, leaving our shoes to weather the night outside. A very small dark room, about thirty of us. It felt like being in a tram at peak hour, elbows in the ribs, an invasion of odours and colours. The idea behind the 'sardines in a tin' exercise was to bring people from different places, different backgrounds closer, as they might never become acquainted in a wider space. Thus we were able to share a moment of our lives with unlikely others.

An hour later the aim of acquaintance was apparently attained, and we were called outside for a reunion with our shoes and a welcome dinner. I signalled to the businessman who had settled beneath my sleeping bag that the time had come for a move, but somehow, he was not inclined to leave his cosy spot to join in the chanting and drumming that had started. The hike up and down the mountain trails had made the most spiritually intense ravenously hungry, and rice, dhal and chapatti disappeared quickly into our many mouths. The stars above shimmered, and peace was with me. 'Bedtime,' said the holy man, 'Off you go, people, back inside.' Everyone got a blanket and I managed to elude my businessman's attentions to take refuge between a retired Sikh colonel, his English wife and their yapping dog.

When I woke up, I begged some morning tea, left rupees on the altar, and moved towards Shivling in a pure, frosty dawn. The mountain's main summit appeared in an opening of the clouds, and I sat to look at it, mesmerised. So beautiful, so unlikely perfect and aloof; no wonder the gods made it theirs. I stood up and slowly walked up the glacier towards the elusive summit. By the time I arrived back at Tapovan, the weather had closed in again, and Shivling had become a memory. Snow by the bucketful was steadily pouring from the sky, making progress towards the mountain practically impossible. To top it all, I got snowblind from not wearing my sunglasses in the fading light of post-sunset. Mohmed told me that the only thing I could do was to close my eyes, rest and be patient. So I did, and soon enough, I was joining the ranks of climbers and friend-helpers making their way with packs full of gear in the general direction of our mountain.

In my desperation to escape the reality of my present situation and find myself, I had resorted to the Belgian way of sorting out relationships, which was to ignore the problem and go away with someone else. I had fallen in love with another man. This soon became obvious to Jon, and oblivious as he had been to my torments, it came as a devastating blow to him. I was destroyed as much as he was, but I could see no way out of it. I had to leave him, and that was that. So much for the party to end all parties. Our friends left on tiptoe to let us sort ourselves out, and Graeme came to the rescue: as we were here, we might as well try to climb our new route and forget about our troubles for a while, he reckoned. We decided that Graeme, Veronique, Mohmed and I would try the Normal Route, while Jon started alone on the new route.

5 May 1986, Meru Glacier

> Little steps, big steps, cat's steps. What colour the cat? My mind jitters as I put little foot after little foot into Graeme's giant steps. The Yeti exists, I met him! If only he had shorter legs, that would suit me fine: goose-stepping in soft snow, I have had enough of it!

We finally established ABC, our Advance Base Camp, a two-tent affair at the foot of that terribly beautiful wave of rock named Shivling. On the Normal Route I roped up with Mohmed, while Graeme and Veronique climbed together. Mohmed was a quiet, proud man, conscious of his class and social standing, and no doubt quite shocked at our casual approach to life. We had had no reason to doubt Mohmed's climbing skills, but when we started on the Normal Route it became obvious that he was not as experienced as he had led us to believe. On one of his leads he took a five-metre fall on a piece of protection which pulled out. I started to feel uneasy about being roped up with him. My altitude headache returned with a vengeance, giving me the excuse I needed to follow my instincts and go back to Advance Base Camp. We all left, fixing the ropes behind us for a quick jumar re-ascent to our high point, and scampered down to camp.

I had to admit that I felt that it would be better for me to stay away from the Normal Route. I hid in my sleeping bag and ignored the rest of the world. Veronique had gone back up the Normal Route with Graeme and Mohmed for a second attempt but returned to the tent after an hour, also uneasy. Jon invited her to go on a walk with him. I stayed put. I knew they would talk about us, and my self-esteem was hitting rock bottom. I settled back in my cloud of feathers and kept myself busy munching and listening to music, gratification and escape rolling into one pleasant moment.

Suddenly I heard Graeme yell. I could not see him; what the hell was happening? Veronique and Jon were on their way back, so I got out and started the stove for a brew. Good old

44

mountain traditions – always have a brew ready for those getting into camp. Automatism saved my sanity. As we discussed harmless topics, snow and weather, a lonely figure appeared on the glacier at the foot of the Normal Route. 'It's Graeme!' Jon recognised the long-legged dot in the distance. He often stopped, and looked a little lost. Then he was in front of us, with the abominable news. Mohmed was dead.

What? Where? When? Why? How? Graeme's voice was partially obscured by Yello blaring in the background on our portable ghetto-blaster. It occurred to me that I should stop the music. 'Mohmed was a long way behind me,' said Graeme. 'I got to the bottom of the fixed ropes and I jumared up to our bivouac. I was hungry, so I ate the chocolate cake we had left there. As I was eating I heard the sound of screams in the distance. I knew it was Mohmed.'

It had taken Graeme a while to get back to the top of the fixed ropes. Mohmed was there, ten metres below, attached by his jumars to the rope and gasping for air. 'Water, give me some water, I am dying!' he cried. When Graeme finally reached him, he was dead. In shock, Graeme lowered Mohmed's body down to the closest terrace, and stumbled down to alert us.

So, the why and the how? The stove had been reluctant to work that morning, and Mohmed had refused to cook, although it was his turn. Graeme, being Graeme, had stormed off, furious, Mohmed following. The bivouac had not been far, and they still had some water left from the previous night. The walk had cooled down Graeme's temper, and he had gone ahead to prepare a brew at the bivouac site. Mohmed's jumaring technique had not been as polished as he had believed. He must have exhausted himself trying to jumar over a vertical section, too proud or ashamed to ask for advice or help. Maybe Jon or I should have paid more attention to the general ill feeling surrounding the ascent of the Normal Route, but we had been too engrossed in the breaking-down of our relationship to notice much outside our suffering. But perhaps the ill feeling surrounding the trip was our own doing, anyway. The pathologist's verdict, two weeks later, was cardiac arrest due to inhalation of cold air.

Graeme and I ran down the valley to advise the authorities. We ran and ran, losing 2000 metres in altitude in record time. My feet were begging for mercy, but at least the action kept my mind off Jon. In Uttarkashi we reported the accident to the police, the Indian Mountaineering Foundation, the local magistrate and the Nehru Institute of Mountaineering. We spent ten days away from the mountains, sending telegrams to the Indian Mountaineering Foundation requesting another liaison officer, writing more reports, eating mangoes, smoking *ganga*, watching the fan slowly turn above our heads as we lay on our beds. Never before had I felt so much like a puppet manipulated mercilessly from above, by a force infinitely powerful. I sank slowly into despair.

The principal at the Nehru Institute of Mountaineering reminded Graeme and me once more that without a liaison officer, the expedition could not legally proceed. We did not tell him that we did not want to give up the climb, that we had gone too far already, that we had to drink the chalice to the bitter end. So one morning, we snuck out to the bus station and caught the next bus to Gangotri, intent on reaching Advance Base Camp, where Veronique and Jon were waiting for us. As we started the walk we noticed that another storm was brewing ahead of us, and it took us another four days to finally make it back to Tapovan. Ganga welcomed us with some rice pudding perfumed with onions left over from the last cooking session. Our climbing permit was due to expire in a week's time. We ignored the possible implications and set our minds on the climb ahead.

The snowstorm which had delayed us on the way back to Tapovan had smothered our high camp: Advance Base Camp was buried under fresh snow, one of the tents was destroyed and all the gear we had stashed at the foot of the face had been avalanched. Still, a fierce resolution to keep going took hold of us all. We needed to climb the mountain to justify the torrent of emotions this expedition had borne in the four of us. In the midst of the torment, a love was slowly unfurling. Graeme and Veronique were spending more and more time together, proving my intuition right and making me reflect bitterly that I was better at organising other people's marriages than sorting out my own relationship.

The first task facing us before we had a chance to get on with the route was to dig out the gear still buried at the foot of the mixed face of rock and ice leading to the ridge we were to follow to climb Shivling. Day after day we trenched our way towards the mountain, day after day we dug around, moving vast amounts of snow to find our equipment. Jon eventually found it in a bergschrund which now looked like Swiss cheese, and Graeme and I were able to fix ropes on the face leading to the ridge. Two months since we had first arrived at Tapovan, two whole months! And in all that time, we had only climbed for four days!

We were more than ready to throw ourselves onto the mountain, but it snowed again and we were forced to go down to Base Camp to fill our shopping baskets. As we walked down the glacier, a helicopter swirled above our heads towards the mountain. We learned later that Mohmed's wife had been on board, but we never had a chance to meet her. What would we have told her if we had?

Leaving Veronique at our Advance Base Camp with a telescope and a bottle of whisky, we jumared up to the top of the fixed ropes, weighed down by huge packs. We had decided to climb the route in yoyo style, which involved fixing ropes to a site suitable for a camp, carrying all our gear up, collecting the ropes as we went, and doing it all over again until we reached the summit. We wanted to take our time, to get to know our route intimately, give her the love we could not share with each other. Jon was filming the climb. The yoyo technique was perfect for us.

Our first camp was on top of the hard face of rock and ice, and offered sweeping views of the steep ridge leading to the summit. Each day we set off, taking turns to lead, with the second climber carrying the gear and the last one removing the ropes. Jon and I had made an agreement to concentrate on solving climbing problems instead of personal ones. The ridge was now free of snow – a sharp rocky blade loosing itself higher up in an overhanging prow of blond granite abutting the summit ridge. There wasn't room any more to erect the tent; at nightfall we would each just find a flattish spot and scatter until the morning came. A horrendous traverse took us to a very small snow ledge we had spotted from below. I scared myself silly following Graeme on it, and swore as I went that I would never ever do it again. So I cooked, brewed, belayed and washed the dishes while Graeme and Jon carried over the rest of the gear on the rope fixed between the ridge and our eagle's nest: those two could recognise a near-hysterical woman when they saw one!

We spent four days on the ledge, four cramped days tied to the mountain twenty-four hours a day.

13 June 1986, home on the ledge, Shivling

> Never-ending herds of white elephant clouds walk the sky behind Meru and Kedarnath peaks. Sometimes, in the afternoon, they jump the summits and engulf us in their cool whiteness. Our little balcony on the pillar receives precisely three hours and forty minutes of direct sunlight every day. I belay Jon during the three hours and fifty minutes it takes him to inch his way up half a pitch of aid-climbing on horrendously brittle rock, which takes us closer to the summit ridge. He tells me that the rock looks better higher up, that the climbing will be hard but in free style. I dare to hope. In the meantime, I belay, mostly in the sun, and I daydream of climbing Sundays with Camille, sweet with the feeling of holidays.

It seemed that time had stopped on our ledge; lost as we were on a vertical wave of stone, where days were all one and the same. Then one morning, Graeme jumared up the rope that Jon had fixed, and ran on comparatively easier ground to the summit ridge. Jon and I packed our gear, but left a cache of food and gear on the ledge that had been our home, including a couple of condoms that Jon had added at the last minute, 'You never know,' eyes burning, me silent. (The look on the face of the next people who get up there when they find them!)

The ridge between the top of the prow and the summit looked like a dragon's back, its proudly outstretched neck rearing at the sky and ending in a crown of stone. The sky was blue, the weather perfect. Graeme led the last pitch to the summit, while I belayed and Jon filmed. Emotions. Tangled emotions of despair and summit fever caused Jon and me to slip into an angry screaming match. Graeme disappeared just under the summit, traversing to the far side to materialise on the very top of the rocky tower. Tears. I saw him throw his arms to the sky, and his words, his words of excitement and elation, echoed in my empty shell: 'Where to now?'

———

Where to now? I could not stay in Natimuk, the place which had become my home in Australia. I would have bumped into Jon every day and that I could not have coped with: it would have hurt too much. In desperation I called James Langley, who had become a dear friend since the '84 Everest expedition: he lived in a shared house in Melbourne, and I was hoping that he would help me with accommodation. I was lucky – a room had just been vacated, and the inmates were looking for a new housemate to share the rent.

Fitzroy, a soon-to-be-trendy suburb near the city centre, was a world away from quiet little Natimuk. I was lost in it and empty, and spent most of my time hiding in my bedroom, poking my head out timidly at meal times. My housemates were nice enough to me, but they had their lives, and little time to extract me from self-imposed misery. James was studying medicine, and Alan Sweetman and Murray Ralph, the other residents, were both working. Al, having finished a law degree, was making ends meet by doing odd gardening jobs, and Muzz was working in a native tree nursery. I met again the wonderful man I had fallen in love with, partly as an escape from the brick wall I had reached with Jon, but guilt had engulfed me so completely that I had to tell him I could not see him any more. Abysmal feelings were my everyday bread, and my self-esteem was at an all-time low. I joined the dole queue and found a four-dollar-an-hour job, putting together mixed flower bunches to be sold at hospital entrances. I invested my too few dollars in chardonnay, drunken oblivion, and chasing another man-crutch.

It seemed that since men had entered my life, back in my caving days, I had become more and more incapable of living my own life without seeing it through theirs. Would I ever be able to stand on my own? Guilt at having abandoned Jon was still choking me, and I found it hard to live without the escape of an affair with a warm-hearted and talented young man moving in a social circle totally different from Jon's. What saved me was the lure of adventure: Geoff Little and Lydia Bradey, a climbing couple I had met in Nati, and who were now living in Melbourne, invited me to join a New Zealand expedition to Hidden Peak, planned for July–August '87. Suddenly light invaded my life again, I had something to work for, a reason to exist in the virtual reality of this great city, and a chance to prove myself without Jon, without hiding through anyone.

Jon occasionally came to stay in my new house, and I never found the courage to break completely with him. But I tended to avoid these meetings, which only intensified the pain we were suffering. Peter Hillary had asked Jon on another expedition to Everest, to take place in September–October '87, and he planned to go back to the Gangotri for a pre-Everest training excursion to the mountains. For some bizarre reason, I let myself be convinced to go with him, Geoff, Lydia, Louise Shepherd,

Vivienne Moore and my housemate Al, with the fact that it would be a good way to get into shape for the Karakorum expedition as an excuse. Sure. But I had no money, and I was not going to get anywhere by earning four dollars an hour. Lydia came up with the idea of looking for sponsors: no Australasian woman had ever climbed an 8000-metre peak, so, full of her natural enthusiasm, she started sending proposals to Australian companies. Australian Geographic responded and we received two thousand dollars, which she decided to share between Geoff and us two. Well, that was a start. I scrounged as much money as I could by living on a shoestring and, in desperation, wrote to my father to ask him for a loan.

He agreed, and I booked a ticket to Pakistan. Soon enough, I would go back to the mountains, where I could feel wild and free, where I *was* wild and free. Al and I talked about faraway adventures in the safety of our Fitzroy den, and he even helped me find a couple more lucrative jobs to bump up my expedition savings. It was a very happy girl who boarded the Thai International flight to Delhi with Geoff and Lydia. We celebrated so well on board that, before we knew it, we were woken from a drunken slumber as the plane landed in Bangkok, and staggered to the next flight holding our temples.

Delhi had not changed. We met the rest of the team at the Tourist Camp, a rather cheap and nasty place near the busy Irwin Hospital, and once again set off for Uttarkashi and the Gangotri. Jon insisted on sharing a tent with me but I had also brought my own along, proud as I was to have been sponsored by Fairydown. I could always retreat to it if the going got tough.

The weather in the Gangotri was appalling, and the snow slopes of 6860-metre-high Kedardome, which we hoped to climb to acclimatise to our further adventures, were deep and unstable. Our group separated into smaller units: Lydia and Jon, who acclimatised faster than the rest of us, went ahead. Geoff and I followed a while later, and dug a snow cave halfway up the mountain to shelter from the coming snowstorm, and to wait for the weather to improve, which it did not. Al and Louise were lower down, on a terrace exposed to avalanches, and while Lydia and Jon were battling down from the summit in waist-deep snow, their bivouac site was hit by an avalanche which sent Louise tumbling down the face, to stop miraculously at the very edge of a gaping crevasse. She was lucky to escape with her life, and had nightmares about the experience for a long time afterwards. She was also reluctant to give mountaineering another go; a top rock climber who had just discovered the hazards of mountaineering, she decided to stick to what she knew best.

I had not achieved much on the expedition, dwarfed as I had felt by Jon's presence, so I was relieved to leave and go on to Pakistan. Jon wanted to traverse Kedarnath and Kedardome, and being the hot-shot that he is, he did it in forty hours, listening to Patti Smith's *Dancing Barefoot*. Louise and Viv went travelling, Al went on to Italy and the States, and as we had gotten on rather well, we kept in touch by writing each other numerous letters, crisscrossing the planet on the paths of our travels.

In Rawalpindi, Geoff, Lydia and I met with the Kiwi team, which was quite large and included four females. We were not to climb as a whole group working together for a summit though: Craig Stobo, our expedition leader, explained to me that the expedition had been organised to allow a number of small climbing teams a cheap expedition to a Himalayan mountain. In theory a noble idea, but one which proved disastrous when put into practice.

Pakistan was totally different from India. Lydia and I, being western, fair-haired women, had a hard time escaping attentions from Pakistani men, who locked their own women up at home but considered us fair game. I found the country beautiful, but I despised the misogynist interpretation men had given the Koran, which reduced women to a subspecies to be exploited and even maimed. The situation became less blatant as we travelled north by bus and rules relaxed a little, but there were occasions where the injustice and inhumanity of it all hit us in the face again.

To get to Skardu, the town preceding the start of the walk onto the mighty Karakorum summits and Hidden Peak (also known as Gasherbrum One at 8068 metres), we drove up the Karakorum Highway linking Pakistan with China. The incredible landscape gave me the impression of travelling in a just-settled primeval world that some caves in France had given me in my teenage years. Except that here, creation was still in the process of happening. A huge landslide which blocked the road and sent a raging torrent rushing over the bridge, meant that we were stuck in a small village for four days, waiting for the road to be cleared.

On the first day in the village, the female members of our group cruised the streets until the town elders came to our camp near the river to talk to our male leader. We had been judged a bad example to the local women, and were asked to remain hidden in the camp until the road re-opened. We were left with no choice but to comply. After all, our expedition had already almost caused a riot: some of us had used convenient holes on what had looked like a vacant lot as toilets, on a small peninsula surrounded by the roaring Braldo . . . that is, until some elders had come and asked us to please stop shitting into the graves of their ancestors! Oops . . .

Well aware of the woman's place in these latitudes, Lydia and I snuck along the river for an overdue wash. We were sure that nobody has seen us, but how wrong we were! Small boys threw stones at us and, as we got down to washing socks, we noticed a mob running along the shore towards us. Forty men had rushed to us in the hope of catching a glimpse of white female flesh. They stood around us, disappointed, while we gathered our washing and scampered back to camp, swearing that being sticky and smelly was better than this.

It was a relief to start the walk towards Concordia, K2 and Hidden Peak. Our expedition was enormous, with dozens of porters to carry our masses of equipment. At night-time, as the smoke of fires and the aroma of cooked dhal lingered on the glacier, the porters prostrated themselves on tattered rugs towards Mecca, and sent their prayers echoing in the cold mountain air. The peaks skirting the glacier we were following had the colours and lines of Sleeping Beauty castles. But this was no fairyland: a war was raging close by between Pakistan and India. Fighting a territorial dispute in this godforsaken land of snow and rock seemed ludicrous, but there were constant reminders, like the telephone line which guided our steps on the glacier, all the way to our Base Camp. As we were negotiating the treacherous icefall between Base Camp and Camp One at the foot of Gasherbrum Two and Hidden Peak, we heard a series of loud bangs. *Look around, fear.* At first we thought it was an avalanche, but no. Some Pakistani climbers had been making progress on a peak located on the border, and Indian soldiers were shelling them!

I did not have a climbing partner. I was supposed to have climbed with Geoff and Lydia, but a violent illness, emptying me top and bottom, had set me back. I ended up spending most of my time in the mountains tagging along with one team or another, or moving on my own. I did not really care that I didn't have a climbing partner; in fact, being at one with the mountains elated me. I was overwhelmed with happiness at being able to look after myself, and enjoyed every minute of the expedition, and also the company of everyone on the team. Who cared if I climbed Hidden Peak or not? Reaching its summit always remained a vague proposition in my mind. I was too busy conquering self-sufficiency, a fragile self-esteem and contentment to worry about such trifling matters.

As it turned out, not much progress was made up Hidden Peak: the season was rotten and the small-team approach did not work as energy was spent in duplicated efforts to climb the mountain. Arguments between teams became a regular practice, to the detriment of the common good.

There were other teams on the mountains surrounding us, and a Pakistani army group on our own Hidden Peak. They were a group of friendly, mostly inexperienced climbers, determined to succeed no matter what. We had fixed some ropes up to 6800 metres on Hidden Peak and retreated to Base Camp to wait for the weather to improve when tragedy struck. Four Pakistani climbers had ascended, spurred into action by an ambitious colonel and their own desire to climb Hidden Peak for the glory of the army (perhaps they also wanted to beat us to it?). They were sitting around at their high camp, waiting for the snow to stop before persevering with their summit attempt – except that one of them had what sounded like cerebral oedema, if we believed the radio reports. Still, the group stayed up, hoping the man would soon feel better. Of course, he didn't.

We were having a bland dinner of dhal and rice in the kitchen tent when Craig's voice boomed over the innocent chatter: 'Fuck! Avalanche!' The four climbers, who had become good friends of ours, had received permission to retreat down the mountain as the sick climber was now in a critical state. As soon as they had left camp, the dangerously deep snow had given way in their tracks, and all four had tumbled down in a monster avalanche. It was a huge shock, and if some of us were still undeterred, most climbers were disinclined to stay after the accident. Our time in the mountains was running short, commitments at home were becoming pressing. Lydia, Geoff, Carol McDermott and I were fiercely determined to stay and try again, if not Hidden Peak, maybe Gasherbrum Two. We could always sort out the minor matter of permits on our return to Rawalpindi – if we were not kicked out of the country beforehand.

We joined forces with a Basque team and while our team was packing, we headed again up the icefall, an experience which was becoming quite shattering as crevasses had opened up greatly with the advancing of the season. As we reached Camp One and scavenged delicious treats from caches left behind by retreating teams, we all looked at Gasherbrum Two. Some fixed ropes had been left by a British team to the site of Camp One on the mountain, and it seemed silly not to use these. The climbing would be easier than on Hidden Peak, and as the route was more straightforward the summit would be attainable in a shorter time.

I gasped as I followed my new climbing companions up the fixed ropes, and it soon became obvious to me that I had already spent too much time at high altitude to be in top shape for the job ahead, while waiting for someone to rope up with on the dangerous icefall between Camps One and Two on Hidden Peak, I had spent ten days at Camp Two, at 6500 metres, before returning to Base Camp for a short stay.

It was too long, too high for me. To function properly in the rarefied atmosphere at high altitude, the body has to manufacture more red blood cells to carry more oxygen around the body (at around 6000 metres the air contains more or less half to a third of the oxygen we enjoy at sea level, the pressure being lower). It takes about three to five weeks at high altitude to reach a peak acclimatising stage, but the body simultaneously starts deteriorating at and above 5000 metres as a result of the lack of oxygen. Although it varies from person to person, usually the best proven way to acclimatise is to climb up to a new altitude, carrying a load of gear to the high point to make the most out of the excursion, then to come down and sleep at the lower altitude before moving up to stay on the next foray high up. I knew this system worked for me, but I did not know how long I could stay at and above 6000 metres without deteriorating. I found out in Pakistan.

At Camp One on Gasherbrum Two, I settled to brew and cook for my tentmates, Geoff and Lydia, as they had been ploughing steps up to camp. This, of course, did not make me feel better, as I kept spending energy working, while they rested, their work done. Carol, sharing a tent with the Basques, kept everyone awake and edgy all night with his continuous coughing. In the morning, as we set off towards Camp Two, I experienced problems focusing on the ground in front of me. Altitude sickness? No. I had lost one of my contact lenses, and found it very difficult to keep my balance on the steep ground. Right. The reality was devastating. I had to forget about climbing an 8000 peak – staying alive is always more important. And even that was not going to be easy: Geoff had my lighter, and I could not wait at our camp at the bottom of Gasherbrum for his group to return from the summit. Without a lighter, and the means to melt snow to drink, I would become dehydrated and useless pretty fast.

There was only one thing to do – pack my gear and descend to Base Camp. Great. That meant I had to negotiate the icefall on my own, with all the risks involved. Without being roped to a partner, any fall, collapsing snow bridge, or miscalculated jump over a crevasse would be fatal. So it was with a certain apprehension that I approached the first visible crevasses. In front of me was a twin crevasse, two bottomless holes each more than a metre wide, with a narrow snow band between their gaping jaws. I was talking to myself by then. *Okay girl, better get this one right. Take your pack off and throw it over, it will be easier to jump without that load on your back.* Easier said than done. My pack was too heavy for me to pick up, let alone throw over the obstacle. I sat on the ground with my back to my pack, strapped it on, and turned around onto my knees so I could use the strength of my legs to get up. Back to square one. Walk back a few steps, run like mad, jump! *Mummy* . . . Made it. One down, only a hundred to go.

It took me all day to come down, my head now cool enough to keep panic at bay, but when I finally arrived within sight of Base Camp, I collapsed in front of the last obstacle of my death race: an eighty-centimetre wide angry slice of water, gushing down a valley between steep ice shores. Fortunately someone saw me, and came with a rope to drag me across. A few days later, the team came down, having climbed Gasherbrum Two, and we all celebrated with gusto, happy that we had made it, and were all back alive.

I had not climbed a single mountain on this trip, but I was overjoyed. It had been so good to find my mountain legs, and to rediscover the person I was deep inside. I had also acquired a taste for being on my own in the mountains, the ultimate freedom. And a sure way to cultivate self-confidence and experience: I could only blame myself if I made the wrong decisions! I started toying with the idea of going solo again. But I was not keen on crevasses, and most peaks worth their names were glaciated, webbed with crevasses to fall into. Soloing would have to wait until I found a high mountain without a glacial coat.

———

Jon had not climbed Everest. He and Peter had been the last to leave the mountain, ducking under the jetstream at Camp Two and finally giving up as winter enforced its presence. He was going back though, having been invited by the Australian Bicentennial Everest Expedition to join the team as a climber, and as a cameraman for the Australian Broadcasting Corporation. He visited me in Melbourne and invited me to accompany him to a meeting with Peter Allen, one of the expedition organisers. I came out of the meeting feeling left out, and jumping up and down. Jon was going to *another* big mountain and I was not! *Aargh! What to do?* We had met Dick Bass, an American millionaire, at Everest Base Camp in '84, and he had explained to our team his goal, which was to climb the highest mountain on each continent. He had completed his task recently, and the seed of an idea started to grow in my head. The Seven Summits. *Why not climb the highest mountain of each continent?* I knew I was no millionaire, but I could work and save money, write to sponsors, travel the world, meet people, climb mountains, and feel the wind of freedom and dare in my hair again.

Where to first? Alaska? I had never been there, but it should be reasonably easy to organise. *Should I climb it alone?* I decided to write to Al, who was in the States, to invite him to climb it with me. I knew I had more experience than him, so I wouldn't feel diminished by my climbing partner's overwhelming superiority of experience for a change. The more I tossed the idea around in my head, the better I liked it. When Jon next called, I announced to him boldly that I was going to climb the Seven Summits, so there. *I was going to climb the Seven Summits.* Had I known then that it would take me nine years to achieve my dream, would I have had second thoughts?

Denali –
First of the Seven Summits

7 November 1988, Liège

Alaska. Me of the Never Ever, I left my heart, a part of it, there. 'There' is a land wild, so wild. It was too much for me; I couldn't deal with the simplicity of it all. I met people who were the land, the sky, the moose crossing the mist of a river at nightfall. I sat on a sandy beach on the shore of a lost lake, I looked at golden curtains closing over magic mountains in the changing light of an Indian summer night. I learned a kind of love and hate, and the in between.

The sun was pounding on my newly cut hair. *Three minutes, no, four minutes, two buckets to go!* I talked to myself as I dived under another grapevine. At one bucket per two minutes, I was going like clockwork. The heat was overwhelming, and red dust had conveniently mixed itself up with sweat to form a total sun-block. I was hoping to fill as many buckets as possible between sunrise and sunset, and aiming to make one hundred dollars a day, which that summer meant filling three hundred buckets to the brim.

The pick-up convoy drove past in a cloud of red dust, preceded by the owner's two German shepherds. My friend

Greg was standing on the back of the trailer, ready to jump off at the end of the row, and to start piling black, hot containers of yellow juicy bunches on the trailer's platform. 'Grape expectations!' he laughed. Greg Pritchard and Phil Wilkins, who had become my inseparable friends since I had returned from Pakistan, had decided to accompany me to the grape country on my quest to earn enough money to go to McKinley, at 6194 metres the highest mountain in North America, as much for the security of the weekly cheque as for the fun we shared. It was great to have close friends, and to be appreciated as one alone, without the constraints of being in a relationship.

Despite the moral support, I positively loathed grape picking: it was synonymous with rising before the sun did, and with spending the hours of daylight shuffling under never-ending rows of vines, knife at the ready to chop bunches in accelerated motion, always on the lookout for red-back and huntsman spiders keen to drop on new friends. Grape picking — the climber's last resort. One of Greg's favourite sayings, often uttered after drunken debauches, crossed my mind: 'I will never, *ever* do this again!'

When I was not picking I was on the phone, wishing Jon well on his third Everest trip, and begging Australian Geographic for food — literally. I had earned enough to buy a round-the-world ticket valid for one year, but once off the plane in Anchorage I was not too sure what would land in my belly. Fortunately, two weeks before I was due to leave, Australian Geographic agreed to sponsor me and filled the gap in my budget. My friends in Melbourne organised a huge party and sent me on my way.

It was cold, and grey, and raining a sad little rain. In the port of Anchorage, a statue of Captain Cook was pointing an extended arm and finger towards warmer horizons. I had arrived from a sultry autumn Down Under, and my mind was still full of the colours and smells of a ripe Australia.

I caught a bus to town. The driver, wearing T-shirt and shorts, asked me, 'You're from out of town?' My nose, poking out of a number of insulating layers, nodded. Up the street, down the street, into a coffee shop, through a shopping centre, amongst Indians stumbling around. My first images of Alaska were of a grey world inhabited by running white people and drunk natives. But for the sub-zero temperatures, it could have been Australia, somewhere between the past and the future.

Life's gearbox took a bit of a trashing when Al arrived from the 'Lower Forty-eight'. My climbing partner! Our room in the youth hostel turned into a whirling store of supplies and equipment where we accumulated the goods we would depend upon to accomplish our climb. The supermarkets were huge, and tequila was dirt cheap.

After a memorable party ('Let me put another moose-burger on the barbie for you, Buddy!'), we left Anchorage and made our way to Talkeetna, the threshold of Alaska's civilised world at the foot of the Alaska Range. Our driver, Big Dave, pointed out bitterly that that lake over there had thawed two days ahead of time; a sign of the seriousness of the greenhouse effect, and of the end of the world around the corner.

In Talkeetna ducks were quacking in the sky, which was grey as usual. Snow was melting in big muddy puddles. I had organised by mail that we should fly into the mountains with Doug Geeting's company. We settled in Doug's clients' cabin and I busied myself with peeling wrappings off various food-stuffs while Al made friends with everybody living within hearing distance.

In between trips to the garage's murky shower, I spent a lot of time looking at pictures of my life in Australia. I wasn't too sure of the way to reach a compromise between asserting myself in my mountain media and growing in a satisfying rela-tionship away from it, in my private world. So I concentrated on what I had to do to get up the mountain. I was feeling uneasy in this town. During the short summer, Talkeetna turned into an international climbing circus. There were too many climbers around and I felt uncomfortable with my level of experience, which I always compared unfavourably with that of anyone else around, regardless of their true expertise.

Al had made friends with Tom Waite, a retired climber and hippie who now ran the Denali Overland bus service and the best curiosity shop in town. I tentatively slid through the open door and discovered common interests and a fascinating other way of life. Tom sang and played guitar. He was quiet and friendly, flirting in a way vague enough to be ignored without appearing rude. I started to relax, and let myself enjoy the newness of life.

One morning the grey clouds left the scene and we were told to get ready to fly in. Doug Geeting's secretary, Sandy, drove us to the tiny Talkeetna airport in an old rattling pick-up. On the tarmac someone was busy preparing a red Cessna called 47 F for take-off. The pilot, David Hicks, complete with moustache, pilot glasses and peaked cap, was filling the craft with fuel. He mumbled a welcome while we piled in and settled in for the excitement ahead. My heart was thumping hard — we were on the way, it was happening! The first of my Seven Summits!

Doug and David flew their planes in formation, playing, each Cessna an image of the other, a reflection on the mirror of the sky. McKinley appeared on the horizon, filling the sky with its majestic bulk. The Great One, the High One. Denali, as nearby Athabascan natives called it. A much better name than McKinley, after William McKinley, once president of the United States. Mountains as impressive as this one need eternal names. Too soon we were turning smoothly over the heavily wrinkled Kahiltna Glacier and descending for the landing. We touched the snow, and the engines roared during the final turn, sending icicles flying in waves.

The door opened onto another world. The sun hit hard, the whiteness flashed at our faces. We had arrived at 'Kahiltna International Airport', a small village of ever-shifting tents and people on the eastern branch of the Kahiltna Glacier. We did not lose any time in erecting the tent and I went in to huddle in my sleeping bag and write my diary. Al, as usual, was outside making friends. I envied his outgoing nature. The time soon came for me to make a public appearance, though, and I found myself not looking forward to it at all. The toilet (pardon me, the bathroom) was a wooden throne in the open, facing the steady flow of people making their way back to camp from the mountain! I tried to be blasé, and thanked the sudden snow shower that allowed me to retain some semblance of dignity while hiding behind my umbrella.

———

Little ants pulling little dots . . . that's what we had seen lining the glacier from the plane. Soon we were two of them, little climbers pulling heavy sleds, slowly working our way along the thirty-five kilometres separating us from the summit of North America. Al had bought a pair of second-hand skis in Anchorage, and slid easily on the powdered snow. I was on foot. The combination proved disastrous – we couldn't get a steady pace with a rope in between us and, in an attempt to avoid heated arguments on the speed of movement, we ended up coiling the rope neatly on one of the gear sleds we were pulling, and travelling at our own pace. It was still early in the season, and crevasses were covered with thick snow – or so I hoped, being more vulnerable on foot than Al on his planks. We were getting closer to the mountain but it was shrouded in cloud and we hardly caught a glimpse of it.

Entertainment in the big white-outs was provided by all sorts of climbers, including ourselves and the wild geese flying overhead on their way to the northern summer. The wind was blowing hard. In that desolate landscape of horizontally wind-blown snow and white-outs, picking up camp sites was nonetheless easy: ghost towns suddenly appeared out of nowhere, with withered blocks of ice forming sad walls crouching in the gale. A snow shovel was a crucial piece of equipment:

digging a hole which would provide protection from the wind was a must before considering pitching the tent and making a brew. And even all the precautions taken did not guarantee that the night snowdrifts wouldn't force the unlucky of the pair to get out and dig the tent up . . . 'Whose turn is it?' . . . 'I cooked dinner!' . . . 'Yes, but . . .'

There were advantages to climbing so close to the Arctic Circle. Of course it was cold, very cold indeed, but the twenty-four-hour daylight allowed the utmost luxury — we could wake up at midday if we wanted to, and climb until midnight if such was our fancy. I loved listening to my biological clock, regardless of rigid climbing time conventions. Early in the mornings, the first trains of guided clients would moan by. The wholeness of the great white emptiness would soon be restored, the wind loudly wiping out any other noises, and then it was time for us to think about a brew and plans for the day.

We did take it easy. By that I mean that we were in no rush to run up the mountain, run down and catch a flight home. We were in the mountains, had plenty of food and didn't feel like carrying it all out again. We thoroughly enjoyed every step, while absorbing every curve and line of the surrounding mountains. Pilgrims of the summits, we were spellbound by their simplicity and power. Social life was quite something — one did not go to the West Buttress on Denali if one wanted to be alone in the wilderness. There were enough solo climbers around, though, and we'd often get together for a brew at the end of the afternoon's stroll.

The presence of so many humans on this mountain created a feeling of false security. It is always too easy to feel invincible in a group, to forget that a single storm unleashing itself furiously on a mountain is likely to have the last word. A Korean climber was coming down on a sled pulled by his friends. He had been lucky: only a broken ankle when a gust swept him off his tracks at Windy Corner and threw him down the side of the mountain . . . something to reflect upon while

I made my way in knee-deep snow behind the flying Al. I didn't have skis, but he didn't have a walkman. Vivaldi kept my morale sauntering on each time my legs sank to new depths in patches of soft snow.

We were carrying so many essentials that two trips were necessary to move our possessions from one camp site to the other. The yoyo system worked marvels, and acclimatisation proceeded smoothly. As we rose in altitude, the temperature dropped. The nights were beautiful but bitterly cold, the whole landscape covered in a silver blanket of light for a few hours. Every evening at bedtime I shivered spasmodically and tried my best to keep warm. I wore a woollen hat and all my clothing, zipped my sleeping bag up to my nose, spread the spare sleeping bag on top of mine and still wished I had another layer of feathers to put on. Al would get in the tent after his digestive night walk, strip down to his earrings and unzip his bag down to his knees, 'A bit stuffy in this tent, eh?' Aaargh!

14 May 1988, Camp Three, Denali

> In the mornings, an early riser flies a kite in front of the buttress. Maybe it is his way of finding a balance between the mountain's breaths and his own energy currents? Looking at him, I see myself as the kite, linked to the earth by my clumsy love for people, and depending on them to find the freedom at the end of the string.

It took a while to walk from the camp at 3340 metres, where we were settled for the moment, to the next camp at 4240 metres. We had decided to make it easier on ourselves by taking one load halfway between the two camps, past the area known as Windy Corner. Al volunteered to go, as I was dealing with a persistent altitude headache and did not want to risk going higher at this stage. How precious to have a few hours alone. I cranked up the stove, and warmed up some water for a wash. My multipurpose eating bowl was soon full of steaming water.

Luxury! I was clean again. A quick rinse for the bowl and it was time for a brew. It might seem disgusting to use an eating bowl for a wash (and I haven't said what else I used it for!) but in harsh conditions anything goes; every bit of equipment has to be used to its full potential. Weight is a crucial factor.

Windy Corner lived up to its name. We didn't fly away, but the wind left me with an unusual souvenir to remember always my days on Denali. I got frostbite on my belly. Of all places. It so happened that the metal karabiner holding my harness snuck through several layers of clothing and touched my skin. The cold and wind did the rest. I did feel pretty silly when I went to seek medical attention, but I shouldn't have worried; between loud 'wow's, the nursing student guiding a neighbouring group was most helpful in looking after my ailment.

Latecomers were working on snow fences and igloo walls. In the first suburbs of the camp at 4240 metres, past the last of the monster crevasses, a fortified camp was proudly flying the Stars and Stripes. We stopped for a look around as we reached the central square. The view was extraordinary: Mount Foraker's tempting curves could be seen past the wooden throne and the queue of wrapped-up customers waiting behind it, the telltale bit of white toilet paper gripped between gloved fingers. I sighed, dreaming of solitary pleasures in fragrant undergrowth. 'Howdy, howdy!' Adrian, one of the solo climbers we had had tea with lower down the mountain, greeted us with a wide smile. Climbing the West Buttress was truly like visiting India on a Lonely Planet guide, always meeting the same people in the same cheap hotels! We were lucky. A five-star trench had been vacated minutes before, so we claimed it as Australian territory and made ourselves at home.

The following morning I went to have my heart pressure checked in the medical compound. Good Lord. There was a woman eating fresh ravioli with avocado sauce outside the hospital tent. 'Yeah', she slurred, 'the chopper has just been in with fresh vegetables and things.' Inside the tent was no less amazing – colour television, cassette player, a lot of electronic machines producing esoteric noises and lights. A doctor put my finger in a plastic clip and announced that I was well acclimatised to the present altitude. *Great! Let's get higher then!*

We agreed to leave the tent at 4240 metres to save us from carrying too much weight on our summit bid. Al had wanted to go to the top from where we were in one push, while I hesitated on the course of action. My head used to give me a hard time when I moved to a new altitude and Al's wish involved a jump of more than 2000 vertical metres without going down. *Oh well*, I thought. *Why the hell not?* and we started to pack up.

It was ridiculously early and there was already a big queue at the bottom of the fixed ropes . . . what was the point in getting up at dawn?! I did not like the sight of all those people enthusiastically scraping bits of ice onto the top of my head. At the Col, the wind hit. I was in a bad mood. I really wouldn't have minded dumping my load right there and running back to the tent, to waddle in the reassuring warmth of humanity in the camp at 4240 metres. Al got the map out and we checked the distance to the next camp. 'Too far,' I said, my usual optimistic self. I was still grumbling when the moon saluted us as we dug a tiny burrow in yellow-stained snow at Camp Six. The sun didn't set much at these latitudes, but when it did, the temperature sure dropped a lot.

We stayed three nights at Camp Six, at 5150 metres, in constant cold and, for me, with a mostly constant headache. The burrow was really too small, so in the morning we moved into a vacated snow cave. The weather was kind to me. It turned bad and gave me the time I needed to acclimatise, although blocking the entrance of our abode proved a mistake – it did keep wind and snow out, but it also kept stove fumes in, which caused the biggest headache of my life. Between two brief moments of sleep I remembered vaguely the story of some Germans dying in their tent on the mountain, suffocated by their stove fumes in a storm. The idea of getting out of my bag, out of my bivouac bag, out of the double bag into the cold of the cave wasn't particularly inspiring; still, it was that or so long cruel world, I thought. I sighed and started to peel off the layers of my painstakingly just warmed-up cocoon. I felt the headache lift as soon as I threw aside the pack obstructing the door. I sighed again and crawled back into my numerous layers to reconstruct the elusive lukewarmness of my dreamless sleep. Al snored all the way through my epic.

———

'Well, what do you reckon, mate?' It was already noon, and a group of guided clients had just left. The sky looked pretty average. We had been told it was a very long day from here to the top and back. 'May as well give it a go, eh?' Once more, roping up was a mistake. Al went straight into fourth gear, while it always took my engine a while to warm up. We unroped. I followed the guided tour and told my toes they were warm, which they only half believed. At the Col between the north and the south summits, engine now going full steam, I overtook the group and shot through. The grey sky was touching the earth. The snow was flying horizontally, and had it not been for the occasional bamboo pole swinging in the wind, it would have been hard to decide which way to go. With no one in sight it was quite wonderful. Alone at last! But it was cold, oh so cold. I did not stop at all, the camera stayed in my jacket. I did not dare expose my hands to take photos of a white elephant in a snowstorm.

Past the last snow plateau, past the ice-axe marking a grave, was the summit ridge. A few silhouettes were walking on the horizon, divers struggling against the currents at the bottom of an ocean of wind and snow. A stagnant moment. The fury of the snow waves rose again and I lost sight of them. I knew, though, that we were going to the same place; I believed that our immodest fight against the elements had the same justification — we were here to get closer, to kneel on a summit, to pay our respects to the one and only power of life, whatever name we graced it with. It wasn't a mountain, it was an act of faith.

They were Koreans. We exchanged a hug on the summit ridge, they on their way down and me a few steps from the top. Al had a big smile on his frosted face. I think I did, too. The smile of my sister flashed through my head. Fingers were cold, we took a few photos. Would the little bits of coloured plastic match the memories of unreality? Reaching a summit can be an anticlimax, because the getting there is what keeps one going. That feeling of climbing to the sky, of getting closer to the impossible star. Then one reaches the last rung on the ladder, and it is . . . what is it? It cannot be satisfying yet, because summiting is only half the job done. It is relief, always, and sometimes an explosion of emotions, but only for a short while. Reality bites. If you want to stay alive, you have to keep your head cool, save the joy for later, for down there, when it is safe.

Coming down. The hard times of going up, forgotten. We were left with the task of getting too much gear and food back to Base Camp. Once again I cursed myself for not having a pair of skis and an iron-woman constitution. There I was, floundering on all fours in deep snow, pulling a sled, carrying a pack! Quite a sight, and no one around to appreciate it. Al backtracked and skied up to rescue me. I sat on my sled, carrying my pack, Al the steam engine towing me. Denali Express. Groups on their ascent stopped dead in their tracks to watch the strange convoy sliding down towards the comforts of civilisation.

Comforts of civilisation they were. When we reached Kahiltna's 'International Airport', Dave Davis, a Canadian climber we had met during the climb, presented me with a cap of whisky to celebrate his birthday. In a haze of beatitude after the second sip, we loaded the plane and were off. I glided on top of the world, at last. David, our pilot, looked pretty bored. 'Are you blasé with it all?' I smirked.

'It's been a long day!' he drawled.

'You bet!!' I giggled.

Suddenly the mountains were behind us, and we were landing in Talkeetna, where we were greeted by nature in full bloom. We all dashed to the Fairview Inn and celebrated success in a wild session of cheers, laughs and dancing, late into the twilight of the never-ending day.

———

Alaska mesmerised me, but my earlier plans of travelling around with Al faded away in the light of my newly discovered passion for Talkeetna and its people. I felt at home in this little town, and did not feel like moving for a while. I was running out of money, though, so finding a job became my priority. The Fairview Inn was advertising a bartender position, which Big Dave convinced me to apply for. The generous man even loaned me a bicycle to help me get around. I applied for the position and, to my surprise, was hired. I had never bartended before, and I had trouble understanding the local accent, but it wasn't a problem; the wild men I was serving were extraordinarily polite and well mannered. I guess it was not every day that a new face showed in town, and women were more valued than gold nuggets in this frontier state.

Talkeetna was a crazy place in summer. Parties succeeded gigs at a frantic pace. I was living in my tent by the river and spent a lot of time drinking cups of coffee at the roadhouse. My heart was aching. The news had just come through that Jon had climbed Everest, on the same day I had climbed Denali. I was uneasy about the mixed feelings troubling my mind. Did I miss him? I was proud of Jon, but I was so immersed in the discovery that people could like me for myself that I was not keen to return to the role of hero's wife. I still wanted to show him, myself and the world that I could do what I had set out to do. I was on a mission, and no relationship could distract me from my goal of climbing the Seven Summits. (I later found out that the Radio Australia news report mentioning our respective ascents had made a mistake: Jon had summited on Everest on 28 May 1988, four days after I had climbed Denali.)

I met Maria Kirwin through a climber from Canberra whom Al had become acquainted with earlier on, and it was not long before we were best friends. Maria lived in a quaint log cabin she rented in one of Talkeetna's backstreets, and worked as a cook and waitress at the Latitude 42 Restaurant. She was a Christian; I wasn't any more. We spent a lot of time discussing our spirituality and the way we related to this violent world. We talked a lot about men, too.

Talkeetna was a small place, where you always ran into the same people. And people were running a lot, from the roadhouse for breakfast, newspaper, gossip and coffee in the morning, to the pizza parlour for lunch, then across to the Fairview for a drink and a chat after work. It seemed to me that the only time spent at home was bedtime. It all made sense though; with the experience of a little bit of an Alaskan winter behind me I can see that cabin fever gets so bad in those dark months that it is only natural to go berserk in summer and live out in the light.

David, the pilot, and I kept running into each other. He hated people smoking tobacco and had a soft spot for women with long brown hair. My hair was fair and short, and I puffed away all day. He thought women should be pregnant and bare-foot in the kitchen, while men should be real men. I thought, *Man, you need to broaden your horizon*, and fell in lust. David showed me the Alaskan way of life, I talked about my world out there. Often after work we'd fly to his cabin on Bunco Lake, right at the border of the Denali State Park, south of Denali National Park. Those were magical moments: I could squeeze my nose against the plexiglass of the window and stare at moose and grizzlies without the fear of a close encounter. Now, that was a thing I couldn't handle! As soon as we'd land on the gravel strip beside the Tokositna River, I'd be looking left, right and behind, spying on the dark forest for suspicious noises. I had a totally irrational fear of big furry animals.

We spent the evenings under the soft light of the sun setting on the Alaska Range, fishing salmon and trout while sipping on Irish coffees and smoking 'doobies'. Then we'd go to sleep with the echoing song of trumpeter swans in our ears. David had one major aim in life. He wanted to complete the construction of a beautiful, octagonal, honey-coloured cabin, facing Denali on the shore of the lake, twenty-five kilometres away from the closest road. I helped him but didn't find the hard life inspiring. Domesticity was taking too much time; I didn't understand it as being creative. At the same time, I revelled in living miles away from civilisation, in a forest alive with a myriad of primeval smells and sounds. I loved cooking with old and new ingredients, and I loved giving.

Did I already know that I could not live in Alaska forever? I did play with the idea, though, living the Alaskan life to the fullest and loving it, and turning it over in my mind. David was the strong, silent type, too busy working away the hours of daylight to have much time to share my thoughts. I started to miss company, and to look forward more and more to my visits to Talkeetna. We did get on well, though, a pair of good buddies at the worst of times.

Talkeetna was a nest of Vietnam vets. I wanted to understand, and spent a lot of time listening to their experiences. The war, why: the answer always, 'I was young and stupid'; how: 'Dope saved me from going crazy'; 'Alaska is a refuge'; 'I got sick of the rednecks in the Lower Forty-eight.' They were easy to relate to. Daniel Mawhinney was one of my favourites in the group. A savage individualist, he played saxophone in the local rock band and enjoyed living. Just living, period. I remember one night I had gone to see him after closing the Fairview. Autumn was approaching, and stars had appeared in the darkening sky. Dan was working night shift on the sewer project. We cruised around dark dirt tracks in the forest, talking our heads off, sniffling occasionally. Through the opened windows the cool purr of the river caressed our ears. I stretched, sending my arms and eyes to the stars. Strange things were happening in the sky above; green waves began flashing and uncurled themselves around us and the night. Aurora borealis. It was so beautiful and unexpected. I felt very privileged to be discovering such a fantastic natural phenomenon with a dear friend, in a wilderness unspoiled by the human race.

My visa ran out as the last fireweeds died, announcing the end of summer and the start of another life. The lakes were frozen – we were now landing on Bunco Lake beside the cabin. The northern lights often changed the dark nights into a festival of colour, taking the shape of curtains, folding and unfolding on mysterious rhythms above my head. It reminded me of those games my sister and I used to play in my mother's kingdom, entangling ourselves in the fresh-scented bed sheets drying on the line, delighted and spooked.

One day, while ice-skating on the frozen lake, I drew a huge smiling face on the thin snow cover. There were tears in my eyes. We took off for the last time in the fading light of an exhausted sun. I glued my nose to the window, taking in every parcel of this beautiful, if unforgiving land. I rang home in Belgium to announce my near arrival. I was shattered by the news: my father had left my mother for another woman. My childlike joy at returning to my family home for a white Christmas vanished. The world fell to pieces.

Halloween was one of my last nights in Talkeetna. 'Trick or treat!' A bunch of burning eyes shone as we threw coins in the extended woollen mitts. Wrapped-up ghosts disappeared, leaving tiny footprints on the new snow. The eerie atmosphere fitted my mood, which hesitated between total crash and obliteration of the facts. I got very, very drunk and danced the pain away with werewolves and fairies until the dawn of a new day put a pink balm on my exhausted mind.

———

There was no one waiting for me at the railway station in Liège. People were moody and aggressive, and the fumes of European life were making me sick. I was back home in Belgium. Another kind of wilderness.

I spent huge amounts of energy trying to cheer up my mum. She simply couldn't accept that her husband had left her after thirty-two years. I could only hope that separation would be beneficial to both, giving them time to bloom in peace, but that would take time. To avoid storms with my mother, I had to see my father secretly. The Seven Summits dream helped me keep my sanity at an acceptable level: I hung to the buoy of a snow-capped mountain floating above the lush African plains – Kilimanjaro.

To finance my trip to Kilimanjaro I ended up once again doing odd jobs, such as painting roof cornices, windows, and the lettering on high industrial towers. I enjoyed every minute, every step taking me closer to the mountain of my dream. I even fantasised about paragliding from the top. Why, it seemed possible, it had been done before: David, whom I somehow convinced to come and have a look at my way of life, was a parachuting instructor, and my Belgian friend Eric Smeets, who ran a bean farm at the foot of Kilimanjaro, was the proud owner of a second-hand Taiwanese-made paraglider. Blooming with renewed enthusiasm, I wrote to Howard Wheelan, Australian Geographic editor, about my plans.

David arrived from Alaska. He had just spent a couple of months working as an 'aerial bus' pilot in horrid conditions on the west coast, in the middle of winter, to raise money for his trip. He enjoyed the utter decadence of Belgian living, matching the never-ending supply of special abbey beers with exotic combinations of old-world delicacies. I felt happy to be sharing my world with him, and even happier that he liked it. I was about to have a surprise.

Kilimanjaro –
Smouldering Passions

'Shhhiiit!' Eric's face twisted around the word. The farm pick-up floated, belly up, in the middle of a sea of dust and bobbing black heads. I looked at Kilimanjaro, floating also, far above the days of our life in Moshi. Half an hour ago we had taken the truck for a tune-up in the garage area of Moshi, where every household specialised in one part of motor surgery. And now, after the tune-up clan had taken it on its ill-fated test run, there was no doubt that the car would have to spend a while in the body-repair casualty yard.

'Always something, always! How am I going to get my beans to Belgium in time? Unbelieeevable!' My friend Eric exported his quality beans from the flanks of Kilimanjaro to supermarkets in Belgium twice a week. Well, he tried to.

David and I were staying in Moshi, Tanzania, at the house Eric shared with Maatje Van Dillen, an 'expat' from the Netherlands. Before coming to Africa I had heard all about expatriates, how they kept the traditions of the colonial age going, not drinking before the sun set but making up for it once it did. Still, I had to rub my eyes hard when I saw Maatje rush to the fridge, take out a full bottle of gin, pour half of it into a pint glass and drink it, all in less than forty seconds. It was all true!

He filled up my glass for me. 'Here, have a drink, it's bloody hot in this country!' So much for legends. It was iced water.

Africa kept throwing me off balance. Nothing was as I expected. The secret was not to expect anything, and things might begin to happen. But not the way you expected it. But maybe I was too stressed to be sensitive to obvious pattern; David was having a hell of a time, frustrated with Africa's unpredictability, and confronted me with regular whingeing. The tension grew between us. I started having doubts as to the wisdom of having invited him into my third-world travels.

———

We had arrived in Dar es Salaam after a five-day trip courtesy of Egypt Air. The plane had been late leaving Brussels, causing us to miss the Dar es Salaam connection in Cairo, and we had had to spend two days in the airport before being transferred to Nairobi and flown to Dar es Salaam a day later. But it had been an instructive trip and an unexpected glimpse of wealthy cultures.

Dickey, a Dutch woman we met at Brussels airport, had befriended us. She had become acquainted with an Egyptian professor on the flight over, and after an aimless day in Cairo's gloomy airport, she resolved to call him for help. Mohammed Ali Sahel invited us on a tour of Cairo and rescued us from the prison we had landed in. We cruised along the currents of Cairo's streets in Mohammed's little black car with a million others. We followed major avenues bordered by palm trees and rickety palaces, narrow back streets festooned by domestic waste decaying on the side of the canals, dusty country roads wallowing through luxuriant green plantations.

The pyramids, mountains of the Nile, threw their majesty towards eternity. But the number of camels and little people tickling their feet was very disturbing. No avalanche conveyed the ire of the gods though; only resignation transpired from the cyclopean granite blocks.

Driving at night-time to an unknown place in a foreign

country has always been to me the ultimate in affordable thrills. Vignettes of a thousand lives flashed in an uninterrupted flow through the car's open windows, becoming alive as their smell hit my face on the wind, and dying as they dissolved in the next combination.

Mohammed closed the day of wonders by taking us to one of his favourite restaurants. On a row of charcoal barbecues attended to by white-gowned men, a few dozen chickens were doing their best to add to the night's rich fragrances. The food was succulent, the conversation stimulating, the beer Belgian. I felt I was losing a friend when I hugged Mohammed before returning to the airport.

———

'Dar es Salaam isn't Tanzania,' everyone said. Just as well. It might have been exotic, but we were tired and suffering from the heat enormously. It was a very noisy place. The hotel we stayed in was a beautiful colonial-style white building, opening onto a lovely square in a popular area of town. There were cobwebs on the room's ceiling, but not enough spiders to keep up with the influx of mosquitoes. Dogs were barking in the street, and disco music, very loud disco music, interrupted our late siesta. The inside courtyard was a nightclub! Night after night we were kept awake by the likes of Michael Jackson. Crowds of beautifully dressed Tanzanians flocked in every evening and danced until dawn. Promiscuity was rampant: prostitutes were standing in every corner, and I learned later that in Tanzania the price of one condom is equivalent to the price of one prostitute – half a day's pay. Most men happily go for the latter, causing the AIDS virus to spread like wildfire. Some tribes, like those from the shores of Lake Victoria who consider frolicking a very respectable thing to do, have been almost entirely wiped out by the deadly virus.

The train journey to Moshi was quite uneventful, with everything going as unexpected. The countryside was lush and green, the earth as red as Australia's own. Shapely hills appeared now and then. As we approached Moshi, the convoy stopped at a tiny station in the middle of nowhere, for no apparent reason. Six hours later, we were still there. Many locals were leaving the train and walking across the fields to the closest road, hoping to hitch a ride to their destination. With a mountain of luggage, we didn't fancy the idea of being stranded with it on an empty road, so we stoically sweated on in our compartment. Eventually the train departed in the early hours of the morning, and the next time we woke up we had stopped at Moshi Station.

Moshi was a lot bigger than I had thought. I didn't have Eric's address, and all my attempts at locating him through official channels failed. Nonchalance was chronic in public servants, as was alcoholism; lunchtime provided an opportunity to top up and wait for the end of the 'working' day in a pleasant haze. Most Tanzanians resisted the stress of the competitive western lifestyle, and I did not blame them for it. Their natural *laissez-faire* attitude did create problems, though, especially concerning race. Indians who had migrated to Africa during the Raj were still regarded as foreigners, and as they had monopolised business and profit through hard work and a commitment to attaining financial success, they were despised by the native population. Even the *musungus* (white men) were generally reluctant to deal with them, for fear of a possible rip-off.

With only five weeks in Africa, we were limited in what we could hope to learn about the continent and its people. Covering a large area would have resulted in only skimming the surface, an approach I have never liked. When Eric found us, we followed him where he would take us, getting acquainted with the way people lived. We did want to see some national parks, though, as in these early days of our stay in Moshi the weather did not allow an ascent of Kilimanjaro.

Kilimanjaro is the generic name of the huge area of high ground rising in isolated grandeur in the Masai country, around three hundred kilometres from the equator. There have been three centres of volcanic activity on Kilimanjaro: Kibo, the highest, culminating at 5895 metres with Uhuru (freedom) Peak on its crater; Mawenzi, now a tangle of shredded rock buttresses rising up to 5145 metres; and Shira, a completely collapsed caldera forming the Shira Plateau. Kibo, towering over the town, played hide-and-seek with thick clouds all day, every day. Furthermore, the heat was oppressive, making the afternoon duties of expedition organising an almost impossible task; stepping out in the dazzling light was like entering a steamy bathroom, turning the shower tap on, and being hit by a ton of hot bricks. I lost my skin three times: to the equatorial summer, my absence of mind, and resignation.

One particularly hot afternoon we were shuffling along the main street by the mosque, discussing safari finances. Our meagre resources didn't allow for the hiring of a car from Moshi, and we needed someone else to share the burden. 'Okay then,' I told David, 'let's find someone. Now!' A young woman happened to be walking in our direction. I crossed the street and asked her if she would be interested in joining us on a safari. Marita Larson was Swedish. She was on a study trip with a group of fellow Swedes, but all of them had taken off on their own to get a feeling for the people and the country. She was to meet with them again in a few weeks, on the coast. She had thought of going up to Marangu to have a look at Kilimanjaro but changed her mind, and we set about organising a safari together.

—

'What's the problem? Did something break?'

'Mmmm, the main leaf springs. Doesn't look good.' David was used to fixing mechanical problems, and his judgment made Marita and me worry about the smooth continuation of our journey. Flies buzzed around as we put on grave, concerned faces and peered over the undercarriage. The noon sun was fierce. We left David and our two safari drivers, Modest and Joseph, in black greasy oil up to their elbows, and prepared a picnic on a nearby tree stump. Our ordeal was starting to attract attention. Two Masai warriors materialised beside the minibus. Marita, who spoke Swahili, chatted away with them. They were very interested in David's bulky muscles, and wanted an arm-wrestle with him!

Modest and Joseph were experts at dealing with break-downs. They retrieved a few ribbons of rubber from under one of the seats and proceeded to tie together all the broken springs. Soon enough we were on our way again, to Ngoron-goro Crater National Park. Our bank balances did not allow us to even consider staying at the expensive lodge, and we drove to the crater's rim where the more affordable camp site was located. As we negotiated the trench called Access Road, two elephants started walking in our direction. They grazed in a field nearby while we set up camp, brushing the air rhyth-mically with their ears. The view from our camp was mind-blowing: behind a solitary tree sculpted by the wind a huge, perfectly rounded crater, hazy with afternoon heat, stretched below us to the horizon. We lost ourselves for a few days in the Eden of Tanzania's national parks, hypnotised by the beauty of the natural world.

———

Chicken juice was dripping from chins and fingers. The bottle of Safari Beer turned into a bar of soap as our greasy hands took turns on its flanks. There were stars above our heads and cats fighting for the bones under the table. We were having dinner with Eric at one of Moshi's local eating houses. This one was a favourite amongst Tanzanians, and we were the only westerners there, gorging on the national dish of roasted chicken and chips. 'Thank God, Maatje is giving us a lift to Umbwe tomor-row. It would have been another six thousand shillings to hire a four-wheel drive from that thief of a Sikh!' I told Eric between two sips of beer. We were discussing our plans for the week ahead. It was time to make a start on Kilimanjaro. Rather than taking the popular Normal Route, I had chosen to take the rarely trodden Umbwe Route, up a very steep forest, and the Western Breach, which was a pleasant scramble to the upper reaches of the mountain.

'Too bad you'll miss the Mardi Gras party at the Moshi Club,' giggled Eric. 'But I am glad you are not coming. I am going to get real drunk, forget about beans and make a fool of myself!'

Park rules made it compulsory and expensive to employ a guide and a number of porters during our stay on the mountain and we needed to hire locals for the jobs, so David and I next took a bus trip to the park headquarters at Marangu Gate, with a photographer friend of Maatje's to translate for us if necessary. We met up with Francis, John and Abel, who were to work for us during the trip up Uhuru, Kilimanjaro's summit. A fair bit of haggling went on to bring the price to a level satisfying to both parties; on top of minimal official wages paid through the park for the climb, guides also required a cash-in-hand salary, to be paid in hard currency. I wasn't sure if we had been ripped off or not when we walked back to the bus stop, but all things considered, the one-week stay in Kilimanjaro National Park was more affordable than a fully organised tour through one of the local companies.

———

Maatje drove like a true local. Porters, dead goat, would-be mountaineers and friends were thrown from one side of the four-wheel drive to the other as he negotiated the numerous turns of the dirt road with a gusto reminiscent of a rally driver. After passing the last of the coffee plantations and small clusters of huts, we stopped in the middle of the dirt track. Getting out was impossible – Maatje had driven as far as he possibly could, and the undergrowth was squeezing the sides of the car, and brushing my hair through the window. We reversed to a more suitable disembarkation spot. *At last, letting us get some credit for the climb!* I could see us on our way to make the first four-wheel drive ascent of Kilimanjaro.

The track ascended steeply through a dense forest, where

white monkeys swung high up in the tree canopy. When lunchtime came in the jungle it was clear there was to be none of that decadent pampering Himalayan expeditions had me used to. The guide and porters (who reversed roles at a whim) dropped their loads and busied themselves with lighting a small fire in a clearing of two square metres. 'Yeah, mama,' Francis informed me, 'We have to eat lots of meat to be strong on the mountain. This really hard work, you know.'

'Yeah, tell me about it.' I pumped the stove and squashed a mosquito that had been bathing in a drop of sweat on my forehead. John, chief guide for the present time, dug in a gooey gunny bag to retrieve a 'thing' which looked like a goat's stomach lining. He impaled it on an improvised skewer. *So that's what they stick on a barbie here, eh?*

'Want some, mama?'

I was drenched with sweat when we stopped for the night at the only reasonable camp site in the forest. While Francis lit a fire under the cover of a rock overhang, I walked down to the little pond which was to be our water supply. Ferns bordered the edges, and funny things were swimming in the murky water. I filtered the mixture through my scarf and hoped for the best.

For two days we swam through sweat and a vertical jungle of mysterious green and black depths. I half expected to hear the familiar cry of Tarzan, all muscles out in mid-air. It wasn't to be. We left the jungle and my unfulfilled fantasy to tumble onto another planet.

The tree cover stopped abruptly, and we walked on short alpine grass to Barranco Hut, at 4200 metres. Dead trees adorned with shredded sheets of fluorescent green moss added to the eerie atmosphere. Kilimanjaro had appeared high in the forest while we walked up a steep narrow ridge to the vegetation border, and it now dominated the sky above us.

Grass trees that looked like pineapples dotted the slopes around the hut, which was to be home today and the next day.

I wanted to get a chance to acclimatise, to be able to enjoy the rest of the trip, and the hut's altitude made it a good place to stop. Barranco was a small, round stone hut topped by a tin roof covered in graffiti. Francis, John and Abel added their names to this unusual logbook. A look inside convinced me that putting up the tent was a good idea.

19 February 1989, Barranco Hut Camp, Kilimanjaro

> The creek is whispering softly and the morning sun washes out colours and feelings. David and I have just had an argument on who was doing what; I was for equal opportunity in cooking and brewing duties, while he still stuck to his ideal of women rhyming with kitchen. I take my clothes off, splash around aimlessly for a while. There are orange and grey cliffs upstream. I hop up the creek, touching and sniffing. Seven days out of the crazy world of down there. I am happy to have a few hours on my own, to find myself again. I talk to the crystal water, to the flowers, to that mountain up there.

The next day saw our safari-like looking group walking up a cloud, through the lunar landscape of an unseen world. Lava Towers camp site was our target for the day. Once upon a time all this had been heat, colour and chaos. Francis and I followed each other's steps on the volcanic ash. 'Tell me, how many times did you climb Uhuru last year?' Francis stopped in his tracks and looked back at me.

'Don't know, Mama,' he replied, 'I stopped counting after thirty-two.' He told me about the poor village he came from, his years as a kid roaming the mountain, his days as a porter. Then the climb up the ladder, the guide course with the national park, his dream of going to Chamonix with John 'to show them over there how the Kili guides can climb.'

Abel was a delight to look at when he was moving. He danced up the track, swinging his body and arms with grace, a stack of branches piled high on his head. At Lava Towers he made for the kitchen, and dropped his load behind the sheet of corrugated iron leaning on the ground against a huge boulder, which was the camp site. Lava Towers Resort must have been popular with prehistoric families on summer leave.

From Lava Towers it was just a long day to the top and down to Horrombo Hut, then another day to the park's gate. I was jumping with the excitement of summit fever when I noticed that David looked far from happy. He had had a hard time making it to the camp, and was worn out. Africa and altitude had gotten to him in a bad way. He spent the night with his head out of the tent, unable to hold down any food or liquid.

I pondered about the different possible courses of action. We could convince the guides to stay one more night here. It would be hard but feasible, and maybe beneficial. Had I felt close to David, it was the option I would have chosen. But sadly, at this stage, I had retreated to my emotional fortress, to protect myself from what I understood to be his lack of consideration. I shamelessly declared as we got up that he was to go down to Horrombo Hut while Francis, John and I went for the summit by the Western Breach Route. Abel would accompany David on his traverse to the huts. It was the most logical decision to make for our expedition to be a success, but I had reached it too easily, I thought.

My heart was ruthlessly lighter after David and Abel left. I finally reached harmony between myself and the starry sky, the tingling of ice in the air and the rhythm of movement. The beloved sound of snow crunching under mountain boots made me want to kiss the ground. At sunrise, the shadow of Uhuru touched the pink of Mount Meru, its dark shape detached on the horizon. We sat on the snow to rest and let the place and moment possess our souls. I thought of David. He could always go up the Coca-Cola Route (such is the nickname of the Normal Route) the day after, if he felt better.

Here I was, on my way to the top of the second of my

Seven Summits. I felt very good. It was funny, though, with one guide in front of me, one behind. Both were so caring and helpful – yesterday it had been everlasting flowers that John had offered me, today it was a helping hand: 'May I push your bottom, Mama?' I was never fast enough on steep ground, it seemed.

There was nothing, nothing but the wind and giant serac steps. We crossed the side of the crater rim towards Uhuru Peak. John took my hand and we walked in that manner for a while. The temperature was remarkably low, the wind howling. We sat for a nibble. No one in sight. I expected crowds up here. 'Where is everyone?' I asked.

'All down at the hut, Mama, they get to the top at sunrise, then down very quickly. They find it very cold here.'

There must have been a view, but I don't remember it. I was too busy slapping backs and being slapped and giggling and embracing to be in a contemplative mood. I was happy to be there, and to be there with Francis and John. No more, no less. At the foot of the summit wand an empty bottle of Veuve Cliquot and a frozen orange told of a recent offering. John took a few shots of us on top, we hugged each other again and kept the giggling up.

I had, with great difficulty as no one there was interested in my project, extorted a World Wildlife Fund flag from the organisation in Belgium, in an attempt to crusade for the sake of the elephants. I left it floating in the wind on the summit wand, lest the world forgets.

> 'This is to certify that Mrs Brigilte Nur (sic) has successfully climbed Mount Kilimanjaro, the highest in Africa, right to the summit – Uhuru Peak – 5,895 metres.'

Well, thank you. The diploma now lives on the wall in our Natimuk office along with the postcard showing the eternal snows of Kilimanjaro, which I had bought because of the

ABOVE LEFT: *On most Sundays our family would go on outings to tourist towns within driving distance of our industrial valley. Veronique and me, Belgium, 1966.*

ABOVE RIGHT: *I remember scrambling to that high point and having to yell for a rope to be thrown to me, so I could complete the climb in safety! Dave, Belgium, 1978.*

ABOVE: *Camille Piraprez and I spent three exhausting but exhilarating weeks together in the Cirque of the Unclimbables. Yukon, 1979.*

ABOVE: *One of the attractions of climbing in Nepal is the ease with which local people share their lives and customs with visitors. Katmandu, 1984.*

LEFT: *Elke Rudolph and I taking a rest in front of Changabang. Garwhal Himalaya, 1982.*

ABOVE: *Peter Hillary, expedition leader for the Everest '84 expedition, is an extremely serious and competent climber — which doesn't mean he takes himself seriously! Katmandu, 1984.*

LEFT: *I hated crossing rivers in the Karakorum, and you can see why! Lydia Bradey flying over the Braldo River. Karakorum, 1987.*

ABOVE: 'Where to now?' yelled Graeme Hill from the top of Shivling. Shivling, 1986.

LEFT: It took Jon (Muir) two days to climb up this horrendously hard and dangerous section, which stretched fifty metres high, of our new route on Shivling. Shivling, 1986.

ABOVE: *Nursing a snow-blind eye – I'd always wanted to know what it felt like to be Mary Poppins. Shivling Base Camp, 1986.*

OPPOSITE: *Bunco Lake was a mirror to the sky and surrounding mountains, and I enjoyed walking and skating on it during the last days of my stay in Alaska. Denali is in the background. Bunco Lake, 1988.*

ABOVE LEFT: *Climbing Denali was a pleasure, involving a delightful scramble up the ridge to get to the last camp before the summit. Denali, 1988.*

ABOVE RIGHT: *The breathtaking view from near the last camp before Denali's summit. Denali, 1988.*

ABOVE: *Apart from Francis, John and me, there was no one to be seen on Kilimanjaro's summit. What a treat! Kilimanjaro, 1989.*

ABOVE: *Half the fun of climbing the Umbwe Route on Kilimanjaro was sharing life with Abel, John and Francis. Kilimanjaro, 1989.*

LEFT: *From rainforest to giant lobelias to a snow-capped summit, Kilimanjaro presented us with an incredible variety of landscapes. Kilimanjaro, 1989.*

ABOVE: Boxing Day at Camp Berlin, after summiting Aconcagua on my own. Aconcagua, 1989.

LEFT: *We'd been climbing Aconcagua's South Face for eighteen hours straight before finally finding a totally unsuitable spot to spend the night. Aconcagua, 1990.*

LEFT: *At our high point on the South Face of Aconcagua the morning after, under the 100-metre-high crumbling ice wall. Jon and Geoff Little munching on our last supplies before our three-day descent. Aconcagua, 1990.*

interesting piece of information printed on the back: 'Kilimanjaro . . . is the second highest mountain in the world, after Mount Everest.'

I had just climbed the second-highest mountain in the world.

———

Howard wasn't impressed. I had told him that I would paraglide from the top of Kilimanjaro, and I ended up walking down the Normal Route. It wasn't entirely my fault. I hadn't received an answer from Tanzania regarding my plan, and it wasn't until I was in Moshi that I found out that bicycling, paragliding or whatever else but walking up or down Kilimanjaro would cost an extra two thousand US dollars. Other expeditions with similar plans faced the same problems. I wasn't the only one disappointed.

Howard's letter was straight to the point, telling me that Australian Geographic had better uses for its sponsorship money than to invest it in people who took their dreams for reality. The words were harsh and painful to hear, but I learned from the experience to plan my goals more carefully to make sure they were attainable.

It was time for David to make it back to Alaska. I was not sure any more of where we would take our relationship. Africa had made it obvious that he couldn't adapt to my lifestyle and that he wanted us to live in Alaska. The Seven Summits quest was the most important thing in my life and there was no way I would give it up. I drove David to the airport in Amsterdam and wondered what to do.

As soon as I arrived back in Belgium, I enrolled in a paragliding course, starting the next day. It was the best thing I could have done. Every day I drove to the Vesdre Valley, where the instructing was taking place. As I approached the small cafe, which was the club's base on the river side, my stomach always turned upside down. I would get so excited and restless that my whole body would tremble with anticipation. Roger Faufra and Jean-Michel Finet were excellent teachers. Soon they had me soaring up in the air, slowly floating down to meet the daisies in the landing field. I was stealing time from paradise. Taking off was the hardest part of the flight – nothing is more unnatural than running towards an open abyss while trying to steady a huge nylon canopy a few metres above your head. I often slowed down unconsciously, grazing the slope with my bottom before soaring up into the azure. Once in the air it was total bliss.

I was working to support my new passion. 'Landscaping', it was called. It meant carting wheelbarrows full of heavy soil up a slippery plank onto a pile. I was working with Jean-Marie Czorniak and Alain Fonsny, two of my old caving friends, making a new garden for a burgher's house in Verviers, a small town near Liège. Just to make things more interesting, it rained most of the time – but then, if you were going to work just on sunny days in Belgium, you might as well forget about making a living.

The twenty-sixth of April arrived too quickly. I had bought a round-the-world flight valid for a year, and suddenly it was time to go back to Australia. I wouldn't be alone there. I had caught up with an old friend in Belgium called Muriel André. She was coming to Australia for two months along with another friend, Annick Leclerq. They were waiting for me at Melbourne's airport when I landed, exactly a year after leaving for Alaska. It had all gone so fast.

Muriel and Annick made their way to Natimuk while I stayed in Melbourne for a few days, trying to adapt to life in the new world again. Jon was in Melbourne, and we met for the first time in fifteen months. It was good and awkward at the same time. I was still vaguely planning to go back to Alaska then. But as time went by I realised how important Australia was to me. It was the only place in the world which would bring tears to my eyes as I first saw it from above on a plane. That must have meant something.

I got a ride to Natimuk with a friend, and stayed at Mount Arapiles with Annick and Muriel. We decided to hitchhike to Queensland so they could see a little bit of the amazing land

Australia is. I was looking forward to it, too; I hadn't travelled north since the first time I was in Australia, in 1980.

We had a ball, and became even better friends. We didn't go very far north, only just making it to the southern part of Queensland. We met wonderful people, lazed on beautiful beaches, trampled around wet national parks and suddenly it was time for my two friends to go back to Belgium. I tried to settle on the Gold Coast by finding a job there, but destiny had other plans. I ended up in Natimuk again, after taking Annick and Muriel back to the airport in Melbourne. It was a very tearful moment as they walked through the passport check gates. It seemed to me then that my life was made of making and leaving dear friends all around the world.

So, once again it was life in Natimuk. Jon was sharing a house with two friends, Geoff Little and Maureen Gallagher. He made it clear to me that if I wanted to give our relationship another go, it was now or never. I had written to David a few weeks before, explaining that I could never live in Alaska full-time, and after a lot of talking with Maureen and Jon, I decided to be game and try to work out the relationship I had walked out of two years before. It wasn't easy. I had been quite happy living on my own for the past few months, so I compromised by keeping a separate room as my own space. May Brown, Phil's neighbour, had a bungalow in her garden, and I spent a couple of nights a week there, too.

I was trying to get to my third summit then: Aconcagua, the highest mountain in South America. There was no doubt whatsoever in my heart that getting there and climbing it was the only important thing to me at that time. In theory I was also Jon's wife again, but time was exactly what the relationship needed. I had applied for a job in Horsham. The work would be quite a challenge for me as I'd have to use my brain in this one, for the first time since I had left university. I was accepted. I think they liked my common sense. For the next three months, I cruised the countryside in a flashy white car, researching transport and human services in the Wimmera region, while plotting my Aconcagua expedition. I had decided to go there alone, because the idea of climbing a mountain without the security of a partner still appealed to me. I had thought of going solo on Denali but I had chosen instead to climb with Al, and now the need for a solitary challenge emerged again. I realise now that I also wanted to experience the feeling which had been Jon's exclusively for so long, although I knew that my projected climb would happen at a much easier level than any of his solo ascents.

Jon, Maureen and Geoff decided they wouldn't mind climbing Aconcagua. I was to leave before them, and they would meet me at Base Camp after I had climbed the mountain.

I booked a ticket to Santiago, via Easter Island. The travel agent, a little man with a slick black moustache, was interested in my project to climb South America's highest peak. Perched on a chair, checking on the wall map that Aconcagua was in Argentina and not in Chile as he had thought, he mumbled to me through his moustache, 'Yes, you are right, it is truly in Argentina. It is the second-highest mountain in the world, isn't it?'

Aconcagua –
Season's Greetings

4 December 1989, Easter Island

> Rapa Nui. Isla de Pascua. Easter Island. A drop in the ocean. A sloping volcanic expanse, its sides gnawed into cliffs by the hungry waves. A grassy desert dotted with volcanoes and big heads.
>
> It does not matter if it was the Polynesians, or Kon-Tiki travelling from Peru on a reed raft, who founded a new country on this little forgotten island. The stonework of the most ancient periods (1300 AD) is extraordinary, and the gigantic heads scattered around the island make one feel to be in a scene from *Planet of the Apes*. Most of the heads are toppled, their noses teased by wild flowers and weeds. Others have been erected again in recent times, and watch over the land as they have done in times past.

A barrage of eager faces was doubling the glass windows of the small Easter Island terminal. Sheets of paper describing the merits of Pension Tahai or Residencial Orongo e Toro Niu were pressed to the windows by anxious señoras pushing each other to get to the front of the line. Maria looked cocky, and I liked the smile in her eyes. Off we went in the rattling four-wheel drive, down the only road of the island to Hanga Roa, its only town. We drove past the tiny market and bought a big piece of fish for lunch.

All of Maria's guests were French – civilians or soldiers on leave from Tahiti. I would not be practising my Spanish here, but it was a treat to be able to chat away in French, my mother tongue. I was alive. Being on my own in a foreign place as fascinating as Rapa Nui was the ultimate way to unwind after the hectic last month of work and pre-departure stress. Maria had a very laid-back approach to business. Chez Maria Goretti was more a family house than a hotel, with all meals shared together around the one table.

Ahu Tahai, a cluster of megalithic buildings and large sculpted heads, was only a few minutes away – a walk up the dirt road through small blocks of heavily forested grounds, with little shacks of every style and material squatting in the middle of the green patches. The road then took a radical turn to the left and ran out of dust on Ahu Tahai. The taste of mangoes comes to mind as I think of it although there were no mangoes on the island – only the wind, the sky, the sea and the giant stone heads fixing their gaze on the ocean. The sunset had the colour of a ripe fruit and the air smelled of salt.

I sat on a stone platform with my diary and a tequila orange. A shrivelled old lady, all smiles, climbed up the steep stone wall to sit beside me. She babbled away in Spanish, showed me some shell necklaces and a little *moai* she had sculpted in pumice. I didn't have any money on me. She laughed at me rolling a cigarette and gave me the necklace along with another smile. I used it to adorn the black hat Jon had given me, starting what would become a fetish. Over the years I collected little presents from friends and attached them to my hat.

After a day in the comfort of a room, I erected the bigger of my two tents in the garden, piled my gear in it, locked it up and started walking north. I had been exercising regularly in Australia but it all seemed a long time ago, and I was bursting with energy and the need to spend it. The lack of water on the island meant a few extra kilos to carry, which would not hurt my training. Clouds were covering the sky; still, it was extremely hot and the light reverberation was extraordinary. It flattened a landscape where no trees were impeding the view.

I found a lava tunnel which had been used in ancient troubled times as a refuge, and escaped the afternoon furnace for a while sitting in a huge, spherical room with dry stone benches on its sides. The walls were dotted with the openings of narrow tunnels leading further underground. I poked the ground, my mind wandering in the past of the place. Shiny slivers of obsidian started to appear in the light of my headtorch. Some were little stone tools, used no doubt by the inhabitants of the cave as domestic implements. I grew excited, the archaeologist in me reliving a present long forgotten. It made my day. I stepped out of the refuge feeling accepted by the ghosts of the Long Ears (the original inhabitants of the island).

The aim of my solitary journey was to climb the island's highest summit, Mount Terevaka. Well, why not? The view would be unlimited from the top and I was keen to grasp the island as a whole, to see, even from a distance, all those hills, valleys, volcanoes, and coastlines that I wouldn't have time to touch and smell. Pleasure, peace and a feeling of belonging to this world of ours took over and replaced the physical and mental satisfaction of the going up, as I stood in the sky, looking down at the ocean all around.

The rain arrived suddenly, with clouds jumping the top of Mount Terevaka. Fumes of sulphur were rising from the grassy slopes, making breathing a chore. I dumped my pack on the ground and fought with the wind to erect my tent. The sun set between clouds on the ocean, while I smiled to no one, happy to be on my own in the middle of such a weird and wonderful nowhere.

Rapa Nui had been a magic first episode for my third summit. I had had the opportunity to let my thoughts wander and unite themselves into a rising excitement for the climb ahead, and it had allowed me to keep working on my fitness as well. Back home, I had been training with Maureen, walking up tracks at Arapiles with increasingly heavy packs, and as much as I hated training as a concept, I had to admit that it had worked: I was a strong little thing. I charged on towards Aconcagua, my mountain, touching my next continent in Chile, on my way to Argentina.

8 December 1989, Santiago, letter to Jon

Hello darling,

Not easy to write to you, as it means opening my shell to feelings, and therefore make myself vulnerable to the outside world. Well, here I am in Santiago on the eve of the first demo-cratic election in a long time. There is excitement in the air, but people don't look like they will become violent over the issue. And just as well I spent time studying Spanish before leaving – at the restaurant last night I ordered a lasagne and ended up with a mixed salad!

Big town, with an atmosphere a bit like Melbourne, but with ten times more people it seems! I have to get out of here, I don't want to be in a big city. I hope I'll get on a bus tomorrow to Mendoza.

I remember the last word I heard before we got cut off on the phone: relax!

Well, I am relaxed. I had a wonderful time on Easter Island and I have got it together for travelling: fifty-five kilos, all neatly packed in three easy-to-carry containers. People are really nice and helpful – no shit to deal with like in India!

I can't wait to be in the mountains, where everything will be in my hands, and I'll be able to feel at home and know where all my things are!

Love,
Brigitte

11 December 1989, Mendoza, note to Jon

Jon,

Mendoza on a sticky Monday afternoon. I am experiencing Argentinian hospitality, and believe me, it is quite something! On the bus from Santiago I was invited by a little old lady to stay at her place. I thought, *Right, a lonely widow.* Not at all! I ended up in an incredible slum-like place, full of kids and dogs, with a fat husband spread on the sofa watching a blurred black-and-white television. All very nice, mind you. Still, I was wondering how the hell to get out of there quickly and politely. The old lady, Delia, turned out to be a good fairy. She took me over the road into a castle (almost), where people spoke English. So, I have been staying at the Jukowezyks – a lovely family. They have been stuffing me with meat and sightseeing. Tonight Sami, the nephew who speaks English, takes me to the Andinista Club, where I hope you will find this. Apparently the Andinista Club will give me all kinds of useful information. If all goes well, I should catch a bus to Puente del Inca on Wednesday (13 December). I saw the mountain on the bus trip here – it is *big*! The only thing I could see at the end of a rocky valley. *Wow* country!

Love,
Brigitte

Last hugs to the Jukowezyks, last waves through the bus window. I sat beside a European-looking guy. 'Where are you from?' The usual polite finding out of superficial backgrounds. I told him I was from Belgium, now Australia, and living close to a town in western Victoria he probably wouldn't have heard of. 'Horsham? I was born there!' The other two western-looking passengers on our bus happened to be from Belgium. Hard to get away from backgrounds.

In the books I had read on the subject, Mendoza was always described as an oasis in the middle of a dusty desert. In reality the desert was far from being a desert, with little towns scattered along the main road linking Mendoza and Chile, and tourists from all over South America visiting the area, which was renown for its ski resorts, mountains and mind-blowing wines. As far as I was concerned, it was paradise on earth. It was so exciting to be discovering a new country, a new continent, on my own. That beautiful mountain piercing the sky, always on my mind.

A huge man wearing a sombrero and a three-day growth met me as I got out of the bus in Puente del Inca. I had organised the transport of my gear to Base Camp by mule through a small company in Mendoza, and I guess he got my description from them, because there was no doubt in his eyes when he picked up all my bags at once. So I trotted behind him, past the posh hotel, to a small, shapeless mud-brick building with junk surrounding its mostly windowless walls. It was called the Parador del Inca. The inside was as warm as the outside was repulsive. There was even a pool table in the lobby! I wouldn't get bored. Two hours later, after a copious meal of steak and steak, I beat a young German climber in a game full of rebounds on the buckled table. I took it as a good omen and went to sleep with my heart at peace.

I woke up with a headache. Ho hum. Altitude problems at 2700 metres . . . what kind of an omen was that one? My bags went up to Base Camp all the same. I would catch up with them a day later.

The sun hadn't risen yet. As I approached the start of the path leading up the Horcones Valley, the sun's rays timidly touched the mountains, stretching velvety golden fingers on their grassy slopes. The South Face of Aconcagua shone fiercely in the distance, blanking my mind. I could only see the top third of its 3000-metre-high wall, and shivered in anticipation; Jon, Geoff and I were to attempt its ascent in the New Year, and it looked very serious indeed.

My aversion to torrent crossing had helped me overcome

my hatred of early starts; the Horcones River had the reputation of being the hardest part of the climb of the Normal Route on Aconcagua, and an early crossing was recommended to avoid the deep waters caused by snow melting high on the mountains. When I reached the other side, knees trembling with cold and adrenalin, I knew that nothing, at least in theory, could stop me now.

It was a long walk from Puente del Inca at 2700 metres to Plaza de Mulas at 4200 metres. Forty-two kilometres that most people did in two stages. I was flying on the dry landscape. I walked on and on and on, along the immensity of an ancient glacial valley. It was all stones and desolation, beautiful in its isolation and savagery of colour. The mountains on either side of the flat valley bed ran rivers of red, purple and ochre rocks in the corners of my eyes.

Plaza de Mulas, twelve hours up the track, was nestling on the lateral moraine of a slowly rolling glacier. It wasn't a very cheerful place, what with the wind sweeping up bits of rubbish. Garlands of used toilet paper welcomed me as I put up my tent. Snow soon started to fall, lazily covering the dusty rocks and sad-looking muddy puddles. Someone was busy digging a latrine for future campers, there was a restaurant where you could buy hot dogs and beer, and already zillions of tents spread over the bottom of the Normal Route. Water was scarce and of dubious quality. Ironically the main danger in climbing Aconcagua would be Delhi Belly.

I was fighting with a stubborn stove when someone knocked on my tent door: 'Tea?' Giustino was Italian, and a little lonely. He had a lot to say, in a happy-go-lucky mix of Italian, Spanish, French and gesticulation. 'What is it like up there?' His hands talked of wind, cold and screes. We liked the same music and scratched our heads together over the stove, which was acting more like a raging wood fire than a well-behaved, dependable cooking implement. It was nice to have a fire to warm up the desolate surroundings of Base Camp, but I couldn't see myself lighting it inside my microscopic nylon tent higher on the mountain. Ominous thoughts were creeping to the surface, voices from my chicken-self: *Well, I'll just have to wait until the rest of the team arrives, and get Geoff to have a look at it . . . Hoy!*, said the other me, *What kind of attitude is this? You are here to climb this mountain on your own, woman, and you will.*

The beep-beep of my alarm just wouldn't stop. Yuk. That time of day. I lit the fire and brewed some stiff coffee. Three cups later, I was raring to go. The sun hit the camp at around ten a.m. Before it did, the temperature was far from tropical. Giustino gave me a hug and wished me 'whales', which is Italian for goodbye and good luck. He was on his way down, running out of time. I switched my walkman on and charged upwards. The ground was far from being exciting, scree after scree after scree, but then what was I so thrilled about kilometre after kilometre? The sky was blue, the air crisp, the music beautiful. The mountains around shone in the morning sun, and I was out to accomplish something satisfying. The tedious going was the last thing on my mind! I was home, exploring my own physical and mental landscape, further and further into the unknown, where questions lay that I knew I had the resources to answer. Fourteen years of mountaineering had not turned me into a super climber, but at least now I had a gut feeling of what was right and what was wrong.

After listening to a couple of cassettes, I was there. 'There' being Campo Antartida, 1000 metres higher up on the altitude ladder. I hid some food and gear and ran back to Base Camp delights.

Giustino's tent had gone, and I felt a little lonely. Strange, when at times I had thought he was intruding on me. I was definitely antisocial after he left – I needed some time and space alone, and couldn't compromise . . . I didn't want to become the focus of social attraction as 'the girl who climbs alone'. I yearned to be alone with the mountain, and acted as if I were.

I even managed to fix my stove, and was then able to consider going up to stay at Campo Antartida. I was tremendously excited, trembling all over as I packed to leave. I guess it was plain fear of the unknown, and it lasted until I got moving, then bliss engulfed me. It was a cold morning. I danced up the scree on Vivaldi's music. Suddenly, the camp was in sight. The last, last switchback, *Come on baby, you can do it, yes.* I shivered all over when I heard the crunch of the snow under my boots and flattened it into a platform. Pack off, tent out, tent up, secured, pack in, stove out, pot out, snow in, stove on, cup ready. Blindfolded, hands tied behind my back, it would have happened all the same. I had acquired a few automatisms during all those years of mountain climbing. It was all a question of survival: looking after yourself and your partners, if you had any, was a priority if you wanted to last the distance to the summit and back.

Up and down I went, scrutinising myself for signs of altitude problems. At last my food was in position at Campo Berlin, the last camp before the summit attempt. The place must have been attacked by bombers dropping rubbish bags by the loadful – garbage desecrated the landscape. The site was sprinkled by a cover of volcanic stones melted into distorted images. Knowing a big clean-up operation was under way was reassuring in light of the view . . . and the smells. Fortunately, it was often too cold for the smells to materialise.

'Your husband has arrived,' someone told me on the scree overlooking Base Camp. I didn't know if I was happy or not about the news. I knew the team had been due to arrive, but had clung to my time as a loner, enjoying its intensity and permanence. When I saw Jon walking up to meet me, a big smile split my face. I could deal with it, after all. Jon had walked to Base Camp ahead of everybody, jumping off the truck which had carted the team to Puente del Inca, and heading off in the middle of the night in the general direction of the mountain. That's dedication.

I set off on my summit bid after a couple of days of utter indulgence. Having someone to say goodbye to made it a little harder to concentrate on the time ahead. Happy memories linked me to the past of the last few days.

———

I remember arriving at Campo Berlin, where there was a little snow. I remember the wind aggressing the tent, the knot in my stomach as a grey light pierced the orange walls of my secure nylon fortress. Listening to the movements in a tent nearby. Suddenly I was up, starting on the last leg of my journey. The fear of getting lost, the breath short. The rhythm setting in, like a forgotten miracle. Music was still filling my head and it gave my day an uplifting force. I gradually overtook everyone on the track except a strong Japanese climber. I offered a lolly to yet another Japanese climber, this one shuffling a mountain bike on the last scree to the summit ridge. That last scree, the Canaletta, was a nightmare scree come true in the rarefied air. Every step up had a price, and that was a step down. As vertical and unstable as you could possibly not wish. What a Christmas day that was. A last effort pushed me onto the summit ridge, for a peep down the dreaded South Face. *Aaaargh!* A gigantic snow wave was deferling on the glacier, 3000 metres below. It was an awesome sight, one which made me think about what it would be like seen from the bottom, the serac wall of the wave's belly.

There was a cross on the rocky top. The Japanese climber I will never know by name shook my hand, we took a few shots of each other and he departed. I was left alone on top of the highest mountain in South America. I walked a few steps around the large sloping expanse, looked towards the Pacific Ocean and burst into tears.

———

Plaza de Mulas resembled the Tower of Babel. An incredible mix of Eastern Europeans, South Americans, North Americans, Kiwis and others occupied tents behind every available nook and cranny. With the arrival of Jon, Geoff and Maureen my tranquil little camp had turned into a four-person base and the magic circle of stones protecting my space was surrounded by an expedition organised by the Australian army, literally.

Jon set off one night to climb the Normal Route on his

own in a day. I watched the light of his headtorch disappear high on the scree. A star had left the sky to meet the mountain. As for me, I was quite happy holidaying for a while – New Year's Eve was just around the corner, and there was no way I was going to miss the party at Base Camp. It started with a flag-raising ceremony, with all the army boys, including Field Marshall Muir and Krondorff, Jon's teddy dog, standing behind the mast and singing 'Waltzing Matilda' in manly voices. They then stumbled their way through 'Advance Australia Fair', and the ceremony of toasting finally started. Someone had been magnanimous enough to buy a slab of beer cans, at five US dollars apiece, thank you! As the evening went on, spirits rose, and just after midnight, army and civilians alike, brothers in arms, invaded a nearby tent of Argentinian guides who were quietly celebrating the New Year with food and wine. It was not to last. We brought the music in, threw the tables out and showed the sedate old world how to have fun the Aussie way. Arm-wrestles succeeded frantic dancing until the early hours of the morning, when a polite Japanese climber camped nearby asked us if we would please turn the music down. We collapsed in bed, covered in sweat and dust from the dancing stampede.

Argentinians are happy people. Their country was in a mess, politically and economically, but this did not dampen their spirit. Ruben was a classic example. He had a tiny shop in Mendoza where he fixed televisions for a meagre wage, while his wife made ends meet by working at the local supermarket. Ruben took a punt on the foreign tourist trade, bought a few expensive mules and hired a caravan to live in Puente del Inca. Jon and I met him at Plaza Francia, then at Puente del Inca, where we were refuelling on steak and beer before attacking the South Face of Aconcagua. The evening we spent with him was full of laughter despite the fact that he didn't speak English and Jon didn't understand Spanish. A few of his mules had broken loose never to be seen again, he explained, but still he was going on. Those moments of happy communication I treasure more than summits. I wonder sometimes if climbing is not an excuse to roam the world looking for kindred spirits.

———

A force deep inside made me feel like running away. The South Face of Aconcagua was *awesome*. Geoff, Jon and I spent hours looking at its glaciers pulsating on unknown rhythms, discarding avalanches of snow and ice with apocalyptic clamour. Plaza Francia, the South Face Base Camp, was a busy place: young French hotshots who aimed to climb the South Face in a day, and ran off at the first snowflakes; Argentinians dropped by helicopters who charged off as soon as they were on foot; and Thomas Bubbendorf, an Austrian hero complete with reporters, cameramen and groupies, made up the crowd. Thomas Bubbendorf wanted to solo the face in one day, as he had carved his reputation by completing such stunts. He was nice enough, though, enjoying our uncomplicated company at times. I remember once when we offered him some salami he replied, 'Beautiful, a good change from the cordon bleu cuisine.' You bet. We had salvaged the salami from a rubbish tip on the way to the face, along with an opened carton of white wine crawling with ants. This we polished off on the spot, fishing the ants out as we went along. We had been walking on air after that. When a dog had run away with the salami at our next camp, we had retrieved it after a growling fight, washed it and declared it fit for consumption.

The dogs. I must say more about the dogs. There was a horde of them, based in Puente del Inca and roaming the mountains. They always walked up with climbers on the Normal Route, stopping when they stopped, starting when they started again, leading parties right to the top. The fiery mob we met was accompanied by apprentices, and they were on their way back from Plaza Francia. Horcones was one of them. I had grown used to seeing him adorned with pink ribbons, courtesy of the Parador del Inca's owner's daughter, and I must say he looked very much out of place in the great outdoors. He felt that way, I think, as he spent the night cuddling up in my sleeping bag before heading off down the valley, his tail between his legs. I felt inclined to follow him.

One can only procrastinate for so long in front of a fearsome mountain. We managed to waste a couple of days observing the contours of the South Face through Thomas's powerful telescope, then one morning there were no more excuses, it was time to start. I understood then the way soldiers must feel when sent to a certain slaughter. Wobbly knees, stomach in knots, heavy pack on the back, and the mountain getting closer at every step. Eventually we bumped into it, clipped on some flimsy fixed ropes and grovelled up an unstable conglomerate of rocks. The next obstacle was a scree steeper than the Canaletta, and far shiftier. 'A walk! Didn't Thomas say it was a walk to Camp One?' We must have lost it somewhere: the ground we were on was anything but a walk. As we were climbing unroped, a mistake here would have meant death. We traversed on horrendous rock pudding, soloed up unspeakable shambles, haunted by the reality of danger. Jon and Geoff, being tough and strong, piled up a bunch of icicles on top of their already huge loads, as we had been told that there was no water available at Camp One. As soon as we reached the camp it started to snow heavily, solving the water problem and making the boys pull their hair in frustration. After studying previous climb reports, we had decided that a tiny Fairydown Assault tent would be sufficient, with two of us sleeping inside and one person outside in a bivvy bag. As it turned out, we encountered terrible weather and ended up squeezing the three of us in the tent, sardine fashion, for days on end.

We spent twelve days on the mountain instead of the usual six days estimated for an ascent in good conditions. Snow fell almost incessantly, provoking numerous avalanches and making us jump out of our skin each time we heard the loud bangs announcing their arrival. When snow was falling we stayed in our camp and did not eat, or not much: a few dry crackers, a cup of soup, recycled tea bags held together by dental floss. Then the weather would clear for a while and we'd be on our way, negotiating horrendously loose slopes and treacherous gullies, usually climbing for eighteen hours without stopping, and when we stopped, it was not always in the most suitable of spots.

Our last day up took us to the bottom of the hundred-metre-high serac cutting the south face at the two-third point, and what a lovely day it was: slopes of sharp ice blades, sometimes more than one metre high, buried in soft snow; steep granite with poor protection and blanketed by unstable snow; spindrift avalanches and alarming ice screams from the serac just above our heads. To top it all, darkness fell right at the foot of it, and we had to make do for the night sitting on a small snow ledge cut into the slope, with incessant avalanches trying to push us off our perch and send us tumbling down to hit the glacier 2000 metres below. Our gear had become wet and we shivered all night, praying to the gods to be kind to us and let us get out of this hell alive. When first light arrived I looked up towards Jon from where Geoff and I had been huddled, romantic thoughts the last thing on our mind. Jon had been leading when we had been forced to stop the previous night, and his night spot had been about ten metres above ours, under a too-small-for-safety overhang. A sizeable snow mount occupied the space where Jon had last been seen, and soon the mount exploded from the inside with Jon, beaming, his moustache white with icicles, his hands sending kisses in my direction: 'Happy Valentine's Day, Brigitte!' It was indeed 14 February.

We did the only thing we could do. We had no food left, the weather was not improving, we still had a thousand metres of hard climbing in front of us. We came down. Easier said than done. It took three days of delicate manoeuvring to reach the glacier at the foot of the South Face. Fear, which had been a constant companion for the twelve days we spent on the mountain, finally left us and, completely exhausted, we wandered down the glacier, hallucinating. 'Well,' said my superhero husband, 'that was the hardest climb I have ever done.' Which made me quite proud to have been part of it.

Kosciuszko –
Paradise Lost

We left Aconcagua a few days later, thrilled to have done our very best in atrocious conditions, and to have returned alive, with all fingers and toes. It was then, happily sauntering down the track back to Puente del Inca, that I came up with the idea of trying to complete the Seven Summits within the next year. Ticking off number four, Kosciuszko – more a bush walk than an arduous climb – would be a formality, and that would only leave another three summits: I could go to Elbrus in September '90, to Antarctica in December, and to Everest during the next pre-monsoon season, in April–May '91. Jon was keen to join me and had some ideas on how to finance the rest of my Seven Summits quest. He had met a Melbourne couple during the time I had spent in Africa, a husband-and-wife team of corporate video makers. They had shown an interest in filming an adventure documentary, and it was to them we turned when we arrived back in Australia.

We met Anne and Wayne Tindall at their Big Time Media office in front of Hawksburn Station in Melbourne, a very convenient location as we did not have a car and did all our travelling by thumb or public transport. I remember being a little shy, slightly intimidated by the exotic furnishings and the huge paintings on the walls. I really felt like a country bumpkin on a mission in the big city. To my surprise, Anne and Wayne jumped at the opportunity to get involved in a mountaineering adventure with a human interest – and female at that, and possibly commercially viable. *Against All Odds* became the working title of the project.

Wayne, the creative genius of the couple, was tempted by the concept of a television series with a coffee-table book to accompany its release. 'Good,' said Anne, who looked after the production side of the business, 'Wayne has always wanted to write a book.' It was also then that Sherry Stumm, a Sydney-based public relations expert who had been recommended to me (by Sorrel Wilby, a photojournalist Jon had met on his successful Everest expedition in '88), came on board to help me secure sponsors.

I was elated to have people helping me raise money. Jon and I had booked places with a French group going to Everest in '91, and to pay the non-refundable deposit we had had to borrow money from our bank, which would only loan it to us if we had a guarantor. Keith and Sally Lockwood, old friends from Natimuk, agreed to be our guarantors, but we had to find a huge sum for the next down payment, and needed all the help we could get. Gone were the days of grape picking, scrimping and saving. With the film solution came the problem of big budgeting, and with the last two summits – Vinson and Everest – lurking ahead, the entry into the world of major expedition finance. Sherry sent me a five-year contract to look at. To get some perspective on things, as well as to do what we loved most, we packed our rucksacks and hitchhiked to Albury, where we were to meet a few friends invited on the Kosciuszko 'expedition'.

———

I opened an eye. Jon was busy with the stove, heating water for coffee in bed. How wonderful. The sky was clear above, and the screech of black cockatoos added to my feeling of well-being. 'Coffee?' asked my delightful husband.

'Sure. What time are we leaving, do you think?'

'How about when we're ready?'

'Sounds good to me!'

Kangaroos emerged from the thick layer of mist covering the huge meadow of Geehi Flats, ears flickering, heads turning this way and that, and dived back in to graze more breakfast grass. Bodies were starting to come back to life, quite an achievement after last night's excesses. It felt rather strange to be mixing my Seven Summits quest with a typical Australian rock-climbing outing. The friends who came with us were all primarily Jon's mates: James Falla, his best friend; Ant Prehn, his oldest friend; Nick Hunt, his newest friend. Karyn, James's girl-friend, and I were the odd addition to what promised to be a boys' own adventure. At the same time, they felt like a support team to my own quaint quest of climbing the highest mountain in Australia. The image of Dorothy and her merry band en route to Oz danced in my mind.

I scanned the sky again, half hoping to hear it desecrated by the roar of a helicopter. Sherry had promised she'd do her best to tempt Channel Ten into covering the ascent, as media interest was alluring to potential sponsors. Nothing. I was disappointed that they had found better things to spend their time and money on, and that this little climb would not serve to further 'the cause'. But I was somewhat relieved, too, as we'd be totally free to be ourselves, without cameras to record our behaviour.

Geehi Flats, at the intersection of the Swampy Plain River and the Alpine Way, was the official departure point for the ascent of Hannels Spur, a long, forested ridge which had once held a bridle trail. It led to high alpine meadows covering the upper reaches of the continent, and offered the biggest vertical gain in the country, with Geehi Flats lying at about 500 metres, and the top of Kosciuszko soaring into the great Australian sky at 2228 metres. We packed our gear, lashed our packs onto our backs, and ambled up the road to the start of the trail proper. The boys acted like schoolboys on camp. So-called grown men, at least the ones I knew, seemed to have that kind of reaction when released in the bush, as if normal life did not allow them the freedom to unleash the child in them. I had a quiet giggle as I followed carefully across the river and up towards the forest.

The smell of eucalyptus oil dilated by the late summer heat pervaded the green twilight of the undergrowth. Red and white fairytale mushrooms poked their shiny hats through the deep mulch covering the steep ground. Huge tree trunks shot through high boughs to hold, it seemed, the ceiling of the white sky above. In Europe I would go to cathedrals when I felt like being in a forest, as their naves, with high pillars so similar to trees, reminded me of the original worship groves of my pagan ancestors. In Australia, I simply went to the High Country. The huge forests covering the slopes were temples to everyone's God, or gods, and in this country lacking in centuries-old buildings soaked in faith, they gave me the peace, love and understanding that my old-world sanctuaries had provided.

That I should be able to enjoy such pristine surroundings – and a feeling of ownership, and of being owned by my country wilderness – while in the course of duty, ticking off number four summit, was an absolute delight. Here and there, wombat holes appeared on the trail, and we'd get on our knees and peer inside. 'Do you know how wombats get rid of foxes if they get inside their burrows?' someone asked. 'They get in backwards, and squash them against the walls with their bottoms!' I still don't know if it's true, but if it is, it sure is an interesting way to eradicate pests!

One thousand metres up the spur, the forest opened into a welcome clearing of lanky grass, and a discreet sign pointed to water nearby. We were sweaty from the climb, ready to call it quits for the day. We established camp, gathered water and dry wood for a fire, and someone found a bottle of whisky at the bottom of their pack. Bush animals had to stick their earplugs in that night as we sat late in the bubble of fireglow, swapping stories and laughs. The boys climbed a summit too, managing to fit the four of them on top of a cubic-foot-sized rock by the blazing logs!

Kosciuszko is the highest point of the Australian continent. Sounds simple and straightforward, but it's actually a point of contention. Since Dick Bass, the millionaire American, was the first to complete the climb of the highest mountain on each continent, a quest which others had entered before him, controversy over the highest mountain on the Australian continent has reigned in the world of mountaineering. Pat Morrow, a Canadian climber, was racing Bass for the honour of being the first to complete climbs of the Seven Summits, and when Bass beat him to it he came up with the idea that Australia was really not a continent, but that Australasia was, and therefore, Carstenz Pyramid in Irian Jaya was its highest summit. It seems Morrow's theory ignores established definitions of *continent* as one of seven major land masses – Europe, Asia, Africa, North America, South America, Australia and Antarctica. What's more, Carstenz does not lie on the Australian Continental Shelf; it is on the Philippine Plate of Asia, separated from the Australian Plate by the Java Trench. And politically, Irian Jaya is part of Indonesia and Asia.

Well, I wasn't racing anyone, and there was no way I was going to Irian Jaya and its forest full of mosquitoes to be continually drenched by downpours, all to climb a summit which was not even on the continent. Kosciuszko was it, and Morrow's theories seemed fundamentally flawed. Besides, the Seven Summits was a totally artificial and subjective goal, anyway. It was something one did to see the world, to get satisfaction from persistence and hard work, to have fun and to be in the mountains. The fact that the Seven Summits as a concept captures so many people's imaginations, in all walks of life, is something which still remains a bit of a mystery to me. But then, anything comprising travel to foreign and sometimes remote parts and the excitement of achieving something measurable is bound to always attract and intrigue. The real reason the Seven Summits has become the quest of so many people not even remotely connected to climbing is that it has become a goal made available to them through commercial guiding companies. It has also been a goal appealing to all of us suffering some kind of identity crisis – from getting over the mid-life crisis to, in my case, finding a way to integrate myself in a new country and a new way of life.

26 May 1990, Moira's Flat

> There is that anguish I live with. Only in my early memories as a child is it not there. A tangle of guilt at the idea that I am enjoying myself and of fear that something bad and nasty may suddenly happen because of it. I am still a stranger in this land. One does not need a black skin to be treated differently. I believe it is hard to relate to a different culture, especially when it seems to be the same in so many ways as the one one has left behind. Thank God for the trees. They feel like home all over the world.

We left the trees the morning after, to find ourselves in thick scrub dotted with enormous boulders. These had to be climbed, of course, and the boys leapt from one to the other, playing king of the castle and brandishing stick swords. After they had exhausted their excitement at the new landscape, and as soon as we had partaken of the chocolate offerings, we force-marched our way through the dense bush section and stopped at Byatt's Camp, another clearing near the foot of Mount Townsend – at 2209 metres the second-highest mountain in Australia.

Mist was hanging about the summits when I started hopping from rock to rock towards the top of Townsend. I had to, for once in this quest, climb the second-highest peak, if not in the world, at least on the continent! I had left alone, to clear the cobwebs in my head, and to better feel my connection with this great land. Since we had left the forest the horizon had dramatically opened, and we had found ourselves in the centre of a blue expanse of hills, endless under the soft light of May. I had needed my own adventure to a summit, away from the noisy joy of our group. I reached the top and swiftly returned to camp to avoid being swallowed by the descending mist. This cleared later, enticing Jon, James and Nick to follow in my footsteps and climb Townsend. 'Well,' announced Jon, when he descended from their successful summit bid, 'I am sorry to say so, but you climbed the wrong mountain!' Indeed. In the partial white-out I had not noticed that Townsend was still above me, and had summited Abbott Peak instead!

The next day was scheduled as our summit D-day, and the tentative plan was to spend the night on the summit. Our spirits were therefore high as we tramped past a string of clear lakes and headed for the final slopes of Kosciuszko.

The rounded ridge roller-coastered towards the sky, climbing higher into its folds. There were rock spines poking through the short grass, and ephemeral flowers waving in the wind. There was also a narrow, truncated concrete pyramid marking the top. Not the nicest summit shrine, but one which did not leave any doubt of the fact — I was on top of Kosciuszko, summit number four, and it was 28 May 1990, the second anniversary of Jon's climb of Everest.

We ran from boulder to boulder, gazing at the innumerable summits below . . . I think this was one of the rare times when I actually managed to savour a view from a summit without having to worry about the difficulties of coming down the mountain! Especially, of course, as we were not going anywhere that night. We pitched our tents nearby, and concentrated once more on 'wowing' about the view. The sunset was spectacular — a fitting backdrop to our little celebration party.

Jon was more excited than I was, I think, maybe because I wasn't used to sharing my summits with larger groups, and could not let emotion flow. Jon and I had never spent the night on top of a high mountain in Australia, and we had an incredible impression of height on Kosciuszko, something we hadn't expected. The shadow of the mountain was surprisingly impressive cast across the landscape, but particularly awesome cast into the atmosphere, like you see at sunrise or sunset on the big mountains of the world. That was the first time we'd seen that on a non-glaciated mountain.

It probably was also the only time we had chocolate stolen from right under our noses on a summit. The offender was a sweet-toothed fox, spotted trotting away with silver foil waving from its jaws.

———

Kosciuszko had been a good break from the realities of making my quest happen on mountains overseas, and it had rekindled my interest in the Australian wilderness, as well as the need to return to its high reaches. I loved the tree-clad hills of the High Country, and was inspired to spend a lot of time over the next few years losing myself in their midst, either on my own or with dear friends. Sharing in small groups, rather than going for the more superficial amusement of large parties.

Now, though, it was time to get back to the grinder. I had a few expeditions to make happen. I was still hoping that Everest might take place before the end of the year, and Anne and I were investigating the costs of going to Elbrus and Antarctica. With our association with Big Time Media also came the prospect of co-writing a book on the Seven Summits quest with Wayne, and I set myself the task of remembering, and writing in a language that was not the one I had grown up with.

25 June 1990, Natimuk

Writing about my own past involves time travelling. To remember is to be once again the Brigitte I was earlier in the canvas of my life. This does not happen without being deeply affected by the people, places and states of mind conjured by remembering. The inconsistency in the interaction of time and space will always boggle my mind. The two elements certainly are not linear.

I read, I read, I read. With the hope that, if I read enough, the art of simple words will sink into my pen.

Chasing media coverage also claimed a fair amount of my time and energy. It was exciting to have the interest of the press, and I gave myself to newspapers, magazines, radio and television programmes, in the hope that someone out there would notice my quest, and be inspired enough to get the chequebook out. Unfortunately, the interest stopped at the curiosity of the unusual; once money was mentioned, people were not curious any more. I remember approaching a women's clothing company based in Melbourne with a full-size sponsorship proposal, outlining the potential advantages to sponsors, and the world firsts that completing my quest would create. I received by return mail a plastic shopping bag sporting the name of the company, with a letter stating that if I brought back a picture of myself holding the bag on top of Everest, I would receive a two hundred dollar gift purchase voucher!

One thing I had decided to draw a line at was the signing of long-term contracts. I understood that Sherry Stumm needed the safety and legality of the written word, but I felt incredibly uncomfortable at the idea of binding myself to any commitment for what was, in my mind, such a long time.

26 July 1990, Natimuk

The beauty of mechanical work. It occurred to me while I was knitting. Thinking, knitting, thinking, knitting . . . I like to have the freedom to think when I have to work, and I always work so that my daydreams can take shape in the reality of hard cash. Work and money have always been a means, not an end – ever since I was a student slaving at night and on weekends behind supermarket check-outs. That's the way it is. I will never ever spend my life slaving away accumulating riches for my retirement. I'd rather be poor, happy and alive, and find comfort in the beauty of my surroundings.

Strangely enough, I find my situation has changed. My dream is turning into a marketable commodity – necessary if it is to become a reality. A sacrilege, if you ask me, but there is a fine line between aborted dream and lucidity. I am becoming a marketable item. I will be wary, to make sure I retain as much independence as I can. No five-year contract for my peace of mind.

Everest did not happen. We lost the deposit money, and kept repaying the loan from the bank out of our dole cheque. All was not lost, though, as Anne managed to secure funding to send us to Elbrus through a Seven Summits coffee-table book deal (which, incidentally, never eventuated due to scepticism over its marketability and the difficulty in imposing a time frame for a book on a quest not yet completed), which would pay for Jon and me, as well as for a film and still camera crew to travel to the Soviet Union in September.

14 August 1990, Natimuk
Do I believe it yet? Someone will have to put a boarding pass in my hand before I realise that I am, at long last, on the road again. I do not know if my cynicism stops me from listening to that little voice saying *it's on, it's on, it's on.* But I have noticed an intensity of colours, shapes and smells which can only mean I am mentally preparing for a departure. Oh. I started training too, riding into the wind on my 1944 model ladies' bicycle.

Six months ago, we were at the highest of our epic on the south face of Aconcagua. Where will we be in six months' time? I guess there is nothing that incredible in being involved in the making of a television series. Some people do it all the time.

Anne and Wayne were up to their eyeballs in pre-series fever. They organised a photographer, Jonathan Chester, who had been recommended by the book publisher, and a cameraman, Glen Singleman, to travel with us to the USSR, where Elbrus lay. Wayne was to come as well, to direct and to help Glen with the filming. In fact, they would be in Leningrad, our expedition departure point, a few days ahead of us. Jon and I were sponsored by Thai Airways International. The airline's closest destination in Europe was Helsinki, so we decided to spend a couple of days in Finland before catching the train to Leningrad and meeting the boys.

It was wonderful to have a team to work with, as for once, I was not the only one possessed with the idea of making the Seven Summits happen. My quest had captured the imagination of a few good people who threw all they had into it and made me feel that, although it had started as a personal enterprise, the Seven Summits was fast becoming the building stone on which mountains of faith, growth and friendship would be built.

Elbrus –

Stars in the USSR

The fireweeds had lost their fire. Under a grey sky, birch trees were still flashing green lights through the train windows, but there was a certain feel of winter around the corner. Men and women, at the slow pace of the end of the working day, were walking in heavy boots along earth paths beside the railway tracks. We passed villages of little old wooden houses and their overgrown, fenced-off gardens scattered amidst the trees. Elena, a Russian art student on her way home from Sweden, was showing Jon slides of her native Kazakhstan. There were colours of the moss on the rock, shapes of tall hills and barren mountains, people picnicking by creeks with horses drinking from the water alongside. It seemed a different land although it was the same country, that almost mythical Soviet Union that we had just entered. I still couldn't believe where I was; everything had a dream-like quality.

I had called Alpinist, the company organising our trip, from our hotel in Helsinki, to tell Vladimir Balyberdin, its director, that we were arriving in Leningrad by train that day. A woman had answered. She didn't speak English; I didn't understand Russian. We had giggled to each other and that was that. How do you say *help* in Russian?

We rode past fewer trees, and a lot of square, bland buildings. More people, too, standing motionless at intersections and stations, and dusty, anonymous old cars. Darkness had fallen upon the unknown. The train finally stopped under the lights of an empty station. 'Do you think Wayne will be here?'

'Sure'.

I volunteered to sit on the luggage while Jon walked off in the drizzle, armed with his only Russian word, *vodka*, to find Wayne Tindall, our film director. Two men were making their way towards him. Both athletic types, they could well have been envoys from our agency, Alpinist, and they were definitely moving with a purpose. Suddenly one of them thrust his hand in his jacket and, with a conspiratory look on his face, pulled out a bottle and apparently whispered in Jon's ear, 'Vodka?'

Alpinist, that is, Vladimir Balyberdin, Soviet Himalayan hero, was waiting for us outside the station. He had booked us into a 'true blue' hotel called the Droushba, meaning 'friendship'. It lacked western sophistication but provided us with insight into the Russian way of life. 'Horrowshow!', we all chanted as we entered the dull rooms, which sounded like the Russian for *good*.

We were really in the Soviet Union! The day started briskly with a queue for breakfast. Irina, our interpreter, joined us. From the glimmer in the boys' eyes when they had mentioned her, I had gathered she was beautiful – which she was . . . and witty, and intelligent, and cultured.

After the breakfast formality it was time for the young western climbing couple to discover the beauties of Peter the Great's city. Wayne, Glen and Jonathan had arrived two days earlier and had concocted a 'see-it-all-in-ten-hours' tour, which took us to all the landmarks – the Winter Palace, the Hermitage, the Admiralty, St Isaac's Cathedral, the Church of Blood, the main drag, and Griffins Bridge. The winter light enhanced the façades of the centuries-old palaces, admiring their own features in the mirrors of contemporary channels.

A 16-mm movie camera, a Hi-8 video camera, seven still cameras and a sound recorder were buzzing under our noses – not the most discreet way to enter a strange new world. 'Your first impressions of Leningrad?!'. A kaleidoscope of colours, shapes and materials versus a cameo of dirt and *niets*. And with the spotlight following us wherever we went, the feeling of being a circus poodle walking on its front legs in a sawdust circle. Maybe I wasn't yet in the skin of my character, that 'me' they were filming and partly inventing. It was a confusing situation.

As a leaving-Leningrad treat, Alpinist had booked a dinner table for us at the Intourist Restaurant. How exciting, anything but Droushba cuisine! Everybody piled into the school bus, which had been one of our taxis in Leningrad, and off we drove into the northern night, to find ourselves in a Russia we hadn't experienced yet.

Dimmed lights, soft music, a banquet table, smoked salmon, grape pyramids, caviar, champagne bottles, heavenly smells welcomed us. It was too good to be true. I seem to remember us all diving on whatever was within reach. It was as if we were scared to see it all disappear without notice. Well, in the Soviet Union, do as the Soviets do. We were soon toasting left, right and centre. Now this was fun, notwithstanding the flashes of guilt at the memory of queues outside shops.

After our feast, the lights disappeared altogether and disco music filled the room. Two solid women in ethereal white walked past the table and ambled towards the dance floor, leading a James Bond (vintage James) sequence. Heavy make-up, glamorous contortions, golden smiles. Dancers, singers and magicians took turns under the flickering lights. I saw a few mouths drop in our group, and eyes widened in disbelief. We giggled madly, and ate and drank some more, until it was time for us to stagger back to the comforts of Droushba. The walk home in the colourless city was nicely vague and curious. I went to bed psyched up for breakfast.

As we stepped out of the hotel on our way to the airport, headed for the south of the Union, I counted one too many video cameras waiting for us. Soviet television wanted to interview the famous Australian woman climber! I struggled to keep my face serious. This was too much! Why would a bumbly like me deserve so much attention? Alpinist had organised the meeting as a nifty way to advertise their service. Irina translated while I did my best to answer the usual questions. I almost collapsed in a fit of laughter when the interviewer asked me how a non-professional mountaineer filming team was going to keep up with me. Jonathan choked and turned red. I assured the interviewer they would probably arrive at the top before me. An efficient-looking woman stood in the background. We were introduced to Llena, Alpinist's official secretary. She was a mountaineer. The calm determination in her eyes told me she was a good one.

A huge avalanche in the Pamir had wiped out a camp a few months before. The death toll had been atrocious – forty-two climbers, twenty-three of whom were from Leningrad, had lost their lives. One of them was Llena's husband, another Irina's boyfriend. Both were very strong women, but I couldn't help putting myself in their minds and screaming mentally with helplessness and pain.

'Niet! Niet! Niet!' Llena could say *niet* ('no') like no one else in the world. I quickly learned the 'Da! Da! Da!' answer which always made her smile in the middle of her frowning concentration, then pursue 'Niet!'. Irina spent a lot of time translating our questions and answers. Llena and I were sisters in soul. We climbed for the same reasons, only Llena's intensity was more aggressively expressed, while mine tended to flow with the currents of my life.

The flight in the 'Russian bus' was uneventful, although interesting. I had never seen a dog (calf-size) in the cabin of a plane before. The duty-free episode had its charm, too – second-hand cassettes, archaic computer games, orange plastic salt-and-pepper shakers. It was not so much that the goods for sale were not available from shops; it was the utter luxury of purchasing items from the comfort of a plush seat instead of standing in a queue for hours on end which struck me as the true privilege of the trolley ritual.

We landed in another night, rich in smells, colours and foreign words. This was the south side of the Union. A man was waiting outside the terminal, a rose in his hand. Flowers were present everywhere, to be bought and given. I sighed with nostalgia at this old-world touch. We were loaded into a bus which took us all to the depths of night and exhaustion.

So much happened in so little time. When I think back, the first memory is the smell of a creek bed in the afternoon sun. It was our first day in the Caucasus, and Jon and I were enjoying a few rare hours alone by sharing a walk up a steep hillside. The team had already gone on an organised acclimatisation tour. With my lack of tolerance for group activities, I had welcomed the situation of everybody out hiking in the great outdoors by indulging in a quiet bath with a good book. The pleasure had been short-lived. The hordes of fit climbers who had arrived to participate in a race up Elbrus had exhausted the supply of hot water in the traditional morning ablutions. I had a cat wash in cold water before Jon and I stepped into the outside world. I remember the song of the torrent, the cars driving up and down the dusty road, the pungent smell of fuel. Some young people were waiting at a bus stop beside a sign warning of huge, mean-looking brown bears in the vicinity.

The sun was high in the sky. So was a sharp snow ridge silhouetted at the head of the valley we had chosen. Our first sight of a Caucasus mountain, it glimmered in a hallucinogenic dance with some small clouds, hypnotising the climber in me. I was lusting for a summit, a corner of eternal bliss. Crowded by activity and people, I had forgotten what lived anchored in my heart. We left the road at a small cemetery for mountaineers, and I made a mental note to query the most common cause of death in the hills. The walk was steep, the grass high. I breathed in the smell of the earth, the flowers and the cow dung heated by the autumn sun. We sat in silence here and there to look at the valley.

I felt my fatigue lifting. Jon had caught summit fever, but mine had turned into a need for peace and quietness, so I left him and strolled down the hill. The bear warning sign was flashing at the back of my mind despite continuous attempts to keep my imagination under control. In the trees at the bottom of the spur I met a woman carrying an empty tin. She told me she was picking berries, but that winter was close and the pickings meagre. She didn't speak English. I didn't understand a single word she was saying, although her meaning was obvious. She invited me to taste some berries from a small tree. We smiled. She kept talking softly, her eyes warm. We waved goodbye. Further down, in the twilight of a fir forest, my eye caught sight of some red dots on the ground. Wild strawberries punctuating a sea of green leaves. They were rare and delicious.

The tourist guides all lied. They all talked of delicacies – borsch of all sorts, shashliks and chicken kiev. Maybe those are the delights awaiting the average Intourist customers. Treated like every other Soviet, we sank deeper into despair and hunger. The climbers were laughing, 'In the Soviet Union the food is very bad, we must climb very fast!'

After another *Niet–Da* match with Llena, it was decided that we would skip the usual gradual approach to altitude. We would catch cable cars and chairlifts to 3800 metres, then walk to the hut, the House of Eleven at 4200 metres, and back to our hotel at 1800 metres on the same day. So we joined the queues of tourists and skiers at the terminal. The work team was having a ball. Glen was his usual mad doctor character behind the camera. An interesting combination. And Jonathan. Ha, Jonathan. Never have I seen someone with such a 'click-the-camera' mania. For him, anything went as long as he could take pictures of it. An old hand at expeditions, he carried even more comfort essentials than me. I was impressed.

Wayne couldn't believe his eyes – a solid, sturdy, smiling woman was bouncing in the snow towards his video camera wearing only a tiny bikini bottom. He lost whatever breath he had left and pressed the button, accompanied by a Jonathan staccato of clicks. Soon, though, such sights became rare. The wind picked up the snow in gusts, and the hut disappeared in a white-out. The temperature dropped, and it was easy to understand how some twenty climbers had lost their way on the mountain and died some six months before. Llena and Jon were waiting at the House of Eleven. Like young puppies with itchy paws, they had raced to the hut, Llena in front. ('Wait a minute,' exclaims Jon, reading my memories of the trip. 'She was only one step ahead, and I was just being polite by following her!') 'Quick! Quick!' they said, 'We must hurry, the last cable car leaves in half an hour! Drop the load, run back down.' Was this mountaineering in the USSR? Where would I find time to adjust? Today was the day of the preliminary race from 3500 metres to the hut. A warm-up, they said.

Only so many hours in a day. The plan now was to visit the school of mountaineering, not far from our hotel. I pondered the spirit of organisation and competition amongst Soviet climbers. This was developed in schools like these, where young girls and boys learned to climb on wooden walls and fall from high towers. Llena and I got into a heated discussion about our future movements on the mountain, our talk punctuated by laughter in the cold of the setting night. The creek echoed its symphony in the freezing air. Vladimir took us back to the dining room.

We were getting spoilt. Many runners had volunteered as porters. This was migration day, and tonight home would be in the mountains. I was looking forward to it. I was always looking forward to it, although I was not too sure about sleeping in a three-storey hut. My relation with the mountain needed to be more direct. I would rather lie on the skin of my love. (Well, on a Thermorest.) I did not like the idea of having stairs and walls between us. Moments with the mountains were always too few.

—

The House of Eleven. Built in 1939, the materials were carried up on the backs of bison. The bison are now extinct, but the hut still withstands gale-force winds. Outside, the wind was howling. I was happy. We settled in a small room on the top floor, with the twin summits of Elbrus visible through the frost flowers on the window panes. At last, time to get organised – to give every piece of junk a home, and remember it. Dinner was courtesy of Alpinist and friends. Chicken, soup – no fancy freeze-dried food here, it was all fresh from the farm or the tin, and Russians can carry mountains. The kitchen was a dark den, with the light of a candle silhouetting heads and shoulders while spoons dived in a cacophony of Russian and English. Two Americans had joined the race. I had thought before leaving that it could be fun to participate, but had quickly changed my mind. Vladimir tried to convince me to join, with 'When you are a soldier, you must aim to be the general!'

'I would rather be the general and the army in one person, Vladimir!' I laughed. Competition was not what I sought in the mountains.

The wind, the wind. Only towards morning did we get a little relief from its attacks. Even my earplugs could not stop the furious screams of the gales. 'We film in half an hour!' *Great. I love plenty of notice.* It takes time to swallow the litre of coffee I indulge in every morning. The weather was perfect, but the wind still strong. It was a good day, they said. The runners were attaching numbers to the tops of their outfits. Everybody was wearing crampons, for although the slope was only moderately steep, the Col between the two summits of Elbrus was icy, and a fixed rope had been installed at dangerous points.

Off everyone went, in a flurry of skipoles and cloudy breaths. It became obvious very quickly that the winner would be Anatoli Boukreev. Anatoli had won the event last year. The weather had not allowed a race to the top then, and the finish had been at 4800 metres. Anatoli was addicted to speed and altitude. He lived in Alma Ata and spent his time climbing and teaching cross-country skiing, a good combination for a speed mountaineer. He was also rather mad. That's what he said! While the Russians were having their fun, we played around, getting used to the altitude by going up and down for the camera, waving sponsors' flags and chocolate bars in the wind.

Most people were going back to the hotel for a rest that night and would be back tomorrow afternoon. We decided to use the time to make a carry to the Col. Jon still hoped to go all the way to the top, but I doubted that we would make it – it would take a lot of time to film, and his wish may have been unrealistic.

Departure time was nine in the morning. As usual, I started slowly. I planned it right, the music filling my ears giving me a perfect rhythm. How blissful! Not only were we going up, but the weather was great and the mountain relatively free of crowds. The climb up the icy slopes proved to be delicate, but it was a real pleasure to have to concentrate on the balance of movements. Soon it was time to sit down and have a look around. Nothing is more satisfying than that quiet evaluation of the surroundings and situation. 'Shall we go this way or that way?'; 'How long do you think we will take to get to the Col?'; 'Do you want a drink?'; 'Turn around, I'll take a picture.' I loved the communion with Jon and the mountain. A *ménage à trois* that worked very well!

The West Summit, the one we had come to climb, was too far for today. We dumped the gear behind some rocks, munched a bit and strolled back down. The hut we were headed for looked too tiny for my taste. I hated going down – it was painstaking and dangerous. And I had run out of batteries for my walkman.

Some dots were moving up towards us. Llena, with a smile, her hand ready to shake mine. 'Summit?' *'Niet*, Col'.

'Ow.' She took her hand back, and I felt sad to have disappointed her. I would have liked to offer her the surprise of a summit stolen in her absence. I tried to explain that work – the film – came first. It felt like an excuse.

The rearguard of our team was still far behind, and that suited the lazy sod in me. It meant that tomorrow would be a kind of rest day, while the mad men and women ran their race to the lower summit. I liked the idea. I wanted to get down to a bit of serious cooking, and I wanted to be in top form to go for the summit. A full stomach was essential. I was hopeless without my fuel, food. Unless I did not have a choice!

Anatoli won the race. While I was sipping a coffee, eyes heavy with sleep, dreaming in the orange light of the empty kitchen, Anatoli was running to the top of a mountain. One hour and forty minutes. I was glad it was him. The American came close, one hour and fifty-three minutes, a beautiful performance.

We were making life very complicated for Vladimir and Llena. We just did not fit the mould. We were supposed to have climbed on the day of the race; there would have been plenty of people to help us on the mountain. A pity we liked solitude, eh?

An early start the next morning; the alarm woke us up long before dawn. Jon won this time. I lost patience before he moved, and stumbled downstairs to prepare the coffee ritual. I was very grumpy, but nothing a kiss couldn't fix. While Jon and I sorted out our minor differences, Glen and Jonathan got ready and made for the door. I followed, adjusting my headphones on the way.

Before I realised it, they had become two specks in the distance. I cringed. The music was too fast for my mind in these early hours. Better switch off and listen to the wind. Jon was just behind me. He liked my pace, found it relaxing! A very bad smell hit my nose. I turned back, 'You go ahead, man.'

'No, you're right.'

'Look, stop farting then.'

'I am not!' I sniffed the inside of my windsuit. When was the last time I washed? The smell again. I got it. It was sulphur. Elbrus was a volcano, too easy to forget. The wind reminded us.

The black of our horizon turned into lines and shimmers. Blue, red, orange, yellow glows set the ice slope alight with tiny waves of shadow and coloured gold. We slid effortlessly on a frozen ocean. I did not even know if it was horizontal or vertical. It could have been anywhere in the universe, in any dimension, it could have been yesterday or in ten thousand years. I was absolutely happy in its present.

'Can you do that one more time?' The familiar tune from the cameramen started the day's work, but it was not always easy to 'take two' on the action. Wayne had asked Vladimir to leave the fixed ropes, but only a couple were left. It did not worry us, but we were concerned for Wayne's safety – after all, this was his first foray into the mountain world. Vladimir and Nicolai, his minders, caught up with us. Vladimir was shaking his head. 'I told Wayne to turn back. Oh, this man is very stubborn, very strong.'

'He'll be right.' Jon's optimism, always there.

Jonathan had a nasty headache. So what, nothing would stop that man from doing his duty. Filming allowed a slow pace, and anyway, there was no rush. It was a beautiful day, the wind had died down, and the mountains were unveiling their shapes as we gained altitude. The low summit of Elbrus was a rocky cone, covered in tracks. Of the higher West Summit we saw nothing, as a ridge hid it from our greedy minds. At the Col we took a lunch break, seated on top of an old wooden hut filled to the roof with blue ice. Curious crows were flying around, sowing their throaty cry in the breeze. Vladimir was convinced that at this pace it would be two hours before we reached the summit.

At Jon's instigation we both followed a rocky spur to the main ridge, while the film team plodded up the snow slope on the side. A holiday! That little spur of mixed climbing, just Jon and me, was like a Sunday outing after a week's work. The crows dived to the valley, respecting our solitude. The spur left its rocks behind, threw a last steep snow sheet to the summit ridge. I became increasingly impatient to reach the top. All those little stops to film were also tiring, and the combination was perfect for a siesta on the summit plateau, with the top of Elbrus in the distance. Now we knew we would stand on that little point. Nothing would stop us.

The catnap had been refreshing. That summit number five, I could almost touch it! Everything was under control, and Jon and I were to climb the last leg alone while Glen filmed. At the foot of the last slope, I had to stop and rig up the sound recorder, then I moved again, in a dream-like reality. The artificial approach inevitable with the filming, the lack of silent connection with the mountain, it all vanished when I made the last few steps. I was suddenly invaded by emotions, laughing, crying, talking uncontrollably. *Elbrus! At last!*

Right on the top, there was a little cairn with a big spanner on it. The incongruity of the object and the place seemed to fit with the absurdity of the situation. Mountains, mountains all around. Silver summits of the Caucasus Range were on one side, while red and orange peaks plunging their feet into deep brown gorges were on the other.

'Turn around!' Glen and Jonathan shot with a vengeance. Nikolai giggled when I gave him a summit kiss. Pictures for sponsors succeeded one another. Jonathan felt very tired, and Vladimir was impatient to start the descent, which would take a long time. We said goodbye to the mountains around, and headed down. Nightfall had well and truly descended. The hut was a lighthouse, calling the sailors off the frozen seas.

24 September 1990, House of the Eleven, Elbrus

Well, another one bites the dust, eh? Two to go. We put Jonathan to bed and had a quiet cup of tea with the hut warden. Celebration can wait until we all have more wind in our sails.

———

The snow was all but a memory, floating between the clouds above the dusty road. Nose out of the window, I was happily breathing in the perfume of yellowing birch trees. The cameras were touring with us, but they seemed to rest a bit more often these days. I was delighted to be a true tourist. If anything, mountaineering is the perfect excuse to play tourist afterwards. To indulge in anything, in fact. Like a bit of shopping, maybe? At Chyget Market spoon carvers and jumper knitters showed a remarkable talent of adaptation to foreign markets, as prices rocketed sky-high as soon as we crossed the iron gates of the market's entrance. Temptation was great; angora wool jumpers were still dirt cheap. Glen and Irina were discovering worlds close and far away in each other's eyes, and the feeling was permeating everything and everyone. Whatever it was, it was intense.

Wherever we went, we were confronted by the same first impression: communism, as a way of life, didn't work for most people. A sense of duty rather than pride, and nobody seemed to care less about what belonged to anyone and everyone. Maybe in the very small villages we visited the feeling was different. Inhabitants here had been massively deported in the Stalin years and had only recently returned to their homelands, and I sensed an attachment, a dedicated adoration of the past.

It was a long ride to Nalchik, and we didn't even really want to go there. The destinations we had in mind were either out of bounds for political reasons (unrest was latent in some areas), or impossible to reach because of petrol rationing. We were crippled by the lack of direct communication. It was the first time I had ever experienced it to such a frustrating level, and I didn't like it. There was nothing to do about it though: we simply couldn't speak Russian and hadn't had time to learn.

Nalchik was oppressive with heat and powerlessness. Wayne tried for the umpteenth time to ring Anne in Australia, to be faced once more with shrugged shoulders. You needed to book a call three days ahead, a little hard to organise when you are on the move all the time.

The lancinated rhythms of an accordion hit the bus as we neared a huge Saracen-looking head on top of a hill on the outskirts of the city. We never figured out what it was or why it was there, but it happened to be a favourite spot for wedding photographs. Dancers stuffed with chicken and vodka were taking turns on the concrete floor. The bride stepped ever so lightly from one foot to the other. She was beautiful, clad in the traditional red velvet robe, damascened silver belt and lace veil on top of her velvet headdress. The groom was performing a rooster dance in front of her with gusto, arms and legs flinging in prescribed directions to an ancestral tune. It was very catchy; soon we were giggling with the wedding party, filming with one hand, drinking and eating with the other. There should be weddings all the time, everywhere.

The groom's uncle invited us back to the groom's parents' place, where the first day of the wedding ceremony was to continue. Getting married took three days in these latitudes, and I believe one wedding is the most a person could take in a lifetime. The groom's family lived in the suburbs of Nalchik, in one of those rabbit boxes that have been compulsory since World War Two. The dancing continued outside the flat, this time with the bride veiled. In accordance with tradition, the groom only uncovers the bride's face for all to admire on the second day of the wedding. I guess that gives him a day to make up his mind.

The accordionist needed a rest. We all followed her inside, up the stairs leading to the flat, which looked like one of the Fitzroy housing commission flats. The table was dressed for excesses in food and drink. We quickly learned to say 'Cheers!' and with the help of our new friends, rebuilt the world on a human base. I don't know who had enough wits left to drag us all out of that den of perdition; maybe the driver wanted to go home.

Vodka soothes the mind. Vodka makes you insensible to the unfairness of the real world. Vodka spaces you out. When you don't know or you don't want to know where to stop, vodka gives you a scrambled head. Spaced-out scrambled brains were what we got as a reward for our efforts to love our sisters and brothers from the other side of the defunct iron curtain. It proved to be very convenient for the task ahead, which was bearing a bus trip back to Mineralnyye Vody and our plane, with a driver nearing a fast car racer's megalomania. There is one on every mountaineering trip, only usually it is on the way *to* the mountains. We were past the panic stage; we let higher powers take care of our welfare. The airport was as we had left it some days before, crawling with characters from every corner of the galaxy, queuing to get their luggage wrapped in protective brown paper, queuing to confirm flights, queuing to get fed, queuing to go to the toilet (with a fifteen-kopeck coin in their left hand). Someone queued to buy us some ice-cream.

—

I can never quite adjust to the change of world brought on so quickly when travelling by air. Zoop, suddenly we were in winter, in the far north, landing upon life in Leningrad.

It was our last night in Leningrad, and Gallina and Vladimir Shopin had invited us to a farewell meal. We were to discover the subtleties of Russian cuisine on our last night. George asked me whether or not I had their address. He had been to their house before, but didn't think he could remember the street. I bought white roses from an old woman in front of a closed supermarket, and as we neared the Shopins' house I understood George's doubts; the house was a flat in a square multistorey building, surrounded by twin sisters on all sides. Without the street and the number, which fortunately we had noted somewhere, we would have been knocking on doors for lives to come.

A huge black fluffy dog welcomed us to the tiny flat. A small kitchen, a dining room which was also the couple's daughter's bedroom, a sitting room doubling as a master bed-room, a balcony opening on a night of mirror lights on the other side of the street. The family cat had never set foot out of its familiar flat territory, and used the toilet like everybody else.

We were directed to the dining room, and seated around the long table. Gallina and Vladimir had organised a real ban-quet to see us off, with pickled mushrooms and garlic chicken accompanied by sumptuous salads, and an array of fruit and preserves ready to satiate the sweet tooths among us. They must have dug pretty deep into the cellar, too, for there was no shortage of toasting substances, and Irina had an increasingly hard time translating for everyone as the evening turned into a chaotically happy night of entangled idioms and laughs. Once again, I had to admire Russian people for their unconditional hospitality.

There is a wooden black and gold flowery ladle hanging in my kitchen, a reminder of the joy and warmth shared in Russia. Thank you, friends.

A Step Towards Everest

The next three years saw quite a few changes in my life, some predictable, some forcing themselves on me. For a start, the Seven Summits quest came to a standstill. This was far from what I wanted, but I was bound by a lack of funds. After climbing Elbrus, with the excitement of ticking off the fifth summit, Anne Tindall and I joined forces again to raise dollars for Mount Vinson, Antarctica, where Big Time Media wanted to send not only Jon and me, but also Jonathan and Glen, as well as Michael Gatehouse, a lawyer and friend of Jonathan's who was going to oversee the sound recording. That meant a big budget, which Anne and Wayne seemed confident they could achieve by pre-selling the series they intended to produce on the Seven Summits.

14 December 1990, Melbourne

> At times I find myself humiliated by the tone of people answering my calls for financial help. It so happens that they have the only commodity I do not have – money – so I must put up with my bad feelings. More than anything else, I want to express myself through the completion of my task, and use its potential to spread the obvious truth of love, respect and tolerance.

Ten days. In ten days' time, our struggle to raise money for Antarctica will be over. Anne and I are not desperate. We believe, along with my always positive Jon, that it can happen. Also that it won't be a drama if we do not go to Vinson this year, only a shame. We are doing our best, and our hearts are pure!

As the summer climbing season in Antarctica approached, we had to admit to ourselves that enthusiasm alone was not working as a fund-raiser in the atmosphere of financial depression choking Australia at the time. Jonathan, monitoring his chances to go to Antarctica, his most prized place on earth, suggested a media stunt which would also serve the more down-to-earth purpose of testing our cold-weather gear. We all packed our mountaineering equipment and boarded a plane to Sydney, destined for the freezer at the Pyrmont Fish Market.

Forty hours we spent in there – forty hours in a huge warehouse full of frozen fish, at minus forty degrees Celsius. In this unusual environment we entertained a number of television crews, newspaper reporters, radio interviewers. We took turns on the exercise bike to give our personal heaters a booster, we cooked garlic prawns on the shellite stove, and we played 'fish' (a modified version of soccer) on the slippery floor. We had a lot of fun, learned a lot from wearing our equipment, made the news everywhere in the middle of the heatwave affecting Sydney at the time, but did not raise a cent.

For a whole year I tried and tried, helped by Anne, and was rewarded with one thousand dollars given to me by Australian Geographic. Although grateful for this contribution, I was disappointed my cause did not attract wider interest. *Get a job*, I thought, *you are a hopeless money raiser! How can you presume to blow your own trumpet anyway?* Clearly I couldn't live on nothing or the dole all my life. I needed a challenge that would get me somewhere, and if possible that somewhere should be my two remaining summits, Vinson and Everest. And so the idea of starting a mountaineering business was born, and I became, along with Jon, whom I had converted to the appealing concept of making money out of something we both liked very much, a proud parent of Adventure Plus.

Well, one can't have a business without a business car. Skimming through the classifieds in the *Wimmera Mail Times*, we soon spotted the vehicle which answered our two prerequisites: it had to be dirt cheap and run on the smell of an oily rag. Three months later, we drove up to Dareton in a rusty 1972 Datsun 1200, intent on earning the three thousand dollars needed for the production of a colour brochure by picking grapes, once again, from sunrise to sunset. My back gave up after three weeks of unrelenting toil, but by then we had the words for the brochure, and the means to see them in colour. Our little Adventure Plus brochure, sporting on its front page a picture of me exhibiting sponsors' logos and a smile on the slopes of Elbrus, invited adventurous souls to join Jon and me on ascents of 'the highest mountain on each continent and more'.

While we were concocting blundering marketing campaigns, fate offered us a chance to join an expedition to Everest on terrific terms; Mark Miller was to lead a commercial expedition to the North Ridge in Autumn '93 and invited me at cost, giving Jon a free spot on the trip in exchange for work on the mountain. We had met Mark and his climbing partner Jon Tinker in the good old days of the mostly British mountaineering camp at Snell's Field, a Chamonix camp site infamous for its lack of facilities and its treasures of ruthless fun. Mark had since started a small guiding business called Out There Trekking and had been joined by Jon as a business partner. We rejoiced at the idea of sharing an Everest expedition with Mark and Jon. Then one morning, my Jon entered the kitchen of the little weatherboard house we were renting in Natimuk, his face pale, his eyes blank. 'I just talked with Louise. Mark has been killed in a plane crash . . .'

Something erupted and died inside my chest. I was very fond of Mark – we had shared some good times together. His flight bound for Katmandu had crashed in bad weather on the side of a hill near its destination. There were no survivors. I cried, angry at the unfairness of Mark's death – to die climbing a mountain one lusted for because one had not read the signs right, that was something, but to die through sheer chance was simply not conceivable for someone as alive as Mark had been.

Jon Tinker decided to go ahead with the Everest expedition, which he regarded as Mark's expedition, and was happy to honour Mark's promises to us. We still had to find enough to cover my participation, and think about getting me reasonably fit for the enterprise. Jon did not need training any more, at all. He had turned into a mutant capable of the most extraordinary feats of endurance after months of drinking beer, playing pool, and opening new rock-climbing routes at Mount Arapiles.

I was given an opportunity of exercise and altitude when Wildwise, a company specialising in adventures for women, noticed our advertising and invited me to lead a women-only expedition to Aconcagua. I accepted enthusiastically, as it would give me experience as a guide as well as a little money. I was also planning a trip there with Adventure Plus. A certain Patrick Kerrin from Adelaide had seen an Adventure Plus advertisement about Aconcagua, and he was to be the sole client on my second trip to the mountain that summer, following the Wildwise expedition. Sitting in cold water in the bathtub which I called my office in the sweltering heat of the Wimmera summer, I talked to him on the phone and assured him that the trip would go on, even with just one participant.

We did not reach the summit in January, although the girls, despite being total novices at the game of mountaineering, did extremely well, getting up to Independencia Hut at 6200 metres. I found guiding the climb tiring and stressful and was happy to see the end of the trip. My second attempt at commercially guiding a climb up Aconcagua was to be completely different in its challenges and rewards. Here I was, with a guy I'd never met before, sharing a tiny tent with him on the mountain, cooking his meals, teaching him high-altitude skills. How many times was he asked, 'Is she your girlfriend?', answering imperturbably always with a twinkle in his eyes, 'Actually, no, she is my guide!' And guide him I did, all the way to the summit. We reached the top in the middle of an electrical storm, and spent only moments there, wary of the yellow sparks encircling us.

Patrick was very tired by the time we started the descent back to Piedra Blanca, site of our last camp, and, to make things more interesting, we were soon engulfed in a white-out. In the white cottonwool at my feet I could just make out the harder snow of a thin trail, compacted by the feet of numerous climbers. I concentrated on following its thread to where I knew it led – Campo Berlin on the Normal Route. I knew that Piedra Blanca was close to it, but I wasn't sure of its exact location as I'd only camped there once before, so I stuck to the certainty of shelter at Campo Berlin. We could knock on a tent or hut door and spend the night inside, instead of huddled in the snow and wind outside. Patrick was not fussed by the idea of a night without sleeping bags or sustenance; he was quite satisfied, in fact, as long as I let him lie down somewhere without shaking him moments later to make him keep going. We shared an icy hut with a couple of young Argentinian climbers who offered us a cup of tea and some space to lie down. Patrick huddled under the tent fly they had given us as a moral blanket for the cold hours ahead, looked at me with mock concern on his face, and uttered seriously, 'You are not going to charge me more for this, are you?'

I returned to Australia enriched by the climbs, and by contact with people possessed by their own dreams and realities. At home, Jon had been attending to the other side of our business, acting as a rock-climbing instructor to experienced climbers and beginners alike, impressing them by his relaxed and cheerful manner, and his complete expertise in his trade. I thought us lucky; we were living in Australia, land of hope and freedom, we were our own masters, and enjoyed sharing our lives with each other and with dear friends. And centre of it all, our lifestyle took us to some weird and wonderful places, abroad as well as at home.

Over the past few years Jon's interest had also shifted from high places overseas to the deserted areas of the Australian continent. He had achieved his teenage dream of climbing Everest, and was ready to direct his love of the wilderness to his own backyard. More and more he immersed himself in books describing bush tucker and remote regions, and this in a way simplified our relationship. There is bound to be some degree of competitiveness between two highly motivated people in the same field; that he had found another outlet for his passionate nature meant I could spread my wings in the mountains without the fear of being with a partner who would always be stronger than I was. We would still enjoy the occasional climb together, like the upcoming Everest expedition, but we would be able to balance those times with other trips shared with other friends or enjoyed alone, taking us to completely different areas and allowing us to grow outside the relationship as well as within it.

With winter came the determination to formalise our business commitments, and we both did a New Enterprise Incentive Scheme course at the Technical and Further Education College in Horsham. This little business of ours had turned into an enthralling challenge to make money: I had always seen myself as someone incapable of making a decent living, mainly because, for me, living was being in the mountains. Now, with years of mountaineering experience, and experience meaning saleable commodity, I was able to have the best of both worlds. We would never be rich in dollars, but we would always be the guardians of invaluable memories, and make enough cash to multiply them as the years of adventure went on.

Make enough cash or know someone dear and talented, able finally to track down a willing sponsor! Anne got on the phone one day and talked with James Hoadley, who was working at that time for what was then called the Wool Corporation.

She wrangled an appointment out of him, and left him speechless on the other end of the line by promising that she would chain herself to his door until he supported my Everest climb! We had even better arguments, fortunately, such as exposure in the media, the documentary and the book I was supposed to write. After the ten thousand dollars the Wool Corporation generously committed, I only needed another five thousand dollars.

Anna Gregory of Channel Nine, whom Jon and I had met a few years before during coverage of our Elbrus climb and the Seven Summits quest for *Wide World of Sport*, invited me to appear on her *Today* show, and mentioned on air that I was still five thousand dollars short. Before the end of the show, Mike Bollen of 'US' advertising plugged the hole, making me a happily dazzled girl.

The day before Jon and I were to leave for Nepal, Mike and his partner, Marcus Tarrant, organised an abseiling session from the top of their Tea House building on the banks of the Yarra, and invited the press to gawk at the blond in a fluoro-pink Fairydown windsuit who was hoping to become the first Australian woman to climb Everest. The story made it into the newspapers, and onto radio and television. Coverage was assured for all the sponsors, which was one less thing to think about. Because thinking I was. I was excited, certainly, but I also saw the enormity of what I had started, and realised that it was for real, that I had better be up to it, otherwise I would look pretty dumb. And hurt pride was not something I could put up with at the best of times. Furthermore, I would be letting a lot of other people down. I swallowed hard, and hoped for a miracle.

———

15 August 1993, Katmandu

Le 15 août a Liège, August the 15th in Katmandu. I had missed the mark by 10 000 kilometres. In my home town, the Day of the Virgin is celebrated with a street fair in the Republic of Out-remeuse, a small enclave of ancient narrow brick houses and sinuous alleyways surrounded by blank commercial streets, on

the other side of the River Meuse. It is a time for joy and feasting, on sausages and fried onions, and for drinking endless shot
glasses of *peke*, the national drink, which the locals sell from
their doorsteps.

Looking at the forgotten stars of the northern sky, I so very
much needed some time on my own, to get back in touch with
myself, and to take it all in. Since we arrived in Katmandu four
days ago, we have not done an awful lot, but it has been quite
enough. There are already six of us here, and I have been feeling
the stirrings of social claustrophobia. I have never been very good
at spending all my time with people, no matter how good the
company, so, here I am, enjoying my solitude, the sky, my thoughts
wandering above the streets of Thamel, the pungent smell of night,
the continual background of traffic sounds, the lights and
movement below. Boy, I needed this. Tomorrow the eleven last
members of our team are arriving. That's going to be something.
A whole new crew of people, of men, that I will have to live with,
pretty much twenty-four hours a day, for two months. Shit.

I hoped there would be someone like-minded in there, someone
I could call a friend, an ally in a world of strangers. My Jon
would be there, of course, but he was so disgustingly strong
that it did not do much for my self-esteem, and finding a more
human companion was always so reassuring. I could compare
myself to them, not to my hero, and come up more favourably
in the confidence odds. Old habits die hard.

Our team was a composite one, with climbers from Great
Britain, Finland, France, Nepal, Poland, Russia and Australia.
Some were experienced, some were not. Most were there to
realise their dream to climb *on* Everest: a few climbed with the
intent to reach the summit.

We left Katmandu and followed the Friendship Highway
towards the border with Tibet. Soon we were swallowed by the
chasms and summits of the Jugal Himal, vertiginous green hills
lost in the clouds and sometimes falling out of the sky, we realised,

as we walked across a sizeable landslide that had cut the road and stopped our bus. Well, we were here to walk and to get acclimatised to the altitude of the Tibetan Plateau, so we got stuck in to it, charging up steep forests dripping mist and leeches and spending a few days in a camp at about 4000 metres. I started looking around for possible allies. Paavo Saarela, from Finland, who physically reminded me so much of my friend Michael Rice from Melbourne, looked approachable in a shy sort of way, and at the other end of the spectrum Pat Falvey, from Ireland, was irresistible in a rather loud fashion. His favourite pastime, to my everlasting dismay, was singing, and sing-along evenings. Being more an avid story listener myself, I dreaded the next rendition of his favourite, 'Who Killed Cock Robin?' with a chorus of male voices behind his earnest effort. Even my Jon was sucked into the cacophonic after-dinner concert, soon to become tradition. The first few notes of 'Who kil . . .' sent me into fast retreat to my tent and earplugs.

———

21 August 1993, Mud in the Sky Camp

Yesterday, when we arrived at our stop for the night, it was raining heavily, and as darkness approached, we found ourselves stranded in a most inconvenient spot to camp – a very, very muddy flattening of the steep ridge which was born, a thousand metres lower, in the steamy forests of the end of monsoon. Two houses here, dark, miserable. Not a nice place to be, I had thought, cursing the porters who had arrived after dark, and the rain which would not stop falling. Then this morning the sky turned blue, the sides of the scrubby hillside dived into faraway darkness shrouded in low clouds, and our little patch of mud soared into the sky. We kept rising towards it, following the ridge, then a suspended valley studded with lakes held in space by a ring of steep peaks and black clouds. Our base for the next few days is a green meadow, on the side of an ebullient creek. On the shore of a lake nearby is a small, peaceful stupa, with rags of prayer flags adorning its wooden sentinel poles.

Jon, who really only came to help me get up 'that mountain', as we usually referred to Everest, was getting into the swing of things. He enjoyed spending time with the boys, but also managed to be attentive to my needs, as always in the mountains. This time, though, I was so petrified by the task ahead that I craved more than the usual reassurance and moral support, while feeling pathetic for still relying on his overwhelming strength. It took snippets of time without him in the mountains to help me cool my head, and appreciate the place I was in.

⎯⎯

24 August 1993, Everest Base Camp

It didn't rain today. When I poked my nose out of the tent, at the early hour of eight a.m., no summits were to be seen above our meadow perched on the side of the sometimes emerald lake, but below, some ridges dark and blue materialised above another meadow, of grey clouds that one. And it wasn't raining! So after breakfast in the mess tent, I put Melanie in my walkman, grabbed my camera and my faithful umbrella, and went for a wee wander towards the lake. I sauntered in clouds of pink, fluorescent blue, and purple, and yellow, and cream and fuchsia flowers, shimmering around outcrops of dark grey slate.

I stopped at a small overhang dripping with water, where some of our porters had spent the night. There were traces of a fire, and a sad-looking green, crumpled plastic bag had been left to fend for itself in the Jugal Himal. It made me frustrated at the immensity of the poverty of the hills people. It also made me recognise that, besides providing them with a job in a place more awesome than Katmandu – but so much harder, in its physical way and so much more satisfying in its spiritual way – there was not an awful lot I was doing to improve their lot on a tangible scale.

Once I accepted that, I felt closer to the country and its people. I had got over my cold, my altitude headache, my sore ankle and my tender stomach, and now I was really enjoying myself. It had taken me two weeks to relax since leaving home –

about the amount of time your average American gets as a holiday every year. Just enough time to let go, and whammo, back
into the productive life. Productive to whom?

It took us three days to walk back down and across to Kodari
and the border with Tibet. I was looking forward to seeing Jon
Tinker again; expedition duties had kept him in Katmandu, and
he would be waiting for us at the border. Characters were starting to emerge, and as diverse a group as we were, everyone had
something in common – a penchant for beer and the lightness
of being. If a few were darkly obsessed with climbing the mountain, it had not emerged yet. I know, because I was one of them,
that some of us were carefully averting our thoughts from the
terrifying prospect of stepping on Everest, *the* Everest;
others, who had been there and done that, were probably just
enjoying the holiday and the freedom of constraints flowing
with it – like the Jons, Maciek Berbeka, a super high-altitude
climber from Poland, and George Kotov from Russia, a wiry,
chain-smoking, moustached mountaineer with whom we had
spent time on Elbrus and then in Leningrad, now known once
again as St Petersburg.

28 August 1993, Zhangmu

> I am so excited, jumping up and down all day! We crossed into
> Tibet–China today!
>
> It is not every day that I cross the border of a new coun-
> try, so everything has been particularly intense today. It was with
> trepidation that I walked the bridge spanning the Trisuli and two
> worlds. On the other shore, below us on the bridge, a platoon of
> drab uniformed soldiers was performing some kind of morning
> ritual, dancing some katas. Another one of the soldiers, standing
> frozen on a pedestal, was guarding the other side of the bridge,
> the new land. I smiled at him and bowed, but he did not move
> an eyelash. Merchants of bright, plastic things and busy pool
> tables were scattered along the muddy dirt road, which we left

behind to walk up a sodden trail bisecting the meandering road to Zhangmu. Plastic bags and wrappers adorned the trickle of a brown seep.

I turned my music on full blast and, happily puffing up the hill, made my way to Zhangmu. There we met David Lee, our young English student interpreter, and a rather shifty-looking character who was to be our liaison officer, and with whom I spent so much time that I can't even remember his name. David was long and lovely, and I looked forward to talking to him some more. Then it was time to hit the town and have lunch. I bumped into Paavo and we had lunch together in a Chinese restaurant (what else?) resplendent in plastic grapes and gold and red plastic tinsel. I was glad I did finally meet Paavo, and it came as no surprise that we all got on well.

The drive from Zhangmu to Xegar ranks pretty high in the hierarchy of my memories. The rain and the mist and the steep hills of Nepal were soon left behind, replaced by the ochres of the Tibetan Plateau. The light gave the dry, barren landscape the appearance of a stone forest. The ruined forts – human brushstrokes on a tableau of eternity – were among the many places I would have loved to explore, but I was on a mountaineering expedition, and the idea of the whole exercise was to climb, not to play explorers in lost cities. The road and dwarfed electricity poles cut strange figures in there, not to mention our convoy of minibuses.

We stopped in the middle of nowhere, and Norman Croucher got off with a roll of toilet paper. I hopped out too, hoping for a quick wee behind the bus. Norman had beaten me to it, and I hurried to a depression in the vastness, while marvelling at the adaptability of the human race. Norman had lost his legs below the knee, having fallen asleep as a very drunk teenager across a railway line on his way back from the pub to his camp in the woods. That had not stopped him from continuing with his passion for the outdoors and climbing. He had achieved incredible feats, such as climbing Cerro Ameghino (5883 metres) in Argentina on all fours, after his artificial legs gave way to metal fatigue and snapped into useless bits. And now, he was going to climb the North Ridge of Everest!

We drove on in the golden light until we reached Xegar, our stop for the night. Jon Tinker, always the caring expedition leader, advised us to keep hydrated as we were quite high up. So we all went to the bar and washed down our insipid dinner with a large number of bottles of Chinese beer, jokes and songs. George Kotov and David Lee, our interpreter, both treated us to a rendition of 'The Internationale' in their respective languages, and Ken McConnell, our expedition doctor, translated for us. Every so often Maciek would exclaim with gusto, '*Piju, piju, piju!*' (beer).

Surprise, surprise, the next morning I had a headache. Four coffees later, I was raring to go. We retraced our steps to the main road and the Everest turn-off. We were to exchange our minibuses for a four-wheel drive and some trucks, as only serious transport could make it to Base Camp. The liaison officer, David, Norman and Thierry Renard, a bearded and diminutive French climber who apparently had pneumonia, piled into the four-wheel drive, and the rest of us rode in the covered trucks. Except that the four-wheel drive would not start. They all got out, with the exception of Thierry who was ill after all, and started pushing the four-wheel drive. Even Norman with his artificial legs!

The Pang La (*la* means Col) was the first place on the drive where one could possibly see Everest. Not so this time. We stopped to stare at the blank horizon and scattered on the stony expanse to attend to more or less pressing needs. A line of small cairns shouldered a bigger one, crowned by a bouquet of discoloured prayer-flag sticks. They were like windmills in the sky.

Impatient honking called us back to the trucks and the wonders of the drive to Base Camp. My hangover got the best of me, and I huddled in a corner of the truck to sleep it off. Next thing I knew, we had stopped on the side of the river beside a couple of big tents that the advance Sherpa party had erected.

The mountain emerged the next morning, as regal as the Goddess Mother of the World could be, white, shimmering and immense at the head of the Rongbuk Glacier. The vision prompted concerned looks and frowning brows, and a pervading feeling of awe, an almost religious intensity. I was blindingly terrified. I could not get understanding from a Jon now too excited to notice, and Paavo had retreated into his own world and was ignoring our former start at friendship. As for Jon Tinker, I'd always felt too inadequately shy to confide in him.

———

3 September 1993, Everest Base Camp.

> We just had a lecture on oxygen and I am absolutely terrified. Scared of not being up to it. I need to relax about it all, I need to talk about my fears. I feel kind of awkward being in a big team, too. I need so much the reassurance of sharing at a deep level. No doubt my fears are related to the difficulty of communication. I am a married woman, and to these men from the Land of the Stiff Upper Lip, I am living with a nice little fence called Jon around me. I feel tired, and I feel like going to bed. Still, I am not the only one. When I look around me, I see people with puffed faces and pockets under the eyes.

After a few days spent walking up very big piles of rocks in the vicinity of Base Camp, the Big Guns decided it was time to make tracks towards Advance Base Camp at the foot of the North Col, and start establishing the route and camps up the North Ridge. The Jons would be going, as well as Maciek, George, Pat, Thierry, Paavo and the Sherpa team of four high-altitude climbers, including Babu, Lakpa and Lama, as well as Ang Dorje and Rita, who would be looking after the camp and never-ending task of feeding everyone. I was not feeling well enough, or so I believed, to join the first wave. I sank into despair and self-pity, and retired to my tent for a heavy session at rock bottom. Twelve hours of despair and one hour of self-love later, I was ready to face the world.

The next day, most of us left behind made for a hill that I baptised Mount Paskakasa, meaning 'pile of shit' in Finnish, with the intention of camping high on its slopes and heading for the summit the next morning. It was lovely to be with fewer people around, and to climb up the unstable screes of Paskakasa without having to rush to meet a deadline of dark and cold. After a two-hour stroll, we pitched our tents and snuggled in. I shared a tent with Farmer Chris Brown and Harry Hakomaki. 'The Young Lions are up there, and the Old Foxes are waiting here to make their move!' Harry said, talking about the team which had gone up ahead. With husband and tortuous friend Paavo away I felt great, and being part of a small group of unpretentious climbers made me timidly confident of my capabilities once more.

In the morning I was welcomed to the new day, the first of my thirty-fifth year, by the boys singing 'Happy Birthday' to me. After a leisurely breakfast of coffee, I took my time getting to the summit, where a snow cake and a happy birthday sign were waiting for me. How kind these people were. We walked back to base, and settled in to an evening of indulgence and loud music in the mess tent.

By the next night, we had heard from the others at Advance Base Camp and decided to join them, taking a couple of days to walk up. There was a lot of snow on the mountain but they were going to push on regardless, and hoped to establish Camp Two at about 7800 metres over the next few days. I had been smoking a lot, because I was scared of not being up to it, and because I had been smoking so much, I was not feeling up to it.

Walking to Interim Camp, at 5800 metres, was a breathless torture, and I collapsed in a heap on the yak dung and rock platform where the tents were pitched, on the side of the East Rongbuk Glacier. A frozen river of ice-fins was visible above: the 'Magic Highway', so nicknamed by climbers, which we would follow tomorrow. And magic it turned out to be. A tongue of rock-strewn moraine led towards the site of our next camp, with hundreds of blue ice waves as tall as trees bordering its left side. I fell into an old, comfortable rhythm and pace, and reached Advance Base Camp after six hours of happy strolling, surrounded by the bells and steamy breaths of yaks bringing gear up. The Tibetan herders were very cheeky, suggesting rolls in the dung with evocative finger gestures. I laughed and declined; they laughed and kept walking.

Jon was in camp when I arrived, and I was happy at the idea of having a partner again. He had done very well since he had left: he and Maciek, the strongest in the team at that stage, had pushed up through deep snow to the North Col, followed by Babu, and in the distance, Paavo and Pat. Jon had taken on another dimension since the easily met challenge, and his whole being exuded intense strength and confidence. My own withered at the comparison, and Jon's little kindnesses to me, such as bringing morning coffee to our tent, made no difference to my self-inflicted state of mind. Confidence was a fragile state that came and went, and only the satisfaction of having done well gave me brief respites in my everlasting quest for the next challenge.

The snowstorm gave me the perfect excuse I needed to rest and get rid of the aches and pains of the walk up. I was so unfit. And here I was, at the very foot of the highest mountain in the world! *Oh dear*. I was so tense that I could not think more than a day ahead, a healthy reflex of self-preservation. I would have died of fright and shame had I been able to actually visualise the scale of the task ahead.

I huffed and puffed my way to the North Col Camp, and was more than a little concerned by the narrowness of the blue clothes line which we jumared up steep ice walls and snow slopes. There were a lot of us going up, including members of Indian and Korean teams attempting the same route. At the North Col I shared a tent with the Jons and Harry. They wanted to go higher the following day to establish Camp Two, and spend the night there. I announced that I'd see how I went, but I had never been this high before, let alone slept there, and could not imagine being capable of going up the next day. I was right, and the next morning I ambled up to the start of the fixed ropes before retiring back to the tent. The Jons, Babu and Lakpa climbed in deep snow to 7850 metres, and erected two small tents for the night. Harry returned, forced to turn back in the wind because he had left his downsuit behind, and carried on to Advance Base Camp. Lakpa and Babu returned to camp, and I settled for the night. I felt quite peeved. This mountain was so big! Its North Face, which was right under our nose, soaring 3000 metres to the summit, was totally overwhelming and drained my energy. I felt insignificant.

It was time to return to the lower altitude of Base Camp. Jon had bronchitis, and spent his days over a pot of hot water with a jacket on his head, and sometimes Jon Tinker joined him. I nursed a bad stomach, feeling tired, and boosted my morale by thinking of hot baths in Katmandu rather than dreaming of getting high on Everest. George and Maciek tried to push on towards Camp Three, but only managed a hundred metres in waist-deep snow before having to turn back. The Indian Camp Two, at 7600 metres, had been destroyed by an avalanche, and the snow kept falling without a break.

26 September 1993, Everest Base Camp

> Still snowing . . . we are hoping that the full moon will bring a change in weather. I feel jittery. I could scream, jump up and down, roll in the dirt. Instead, I am trembling, mentally and physi-cally. I probably need a staccato of orgasms, but I can't cope with the idea of making love. I would fall into bits, burst into wailing. No, no, no, I need to keep in one piece, even a trembling one.

The sky was blue again the next day, and the mountain, hidden behind thick veils of silver clouds, treated us to a tantalising striptease which took all day, and ended in a glory of blue and yellow snow at sunset. The British team which was to share our permit for a scientific experiment on the North Col had timed it well. The mountain had never been that resplendent. Harry Taylor, ex-SAS and friend of Jon Tinker, was the leader of a motley team: Doctor Carl Henize was a sixty-eight-year-old American astronaut who, at fifty-eight, had been the oldest man in space when his capsule circled the earth. Colin Bruce, better known as Nish, was hoping to dive from a balloon at the edge of the stratosphere, and Brian Tilley was there to help where help was needed. Carl would do experiments on the North Col, measuring the effects of cosmic rays on the body, as part of the research for Nish's project. Carl had the effect on us of a honey pot on cubby bears: we glued ourselves to him, asking never-ending questions on space. Jon particularly welcomed the opportunity to further his knowledge on the universe, and, his eyes intensely focused on Carl, asked, 'Did you say *wow* when you first looked out of the window?'

'You know what,' answered Carl, his calm blue gaze hooking Jon's, 'I think I did.'

Once again plans were made to move to Advance Base Camp and to carry some more gear up the slopes of the North Ridge. I went up with the first group this time to assist George and Maciek, who were to attempt the summit. Thierry, despite having gained experience at high altitude when he had climbed and skied down Cho Oyu a few years before, managed to help as little as he possibly could. There were complaints from others: I must say I hadn't noticed, but the episode gave everyone an excuse for jokes about French work ethics. We settled on the North Col and eagerly awaited news of our friends' attempt, and were quite disappointed when we heard that the wind had turned them back. There was still a lot of snow around, and during the night Babu and Lakpa, who had been supporting Maciek and George, returned to the Col with the news of the destruction of Camp Two. In the morning, we descended to

Advance Base Camp to rest and wait for milder weather.

Carl and his group had just arrived in camp, and we shared the evening meal with them. Ken, who had been preoccupied in the last few days, announced his decision to go back to his Tasmanian home. Harry had given Ken a letter when he had first arrived at Base Camp, and Ken had been agonising over its contents ever since. The news from home was not good; he had to go. We were all sorry to hear it. He had been such good company, his past travels an endless source of entertainment.

4 October 1993, Everest Advance Base Camp

Major epic today. It was too windy to go up, so we hung around. Just as well. Carl has not been feeling too well recently, and this morning after breakfast, Brian and Harry had him in the Gamow bag for a few hours. He felt better, he said, back in the mess tent sharing stories with us, but to me he looked quite drawn and grey. Then he had to go in the bag again and afterwards on oxygen, and it became obvious that he really should go down. He prepared to descend, staggered and stopped. He could not walk down. Everyone in the team ran around improvising a stretcher, packing packs, counting helpers to carry the stretcher. I, not being Superman, would stay at camp and relay talks with Ken at Base Camp from the base station to the rescuers' handheld. The plan was to take Carl to the British Camp Two, 500 metres lower, to have him spend the night in the Gamow bag, and to be met by another team coming up from Base Camp to help. The doctor of a Spanish team who had been watching the proceedings with arms crossed on their chests told us: 'You must take him all the way to Base Camp now, you know.' Well, we knew. But we couldn't. The stretcher system was too tiring on the uneven terrain and the boys ended up carrying Carl piggy-back style. They returned a few hours later, exhausted. Carl had appeared very feeble when they left him with Brian, Nish, and Babu. Jon Tinker exploded after dinner: 'No one is going to die on my expedition!'

Jon unzipped the tent door and gave me a cup of coffee. His voice was tinged with sadness. 'Carl did not survive the night,' was all he said.

There were a lot of red eyes in the mess tent that morning. Talks about Carl's earlier references to dying. 'He told me,' said someone, 'that if he died, he'd like to be buried at the foot of the mountain.'

'Yeah, same here.' We looked at each other. Well, so be it. Carl would be buried near the old British Camp Two, with the highest mountain in the world as a headstone. Ken, postponing his departure, was on his way to declare Carl dead. He found a huge scar on Carl's chest, a souvenir of major heart surgery that had carefully been kept in the dark by our friend. Worried that he would not have been invited along?

5 October 1993, Everest Advance Base Camp

> Jon, Maciek, Ian and Pat went to Carl's burial. I could not face it. After losing it this morning, what with the sadness and anger of his unnecessary death, I have put him to rest at the back of my mind. I couldn't have gone down. I don't have the energy. Ten days before the yaks arrive to bring our stuff down. Can I do it? Sometimes I feel like screaming.

If we wanted to get to the summit, it was to be now or never. Maciek and Lakpa had been selected as the first summit team, and made their way in high winds towards the camp at 8100 metres. They found that the wind's speed eased as they approached the 8000-metre mark, making it obvious that anyone wanting to climb the mountain in the present conditions would have to be able to climb from the North Col to Camp Three in one go, skipping the overnight stop at the 7600-metre camp. A few members were becoming unhappy with the organisation of climbing teams, thinking that only the big guns were going to have a shot at the summit. Jon Tinker was very keen to be part of the second attempt, making Harry, Paavo, Pat and

Thierry furious that the leader should come before the paying clients. It was Jon's and my turn to go to Camp Two, and to possibly try to get higher. There were a few tents lying around at the camp site, but none of the complainers volunteered to come up and erect one of them, preferring to stay at the Col to wait for the tent that Jon, Pat and I had set up a couple of days before to become available.

Jon and I moved in howling wind to Camp Two, and soon received the news that Maciek and Lakpa had reached the summit, opening a new path from Camp Three to the Second Step. Well, it was nice to know it could be done, even if one had to remember that they were probably the strongest members in the team. The temperature rose at the North Col Camp as Jon Tinker and Babu stormed off to Camp Three on the second summit attempt. Lakpa, flying on elation, stopped by at our tent for a cuppa and kept going to Base Camp. It was almost dark when Maciek, coming down at a more human pace, staggered inside and spent the night with us. He looked ten years older, totally worn out. Not much sleep was possible in the little tent buffeted by the wind, and I was troubled by the insidious question . . . *Will I be able to keep going up?* I had been at high altitude for too many days, and must be getting weak. I hadn't been sleeping . . .

In the morning Maciek went down. He was replaced by Norman, who was intent on reaching 8000 metres for his charity fund-raising. At the North Col, the atmosphere was becoming decidedly hostile. Harry brought up some more food for us, but not the gear he would have needed to spend the night in the other tent, and accused us of obstructing and robbing anyone below of a chance to climb higher. Thierry packed in a huge pack everything he needed for an attempt and almost made it to our camp, but he did not quite have the stamina to get there. Jon Tinker and Babu summited, and Norman, Jon and I squeezed in for another night at 7600 metres.

It was going to be our last night at that altitude. Early in the morning Norman tried to go higher, and soon turned back: the wind was just too fierce. He wanted to stay another night and try once more the next day, but as he had no intention of attempting the summit, Jon asked him to go down; some room in the tent might give us a chance to actually rest and be ready for going higher. Norman saw the sense in this, and started the descent to the North Col. I had great admiration for his strength and determination: to climb up to 7600 metres in less than ideal conditions, with artificial legs weighing a good fifteen kilograms, plus the gear he needed on his back . . . well, that said a lot about the guy.

The wind was playing with clouds high on the North Face, and soon they formed a menacing dark blanket slowly sliding down the mountain and threatening to engulf our camp. 'Let's go,' said Jon. We packed our few belongings and started down the slope towards the North Col. I felt very strange, losing my balance and having to be held on a short rope by Jon. At one point, I sat down in the snow and burst into tears. Jon was less than sympathetic: 'Get your shit together, will you!'

I felt awful. I had enough on my plate, I thought, without having to put up with his anger. None the less, his ruthlessness achieved its aim: the harsh words penetrated the mushy mess my mind had become, and I managed to whip myself together for the rest of the descent to the Col. Jon was not in a happy mood, and I interpreted this as disappointment to have missed out on the summit because of his pledge to climb with a wally wife. I cried myself to sleep, hiding in the loft of my sleeping bag.

At Advance Base Camp, packing was in full swing. The angry North Col team had disappeared down valley, and it was left to a few of us to sort out a huge amount of gear. After breakfast the next day, as I was helping to take the mess tent down, I suddenly felt very strange indeed and had to sit down. Light spiralling in staircases danced in my eyes, and I had the distinct impression of watching a movie of what was happening around me. I retired to our tent, lay down, and looked at my face in the pocket mirror I carried around to deal with my contact lenses. I found myself staring at a complete stranger. Jon came to see me, quite concerned, and soon had me on oxygen. After a while I started to re-enter reality, and realised that I had probably been affected by an attack of cerebral oedema. It was definitely time for me to get to a lower altitude. It had been almost two weeks since we had moved to the 6400 metres of Advance Base Camp, and obviously it was too long a stay at high altitude for my body. The same problem had weakened me physically in Pakistan, but now the seriousness of it hit me, and I swore to make sure to take it into consideration if I ever got high again.

Coming down to Base Camp was long, tedious and a little sad. I had not exactly been up to climbing the highest mountain on earth, and realised that I needed a summit, an 8000-metre-high summit, to re-establish the faith I required to complete my Seven Summits quest. Eight thousand metres had always been a landmark in high-altitude mountaineering, with only fourteen peaks culminating higher than the 8000-metre mark. I had come to see 8000 as a magic number which, once reached, could become the mental key to success on Everest. Jon just sniggered and wondered why people wanted to climb the big fourteen. 'So artificial,' he tut-tutted. I brooded over my prospects and was agreeably surprised when a four-wheel drive, with David and Farmer Brown as a welcome committee, drove up to the terminal moraine of the glacier to give us a lift to Base Camp.

'We did it!' exulted Chris. 'We got someone on the summit.' Yes, we had done it, I reflected, having helped the people who summited to make it possible. As a whole, the expedition had been a success, even if some of us were not of that opinion. That night, Graeme had us all in stitches imitating Thierry, who had already disappeared, having hitched a ride out with another expedition: 'I do not carry anything up, so why should I carry anything down?'

---

19 October 1993, Katmandu

Hotel Manang – princely view on the outskirts of Thamel. The delirium of being back in a place full of people, buildings, streets, rubbish, noise, funky smells and stimuli of all sorts. More than anything I feel like being on my own, with just the wind in my hair. I look forward to sleeping tonight. Jon Tinker has told me about a trip he plans to Shishapangma, a mountain in Tibet which happens to be just over 8000 metres . . . I am going to lie down and dream of ecstasy on high summits.

Both Harry and Paavo have found out tonight that they are to become parents! I am glad to know that no letter containing such news will ever reach me! Not for me, child-bearing. No, it is of a mountain that I am dreaming, and it even has a nice name. Shishapangma . . .

The Magic Number

28 April 1994, Nyalam Heights, 3800 metres

The wind and the river, words whistling a sweet tune in my ears. Shining mountains skirt the southern horizon. Up valley lives a big cloud, and in that cloud, a mountain called Shishapangma.

Nyalam, in Tibetan, is 'the road to hell'. The name must refer to the descent towards Kodari, the awesome gorge establishing the link between Tibet and Nepal. Yesterday we drove up it, the road from hell, to where one can touch the stars. The sides of the gorge were sprinkled with pink and white patches of rhododendrons. Higher up it was snow which dusted the steep walls. Today the sky is blue, and spring is in the air. Once again I am the only female, this time in a group of twenty. Integration should be easier though, because Jon is not with me and therefore I am not the fenced-off married woman, and can be talked to. The wind brings to me bribes of conversation from higher up. Most of the boys seem to be on their way to climb a hill towering nearby. I am content running around at this altitude. A pointy summit has emerged from the cloud. Maybe it's Shish, maybe it's not! It feels good to be here and now.

I gave Jon a last hug, then a last, last hug. I stepped out under the stars, looked up and sighed. I would miss the southern sky. I drove to Horsham in our twenty-two-year-old Datsun, blowing on my fingers as I went along. The heater was only a memory, and if the gurgles emitted by the engine were anything to go by, the car would soon be one too. The overland train to Melbourne was crowded and smelled of sleeping bodies and confined spaces. Through the night we glided, from the mist of the countryside to the bustle and smog of the big city.

Two taxis and two planes later I was in Katmandu, rally point of the Out There Trekking (OTT) Shishapangma expedition. Customs finally spat me out into the crowds waiting outside the airport. I heard my name yelled and at the same time I caught sight of Jon Tinker, waving. We laughed, kissed and hugged. Jon always had a special aura about him, the air of an island full of mysteries and treasures. He also had a mild case of stiff upper lip, which seemed in remission at the present time, and a slash-and-burn sense of humour. With him were Bill Pierson from the States, who had arrived on the same flight as I had, and Andy Cave, climber extraordinaire and socialist from the United Kingdom. Andy was going to help on the expedition. Another climber called Mike Smith would also serve as a sort of a guide to OTT. We piled into the hotel courtesy bus and drove off towards the city centre and Thamel.

Katmandu was as polluted as I remembered it — taxis, cars, jeeps, motorcycle rickshaws, trucks, public buses and private buses all did their very best to render the air unbreathable, and the more deafening.

Two days later all the other members of the expedition arrived. Once on the road, the trip was studded with frequent 'run for the dunny' breaks. It was hot and dusty, and we were already dirty and smelly. We were to stay that way as our stop for the night was Kodari, border town on this side of the Friendship Highway to China. Kodari was dirt and smell. A real frontier town, and, if at all possible, a poor sister to its counterpart on the Chinese side, Zhangmu. Dogs were barking as we settled for the night in a rudimentary lodge. The river's voice was mounting in the evening mist, and echoed up the steep walls of the narrow valley. It gave the cold air an eerie dimension.

In the morning, after a quick breakfast of fried eggs and *chapattis* (flat bread cooked on a hot plate, or by being stuck to the inside walls of an earth oven), we patiently overcame the not-so-quick border formalities and walked across the Friendship Bridge. I was as excited as last year, when I had sauntered into China for the first time as a member of the North Ridge of Everest trip. Zhangmu was Zhangmu. 'A toilet,' as Jon put it.

The Zhangmu Hotel must have been a grand place in the Middle Ages. Its carpets were now threadbare, held together by grime and memories of better times. The bathroom looked at first glance like a bathroom, until closer examination revealed that the toilet didn't flush, the hot water system didn't work and anyway there wasn't any water to use, hot or cold. 'Hotel not so good,' translated Jack, bowing slightly. He was a twenty-year-old university student working as an interpreter for the liaison officer, Mr Li Feng Wu. Mr Li was a lovely man, always ready to help with solving problems. In this case, he could only acknowledge the fact and raise his shoulders.

From Zhangmu we followed the deep gorge linking those two different worlds, Nepal and Tibet. We were to stop for two nights in Nyalam, the town crowning the entrance of the gorge. The idea was to acclimatise to the already high altitude (3500 metres), before moving up to higher ground. Nyalam was also uninspiring, although the Tibetan part of town was its best kept secret: the back streets were a rainbow of traditional Tibetan houses shining in that pure light I have only found there. The Chinese part of town, where commercial and administrative life happened, was far less appealing.

As dusk fell, a few among us would overcome the bitter cold of the evenings to share a beer and a chat. That included me, of course. I had not been brought up in Belgium and adopted by Australia for nothing. I could drink beer all right, even on teeth-shattering Tibetan nights.

———

The bus drove through an endless landscape of vast plateaus and rocky hills, past scattered villages, a few infant trees, children in rags wiping their runny noses and waving at every passing vehicle. Dust. The drive to Shishapangma took only a few dream-like hours, which gave me two occasions to regret the amount of tea I had drunk before we left Nyalam; bushes are not that common on the Tibetan Plateau. I improvised, using my umbrella as something to squat behind. It was still a bit early on the trip – I didn't want to offend British male sensitivity by squatting openly on the featureless plain. There would be enough time for that on the mountain. I could imagine eyebrows raised in horror as I peed into my cup to avoid a trip in the cold of the night. ('For God's sake, Brigitte!')

We never saw our mountain that day, as it was obscured by a thick layer of cloud. Goats and sheep wandered aimlessly on the grassless expanse of the valley. Suddenly we arrived at Base Camp. Prayer flags, cairns and camouflage mess tents. A creek bubbled and gurgled nearby, with plastic bags and empty cans bobbing against the pebbles of its shores. The trucks arrived with all our equipment, and we worked at establishing the camp, putting up mess and kitchen tents, Chinese staff tents, the nylon bedrooms for members of the group and, of course, the official outdoors dunny. I had my own room – an advantage of being the only female. I had travelled with my tent from Australia to be sure that I wouldn't have to share a tent with someone I didn't like. It was great for a while, then I missed the company and the light-hearted chats I could hear twin-share members sharing together.

We were to split our big group into two teams. The first team would leave Base Camp in two days to establish Advance Base Camp and the first camps on the mountain, and the second would follow a week later and take over from wherever the first team had got to. I had been part of team number two the previous year on Everest, but this time I wanted to be where the action was from the start, so I volunteered straight away to be part of the first group.

That afternoon, our yaks, organised by the ever-efficient sirdar and cook Ang Rita Sherpa, materialised in the middle of the camp, along with smiling Tibetan herders mentally taking note of what would be worth grabbing if they ever got a chance. We had been warned that the people of the area were 'thieving gipsy bastards'. We kept our eyes open and our tents zipped up.

Shishapangma appeared one morning, shaking its cloudy veils and revealing its gorgeous lines. I had to squint to see it properly; it was an awful long way from Base Camp. It would take us two days of solid walking to get to the site of our Advance Base Camp, not even at the foot of the mountain. The walk was sprinkled with numerous stops as the yak herders had deliberately tied our loads loosely onto the animals, hoping for the opportunity to rummage through our equipment. But we stuck with them, ruining their cunning plans.

It was exhilarating to be walking towards Shishapangma. I caught up with members of our group here and there, chatting away for a few moments, then fell back and listened to music on my walkman. I was the only one in the group who couldn't leave all the comforts of Base Camp behind, and carried a folding chair on my pack (well, I was doing without my tequila and massage oil!). It attracted a little scorn from the other members of the group, a few laughs, and later a lot of 'well, I might as well use it while she's not' while we were waiting for the rest of the gear (including twenty-four cases of beer and the chairs) to come up with the second group.

The next day we reached the site of our Advance Base Camp. Ang Rita had left in the wee hours of the morning to scout for the best spot and had settled his sights on a low camp, thinking that the higher alternatives were too windy to be worth it in the long term. We were happy with his choice, and stayed – only it meant that every time we carried a load to Camp One, we had to tramp up the most disgusting moraine one can imagine. I didn't mind it too much, because I loved playing mountain goat, hopping along on rocks, but most people absolutely loathed it. I was thoroughly happy, flying through the days and getting closer to my dream: to climb an 8000-metre peak.

But it wasn't always easy. I had thought that I could mix easily into the group. It turned out that nothing had changed for me; I was still someone who needed to have heart-to-heart conversations with people, and that was apparently not the norm in a group situation. So I chewed my fingernails and read a lot in my tent, feeling alone and miserable. I was concerned that if I spent time with any of the boys on a one-on-one basis, both of us would be ostracised by the wider group. After a while, I didn't give a damn any more. I needed a friend, and if I found someone willing to share some of my time and conversation, I was going for it.

8 *May 1994, Shishapangma Advance Base Camp*

> Ups and downs . . . went up to Camp One yesterday for another carry, and realised that I am not very good at contemplating climbing a mountain on my own. Bit of a problem for someone who doesn't mix well, eh? It was only three days ago that I declared at the intermediary camp, 'No way am I waiting for the slowest, I am here to climb this mountain!' And I find myself slowing down at times to wait for Mike Brennan, our expedition doctor, because, well, I like being with him, and we move roughly at the same speed. Funny that he reminded me of my words yesterday, as I was sitting on top of that steep ice slope at the end of the glacier. I am hopeless at working on my own, unless I am on my own.

As things turned out, I teamed up most of the time with two of my favourite companions, Mike and Billy. Billy was living in

California and worked in the film industry. He sported a pony tail and a goatee ('Billy's Charles Manson impersonation,' said Jon) and had a shameless taste for obscene T-shirts. He entertained us with endless stories which could only have really happened, because they sounded too outrageous to have been invented. Like the Los Angeles riots. Billy was there. He actually drove downtown to take photos of the action. He lost his camera, his car was stolen and he was held at knife and gun point. He had us enthralled on those cold, snowy afternoons, when one thinks that really it would make sense to go and snuggle up in a sleeping bag, but finds it hard to leave the warmth of the exchanged word.

The weather had taken a turn for the worst. It wasn't all that bad really: one only had to be prepared for hours of plodding in white-out and howling winds between the camps. After having done two load-carries to Camp One, we were ready to go and sleep there. The crevasses skirting the Camp One area were definitely getting bigger and we were moving unroped, so we had to tread carefully over the gaping holes. The worst crevasses were those that one knew were underfoot, but could not see. The tactic here was to move as fast as possible and to rest, bent double over the skipoles, on the other shore. Why we ever moved unroped, I don't know! There was perhaps a feeling that nothing bad could possibly happen, a feeling of unreality.

Eating was a chore. I couldn't stand the mountain food, which consisted mainly of cooked meals – 'boil in the bag' catering, it seemed, for the British taste for hearty fare . . . Yuk. Despite the variety, the smell of the stuff was enough to make me feel ill. Instead, I thrived on a diet of dried water-buffalo meat, cheese, *tsampa* (roasted barley flour) and hot drinks with lots of sugar.

In the next few days, our team carried a load to Camp Two in horrendously windy conditions (I was on all fours for the last hour to avoid being thrown around by the wind, crying in frustration and anger) and then moved up to acclimatise to the higher altitude. Camp Two was at 6800 metres. I felt very tired when we came down to Advance Base Camp for a rest, and slept in the morning after. Jon woke me up with a coffee . . . just in time for lunch. I had the impression that I was floating; I was completely unfocused and a little panicky. If I felt that way after a couple of days above 6000 metres, what the hell was I going to feel like higher? It became more and more disturbing. I had decided to come on this expedition, having failed to reach 8000 metres on Everest, and I had come without my Jon, to prove to myself that I could do it without the help of one of Australia's best mountaineers. Well, well. I didn't fancy going home with my tail between my legs. I opened a can of beer and tried to forget about it.

14 May 1994, Shishapangma Advance Base Camp

It snowed today. In the distance, the hills of Tibet are sand and shadow. The sky is turning blue again and Shishapangma shines on a pearl-grey horizon. The top is not there though. Going up tomorrow, en route for the summit if all goes well.

The wind, the wind, the dust. All the dust in South-central Tibet is dancing with the wind. My tent feels like it will take off any time now. My knees are cold, I shiver. Could it be that, in a few days, I will be on top of this beautiful mountain? The goddess will do as she pleases.

We didn't go up the next day. I was happy with this outcome – I needed the two days' rest before tackling the summit and my fears. I also wanted to go up with Billy and Mike, and I think they were quite keen to keep our little team going as well. We kept asking each other, 'And how are you today? Think you will be going up tomorrow?' Somehow, we synchronised our wishes in time to communicate them to Jon at the six p.m. radio bulletin. We planned to follow Alex's group (Babu, Lama and himself), catch up with them at Camp Two and all attempt the summit together. *Alea iacta est.*

15 May 1994, Sunday night, Shishapangma Advance Base Camp

I am listening to the piano, Michael Nyman. A musical score which, like the movie it accompanies, sends shivers down my spine, makes me short of breath, happy, and gives me the irresistible envy to start running under the stars, cartwheeling and dancing and yelling to the sky. It is so beautiful, so powerful, so unique. It is life. I feel like making love to this, somewhere warm and huge in those majestic Tibetan hills, on a hot summer morning, windless, with slow clouds caressing the mountains, and the light catching turquoises in the frozen waves of the glacier.

Tomorrow we are going up. Tonight there are candles and flickering scarves dressing my tent, and soft voices making their way through the music which has invaded my head. I am ready, and I am overwhelmed. So many emotions, so much give and so much take involved in this business. Life is strange. I don't want to be alone, I want to share that life tumbling through me. How could I sleep with all that energy inside me? My skin feels the touch of the music, travelling in bursts along those roads which soft fingers have followed. I am awake, I am aware. Too alive to be alone, here, in this tent, with this music which is me, and nobody to share it with.

We were going. *Alleluia. Must get it over and done with.* My blood pressure was getting too high. Same old plod with the same old heavy pack to Camp One, then Camp Two. Nice to see Jon again, and to share a tent with him, Babu and Lama. Good Lord, I had forgotten how much men can smell!

18 May 1994, Camp Two, Shishapangma

Snowed lightly all night. No headache, no visibility. Hanging out, waiting for the weather to clear. Have a good feeling though. Maybe this is the necessary rest day for a comfortable summit attempt?

At around ten a.m. the mountain showed its nose, and our first wave split in two, with Alex, Billy and Babu racing up to the last camp, while Jon, Lama, Mike and I prepared for an early-morning start the next day. We were up too early for my taste, to make the most of the cool weather: we had to plod up an endless valley to the foot of the steeper slopes leading to Camp Three, then climb up a long couloir towards the summit.

At the top of the couloir I met Babu on his way down to Advance Base Camp. The strong bastard had climbed the mountain in six hours return from Camp Three, and was now happily strolling back to civilisation. He told me that Billy and Alex had summited, and left me with a 'Be careful'. I liked Babu, his guffaws and sparkling eyes. Tents appeared in the misty air, and I was at Camp Three. Billy and Alex were back in their tent, a roomy Himalayan Hotel. I dropped in to give them both a congratulatory hug, happy that they had made it. 'You'll have no problems,' said Alex in his cute Scottish accent. I hoped he was right. Mike arrived in the camp late in the day, and was told by Jon that he'd have to go in the next group. I settled in a tent with Lama and Jon, tomorrow's climbing partners.

———

Jon stood upright in his sleeping bag, violently and noisily gasping for breath. Was it really already time to steer away from dreamland and to show some vague interest in the hours ahead? Yuk. I took my earplugs out just in time to enjoy Lama's loud rendition of a dying sea-elephant. After having successfully cleared his throat, he lit the stoves to melt some snow, and settled back in his bag. I managed a sigh and closed my eyes again. Right. Today was the day, everything was quiet outside, a good sign I guess. It meant that this was not a false alarm, that we did not have to sink again into the delicious warmth of our sleeping bags and wait for a better day. Sigh. It was not even one a.m. yet.

Soon the tent was full of three people sipping milk tea, in an uncertain mist of early-morning breath and water vapour.

Contact lenses in, downsuit on. My automatic pilot had taken over, while I lubricated the manual controls by ingurgitating my usual litre of coffee. I was still cringing a little at the idea of moving, but it had to be done. This was why I was here in Tibet, far away from husband and chooks. Nonetheless, it always seemed so cruel and painful, the birth of a summit day. Like a foetus being kicked out of the familiar womb (the sleeping bag) to land on the dark side of the moon (out beyond the tent door). Once the compulsory four cups of brew were consumed nothing stood before us except the zipped tent door.

Soon we were outside, peeing, pooing, putting crampons on boots, blowing on fingers to bring them back to life, putting pack on, headtorch on, mitts on, ice-axe in hand. Out of breath, already. In the complete darkness we could hardly guess the mountain, let alone the way to the summit. Alex had told us to stick to the left of the rocks, that there were wands here and there. Around the corner, the snow slope steepened considerably to the top of the first buttress. A wind slab, prone to avalanche. I hyperventilated like a non-swimmer in deep water. It was cold, oh so cold. My toes were numb inside my new super-duper high-altitude boots. I wiggled them, I breathed, I breathed, I moved.

The route out of darkness followed a slender ridge straight on to the summit, hours away. I discovered that I was hungry. I had never been one for baked beans and sausages at unspeakable hours, but now was the time to force something inside me – my energy was fading. At the next stop, I got my banana chips out and managed to send some down my throat. Sounds simple like that, doesn't it? *I am going to have some banana chips because I am hungry.* In reality it is a circus act: nose dribbling, mouth mask to be pushed down to facilitate entry of chips in mouth, mouth mask doesn't want to go down, left hand out of mitt to pinch reluctant mask and force it down to chin, blow on left fingers to thaw them, unzip plastic bag while I think of it, blow on fingers again, tuck them back in mitt, bend head backwards, shake plastic bag in the vicinity of estimated mouth location, choke on banana chips tumbling down throat. Success. Jon put his arm around my shoulders as I munched on contentedly. 'Are you all right?'

'Mmm . . .' Our headtorches touched. 'Want some banana chips?'

'No thanks. Shall we keep moving?'

'Sure.' Colours appeared on the horizon. I thought of taking a photo. Only thought of it. I was still getting over the banana chips act, and could not cope with an 'encore'.

It was like being there the morning the world was born. There was a lake, intensely turquoise, and brown hills and blond dunes, shining sharp summits, and darker ones in the distance. There was Lama and his gentle smile, there was Jon, so strong, discreetly caring, looking at his watch: faster, come on, let's move. He reminded me of the rabbit in Alice's wonderland. He was right, though – speed is safety in the mountains, as long as one can move fast safely!

The snow was deep. As the sun started its ascent through the rarefied atmosphere, the temperature shot up. Jon and Lama were in front plugging steps in a steep snow slope. The ridge was at times icy and sharp, or it lost itself in rock formations that we skirted on the left slopes. I looked down. Right. Not the place to choose for a faux-pas. I kept thinking, *God I am so hot, I wish they would stop so I could cool down.* Gasp, gasp. With the heat of the morning getting on its way, the snow had become softer.

We were getting close to the summit – I could see a couple of flags wavering in the heat. I felt vaguely worried. I had heard so many stories of people hallucinating at altitude that I was expecting to see pink elephants in tutus pirouetting up the summit slopes. Nothing. My brain was in perfect working order; I could have said the Act of Contrition without stuttering once.

Up the last snow slope, steep, deep snow, onto an icy crest littered with old fixed ropes and buried player flags. Jon, in front, was seconds away from the summit. I was empty of feelings. I took photos, cold-headed, almost businesslike. The summit was a narrow ice ridge, and Jon had to slash around with his ice-axe to make it fit for three people to sit on. Lama got up next, then me, still clicking away. We were mounting the summit like riders on a frozen white horse. No room for extrovert summit indulgences, we just grinned at each other, took a few more photos, tried to spot Everest on the horizon, called Base Camp to say hello and to tell them we had made it, and it was time to go down.

I felt a little tired now, relieved to have made it and concerned about going down those slopes of what looked now like melting lemon ice-cream. I watched every step, making sure that my crampons bit the ice just so, or plunged my arms in the ice-cream and wiggled down the steep snow slush. We were all tired. Lama stayed with me, while Jon moved faster in front. Camp Three appeared in the distance, the Promised Land. I could only think, *Gee, it is so hot.* Only about eleven a.m. and it was tropical. Another stop to cool down. I was starving. Not elated or anything – that would come later, when it was safe to feel the emotion. Just down to practical and vital matters, left foot here, right foot there, ice-axe in, ice-axe down, repeat. Eventually, we reached the bum-slide close to camp, where Jon had just arrived. I sat on the snow and slid towards Camp Three. Slowly. I wanted to stay in control and I was not sure I would if I went too fast. Last steps to camp. I sat outside the tent, dog-tired. Mike got out. 'Two things,' he said. 'First a photo,' he pointed at the giggling mess on the ground, 'then a hug. You have done well, grasshopper.' I thought so too, but right now all I wanted was to stagger into the tent and get spoiled. Jon Tinker was already spread in there. He looked happy. I bent over and kissed him. 'Thank you for a wonderful day.'

He smiled back. 'I am chuffed, real chuffed!' *Qué?* Those Brits and their funny language!

22 May 1994, Camp One, Shishapangma

The summit tears finally came, listening to the Moody Blues. Up here, where I had stopped on the way down to Advance Base Camp, I caught up with my feelings, and allowed myself to be engulfed. A big warm white wave toppled me on my back in a mountain of feathers, my hands contoured slowly the map of my body, bringing to the surface the burning emotions of the last few days. I sang to the mountains and the blue lakes of Tibet, to a universe of love and friendship. Smell of damp forest smeared on my face by moist fingers. Smile and tears in my closed eyes. I had climbed Shishapangma. What had started as a magic number – 8000 metres – to be reached by all means had ended up being a flowing dance on a mountainside, perfectly orchestrated because I accepted the next move without knowing what it would be, and danced it through with a smile on my face. I didn't climb this mountain on my own, though: my Jon was with me when I was tired and needed to concentrate, and I drew energy from Mike and Jon as well. How couldn't it have been? Reaching the summit has been the inevitable outcome of all the care and mental support I have received and given during the course of this expedition.

Back at Advance Base Camp, I floated around, on a real high after climbing my beautiful mountain, wanting more. I could have gone and climbed another one! It was then that Jon invited me to join the small team going to attempt Cho Oyu in alpine style . . . I tossed and turned all night.

29 May 1994, Shishapangma Base Camp

The walk back from Advance Base Camp was long and tiring. Today I feel really flat. Maybe due to the fact that my period is approaching. Feel like crying too, so it would make sense. What am I going to do? Go? Not go? Nothing ventured, nothing gained. But if I fail? . . .

I tossed a coin. I am going.

The truck bolted over the top of the pass, and we were airborne once more. Dust in streams followed the smell of the exhaust. I sang my head off in the wind, to the great amusement of my companions. It was so exciting to be on the way to Cho Oyu, which we could see, resplendent in the distance, at the head of the narrow valley we were now entering. The sun covered the bare earth with a carpet of yellow velvet, enhancing the slopes with the stage lights of its rays. Going full speed in such a land-scape, standing in the back of a truck, being tossed around at every bump of the track, breathing in Tibetan dust and the smell of the unexpected was total bliss. I felt like screaming my joy to the world.

Tibetan herders were leading hundreds of goats and sheep to their grazing grounds, moving along the road at a casual pace. Automotive traffic was the last thing on their minds. Our Chinese driver took great pleasure in accelerating each time he saw long-legged herders in their black woollen pants, spinning wool as they went. He would toot at the last possible minute, sending the poor guys up in the air with fright, diving for the side of the road. Roars of laughter came from the truck's cabin. We couldn't help laughing too, the sight was simply too hilari-ous. The Tibetans, once they understood what had happened, broke into big grins as well. They had left their villages further down in the valley to come and stay with their herds closer to the mountains, where the rains of the approaching monsoon would cause dormant seeds to germinate and spread a bright green cover over the whole countryside. Well, bright green compared to the usual stoniness.

We crossed a river, passed more herders with their yaks, and stopped near a spring nestled in a small meadow. From our high viewpoint on the truck's apron, we were looking down at the ruins of a small town. Dusty courtyards were enclosed in a labyrinth of crumbling mud-brick walls, opening onto small, one-room roofless houses. The wind was howling, hurtling dust gathered throughout the countryside at the walls in a fury of destruction. This was going to be Base Camp, our home for the next two weeks.

We were still at least a couple of hours away from the start of the glacier leading to Cho Oyu, so why did we stop here? Mr Li was extremely concerned about illegal emigrants roaming the area. I caught fragments of conversations about people getting killed. Ang Rita had to explain that the Nangpa La, the pass at the head of our valley which had been a trading road between Tibet and Nepal since time immemorial, was now the favourite escape route for illegal Tibetan emigrants wanting to cross Nepal and get into India to join the ranks of the faithful in Daramsala, where the Dalai Lama lived in exile.

Some of these poor people, no doubt pushed by desperation, had a reputation for being gun-carrying bandits. From the stories told by Mr Li, in a flurry of raised eyebrows and flinging arms, they used their weapons, too. His first preoccupation after we had erected our tent city was to find a bodyguard. In Tingri, the town serving the pass on the main road to Lhasa, he had tried without success to get a policeman to come with us and protect us all from the *banditos*, but no one was keen and Mr Li had been left to his fears. The next morning a solid-looking Tibetan man, sporting the usual tresses and turquoises, started loitering around our mess tent. As it turned out, he was the bodyguard employed by Mr Li to protect our precious lives and material possessions in the Base Camp I had now baptised 'The City of Thieves.' Considering he only had his body to put between us and potential trigger-happy assailants, I had doubts as to how useful he would really be. Ang Rita soon found a more practical occupation for him, and had him running to the spring to collect water and doing the dishes after every meal.

We had neighbours, too; at the end of their hard working day, herders and their children flocked with hundreds of goats to the courtyard next to ours and settled for the night. The goats were gathered in empty houses and closed in with stones piled up in the door spaces. Dogs made themselves comfortable in the dust outside the doors and growled each time one of us walked a little too close on the way to the toilet. We made a habit of carrying a stone on our errands, just in case western calves proved too appetising . . .

The Tibetans usually came and visited us once the goats were safely away. There was often a group of Tibetans in the kitchen, orchestrated by Ang Rita, and more of them framing the entrance of the tent. Questions fused. Ang Rita, laughing, told us that two of the men were brothers and were married to the same woman, who was in one of the nearby villages with their other brother, husband number three! A very convenient arrangement, it seemed, to keep wealth in the family. He added that one of the brothers had asked if Jon, Mike and Billy were my three husbands! Babu was listening to his favourite tape once more, and practising playing the *domien*. I had thought when I saw him proudly carrying the home-made guitar he bought in Tingri that it would look really nice in the hotel he was building in the Khumbu. Ha! The thing was actually a real musical instrument, if one can call the dull repetitive noise that our future rock star managed to extort from it 'music'. Mind you, it went quite well with the dull repetitive drumming and humming of the Sherpa tape he played constantly on the expedition music box! Jon was the first one to crack. 'Aargh! This is shit, I never want to hear it again!' And off he went, confiscating the ghetto-blaster and retreating to his tent with it. Babu, completely unaffected, walked to his tent and returned with another stereo that he had bought in Zhangmu. The quality of sound was appalling, but went quite well with the already distorted recording of Sherpa bangs and clangs . . .

2 *June 1994, City of Thieves*

> A huge front closed in on us tonight, illegally entering Tibet over the Nangpa La and Cho Oyu. Ugly clouds cover our sky from horizon to horizon, and spit a nasty little snow. Still, we must go on. We have packed food and gear for two weeks; the pile looks

quite impressive. I am glad we will have some help to carry it all to Advance Base Camp; Ang Rita is coming with us, as well as a yak and its herder.

Cho Oyu is a beautiful mountain. The climbing on it looks interesting. A lot of rock appears in the upper slopes. I feel quite fit and rested now. I went for a walk up to the fortress crowning a rock outcrop nearby and even had a little run up the hill, just because I felt like it. All that unknown history surrounding us appeals to me greatly. I could ask questions, find out when our City of Thieves was built, what the role of this fortress was. I prefer rummaging around, finding old fragments of pottery, to feel the atmosphere rather than to reconstruct harsh reality with possibly erroneous facts.

There was a feeling of Christmas Eve in the air as we started the walk towards the foot of Cho Oyu. The yak carrying the bulk of our gear looked terribly small. We pondered its origin; maybe it was a dwarf kind of yak, bred for sturdiness? It was not moving very fast, but maybe it would be steady? We had a long way to go, as we would be packing two days' walk into one, in our rush to get there and beat the monsoon to it. The sky was blue, windless. We strolled happily alongside the river, crossing it to reach the left side of the terminal moraine of the glacier leading to the Khumbu. Along its flank lay a beautiful valley of tiny flowers, with a sandy floor and a creek meandering down it. We found ourselves sitting around more and more, waiting for the yak to catch up with us. At the last stop, as we were departing, I looked back and was a little concerned to find the yak standing motionless in the middle of the track, and its minder bowing towards it, hands joined in an attitude of prayer . . . Once more we stopped and waited. No yak materialised on the horizon this time; only three men, stopping very frequently. As they got closer, we could see that they were heavily loaded. 'Yak won't move' said Ang Rita, very matter of factly. So we shared the yak's load between us.

I was given eight kilograms of 'boil in the bag', the dreaded mountain food I couldn't stomach any more. 'Poetic justice,' giggled Jon. We still had a long way to go, so we kept moving. Every so often, we would meet the occasional yak caravan on its way from Nepal to Tingri. The Tibetans would greet us with *Namaste* instead of *Tachi Delai*. It was getting late in the day, and I was feeling grumpy. I found my pack too heavy and lagged behind. We crossed a side glacier. Cho Oyu was now a tangle of ridges we could make no sense out of. Eventually, we stumbled upon a camp site. Plump-looking pigeons pecked at the edible rubbish left by unscrupulous previous groups. We erected the tents and huddled around the stove for some welcome brews.

We left at first light, hoping to make it to the first camp on the mountain that day. From the side track we now followed, we could see yak caravans coming over the Nangpa La. I loved listening to the lullabies the herders were singing to their yaks to keep them in line. The melodious tunes were carried by the wind, and caressed my ears and heart.

After a couple of hours, we reached another Advance Base Camp — the real one this time! I organised a brew while Babu and the boys sorted out gear and food. Ang Rita and the yak minder left us, in order to go back to the City of Thieves, hoping that the yak would be where it had been left on the moraine.

We took one week's supply of food with us, and an impressive array of gear: snow stakes, ice-screws, climbing ropes, static ropes to fix the icefall, a five-person tent, pots, stoves, a stuffed koala (my Sheila Koala, who had ascended Shishapangma snuggled up in the lid of my pack, and hoped to tick off another 8000-metre peak), a toy gorilla (Billy's Murf, who had climbed Shishapangma twice in different packs, always to be forgotten in the summit shots) — you name it, we had it! The moraine went on and on and on. We were carrying absurdly huge packs. A funny thing is that the kind of expedition we were having — a one-push alpine-style attempt without major support, was known by mountaineers as a 'lightweight expedition'. Ha!

It was hard work, very hard work, although it did not blind us to the surrounding beauty. We were now walking towards Cho Oyu's base, gradually gaining altitude up a secondary glacier hugged by the most amazing peaks. I was salivating just looking at them. Most of them were probably unclimbed, as happens when there is a popular peak in an area. The glacier itself was covered with flat rocks which, when the light of the sun touched them at the right angle, would suddenly burst into miniature fireworks. We camped in a forbidding lull at the foot of our route. Or so we hoped, as the weather had closed in once more, and we could not tell where we were.

The alarm went off at four a.m. A look outside. Yep, she'd be right today; the sky was clear, the air still. Really quite thrilling to get onto the first scree leading up to the snow ridge we could see petering into the serac wall up there. We were hoping to reach its foot today, at 6750 metres, the site of Camp Two, and to climb it and establish another camp at around 7400 metres. That would put us in a position to go for the summit in only three days. Speed was of the essence now. There was a race on – the monsoon could not be far away.

Our packs were heavier than ever. The ground we had to cover to reach that snow ridge was horrendous. I thought I had seen it all when my Jon, Geoff and I had grovelled up that almost vertical scree on the South Face of Aconcagua. Wrong. This one, as impossible as it might seem, was even steeper, even looser. Stones kept rolling underfoot and plunged towards those following behind. No fun. Babu and Jon, the fastest in our little group, had gone ahead to find a camp site and reconnoitre the route through the serac. Mike was in pain – he had hurt a rib on the bumpy minibus ride to Zhangmu, when his chest had collided with his pelvis. He thought one of his ribs was broken. I hung around, knowing that company made torment easier to endure. Billy was waiting for us at the start of the snow. There were huge crevasses around, which meant that we would now have to rope up. Roping up was a bit of a concern, because the snow was of the very hard type – not quite ice – and as we were moving together it meant that if one of us fell the rest were likely to be history.

Jon and Babu were returning to the site chosen for the tent as we arrived there. They had encountered fixed ropes on the serac wall, but had not been able to use them as their attachment points were popping out of the ice. Tomorrow we would have to leave very early, as it would take a while to fix new ropes up the ice wall. We would also take a roll of clothes line (the blue plastic-looking rope we used to leave fixed-roped in dangerous places), in case the serac toppled while we were above it. That would allow us to fix a new line to descend, instead of being left on top of a new ice wall with no means of escape. Just to make things more interesting, Mike sneezed violently and hurt his rib even more. He could hardly move now, and groaned with pain. The wind shook the tent with mounting anger.

We huddled up, joking about the situation in an attempt to forget our concerns. Murf the gorilla presented the weather forecast, while Jon and I made furious gale noises and rolled around the tent to help capture the storm atmosphere on film.

I had been worried earlier on about sharing a tent with another four people, but I could have saved the energy; we all got on like a house on fire. There was a lot to be said for sharing a small space in difficult conditions while trying to achieve an ambitious project, such as climbing an 8000-metre peak in a few days. Our advantage was that we had already been through a lot together on Shishapangma and Everest and knew that we could get on all right, as we cared for each other. Mountaineering is often compared to war. I do not like the idea implied in the comparison of setting off in an aggressive way to conquer a peak, no matter what. I am more inclined to flow with it all, to accept the moods of the mountain and to act gently, accordingly, but I understand that the whole experience bonds people who share it, beyond the comprehension of anyone who has not been in a situation similar to it, for example, a war fought alongside others. One thing is for sure: screens fall down and the true nature of the individual is exposed, revealing ugliness or beauty.

7 June 1994, Camp 6750 metres, Cho Oyu

> White-out as the alarm goes off this morning. We won't move up until the sky clears completely, which is unlikely today. To save time for tomorrow, Jon and Billy went and climbed the serac, fixing a new rope up the vertical wall. They came back tired, their faces puffed up by the altitude and the hard work. Mike is not getting any better, and Babu seems to have lost interest in going up. I am glad we all had this day of bad weather to rest before continuing on. Jon has doubts as to the value of rest at this kind of altitude. I keep hoping that tomorrow will be good and everything well in a perfect world. We have six days before the truck is due to arrive at Base Camp.

The wind blew like mad last night. 'Showing off,' said Jon. It lulled for a few hours, then started again, more violently than ever. I had images of the tent making the first parasail descent of the mountain, with us inside. It was time for a powwow. We all agreed, although reluctantly, that we would not get the three days of good weather we needed to climb the mountain. That meant that today, we must go down to Advance Base Camp. I risked an eye outside, praying for a miracle. Not this time. The sky was black over Nepal, the wind threatening to destroy our tent and leave us without shelter for the descent.

We did not rope up this time. Instead, we stayed close to each other as we ran down the mountain, over gaping holes, down steep slopes. As we lost altitude, the sun came out of the cloud and it grew quite hot. We knew it was a nasty trick: higher up, the clouds moved at a speed which left no doubt in our minds as to the rightness of our decision. That kind of wind can freeze and tear a climber off her feet.

Going up was one thing, coming down another. At the top of the steepest slope, not trusting my big clumsy boots for downclimbing, I had no shame in asking for an abseil to be set. What good would it do me to have failed, and to die on the way down? It all went so fast. The hours we took to climb up the snow ridge we reversed in instants. The crevasses looked a lot more menacing, their opened jaws ready to swallow the foolhardy. I climbed down carefully, taking my time in the rushing wave of energy generated by the descent. Jon and Babu had already taken their crampons off, and were running down the scree towards Interim Camp. Billy looked up the mountain and raised his shoulders. With a contrived smile he too was on his way. Mike took his time – he could hardly stand for the pain – and slowly started on the scree, trying to avoid jolts which sent little exclamations of pain to his pursed lips.

I sat on my pack for a while and took my crampons off. I wandered behind some rocks for a pee. I did not dare look up. I sighed, zipped up and returned to my pack. I squinted as I let my eyes glide over the ridge in front of me, the growling crevasses, the smooth domes leaping to the blue walls of the serac, the curve of the rocky face towards the hidden snow of the summit. There were tears in my eyes. It must have been the wind.

Antarctica, at Last!

The Hercules banked steeply, and the ear-splitting drone of its engines drowned my dream. Holly, the Adventure Network International (ANI) representative on board, shouted in Guy's ear, and I gathered that it was something worth hearing about. Not that I hadn't guessed: the steep turn had brought home the reality of our turning back to Punta Arenas in South America. An icy fog was taking over the whole landing area at Patriot Hills, Antarctica, making take-offs and landings impossible. I remembered with some bitterness my joke about it all being a dress rehearsal as, late into the starless Patagonian night, we piled into the bus taking us to the airport, ensconced in our downsuits. After eight days of standing by in Punta Arenas, and a two-and-a-half-hour flight towards Patriot Hills, we were back at square one. Antarctica remained as elusive as ever.

My first attempt at raising money to go to Antarctica had been four years earlier, when a group of us had spent forty hours at minus forty degrees in the freezer at the Pyrmont Fish Market in Sydney. It had led to nothing at all, and life had taken me away to other places. Then, when I was on Shishapangma, Jon had received a call from John Colls, a Melbourne actuary and orienteering enthusiast. John had never climbed a mountain in his life, but he had always wanted to visit Antarctica and to take part in a mountaineering expedition. He had noticed our 'climb Mount Vinson' advertising in *Wild* magazine and thought, *Well, why not?* I was thrilled. At last, a chance to climb Vinson!

I wrote to Anne Kershaw, the managing director of ANI, which was the only airline in the world flying commercially to Antarctica. In fact, the company had been created specifically to cater for climbers wishing to tackle Vinson and other Antarctic summits. Anne pencilled me in, and we agreed on a deal: if I did not find the fifteen thousand dollars still needed (on top of the expedition fee charged to John) for me to make it to Antarctica, ANI would allow him to join one of their guided groups, so he could still climb Vinson, albeit without me as a guide. John was happy with the arrangement and I embarked once more on the sponsorship hunt.

The economy had made a hesitant recovery in the last few years, improving the odds of raising money. James Hoadley and the Wool Corporation came to the party again, and through a mutual friend, I met the man who was going to change the face of my Seven Summits quest. Ian Darling, his wife Min, and their friend Roddo O'Connor had booked to join one of our 1995 Aconcagua expeditions. As we met in the months leading up to the expedition, Ian realised that although I was totally dedicated to making my dream happen, I lacked the necessary contacts and ability to secure sponsorship from companies swamped with similar requests. Ian was a delightful stockbroker who would offer jelly beans and red cordial to his clients. He was a natural at business. He also happened to be very good at blowing trumpets. With a heart of gold, he was prepared to commit the time and energy to help me find the money to go not only to Antarctica, but also on to my next Everest attempt. A gift from the mountain gods. Two weeks before the scheduled date of departure, HIH Winterthur Insurance and Woodside, a couple of the

numerous companies Ian had approached, agreed to sponsor me.
I was able to stop chewing my fingernails, and send Anne Ker-
shaw a fax to say I was coming. Reality took a while to sink in.
Soon I would be in Antarctica. Wow!

And now, after ten days in Punta Arenas, a godforsaken
little frontier town in the forgotten Straits of Magellan, it was
just as hard to believe. John and I were not the only Vinson aspi-
rants on the aborted flight to Patriot Hills. We were joined by
Ross Nichols, a former ANI accountant, who was being
rewarded for his services by a free trip to the ice; Guy Cotter, a
New Zealand guide working for Rob Hall's company; and his
client, Yukimitsu Okubo. Ours was a strange little group – an
eclectic gathering of mountain lovers shipwrecked at the
southernmost part of Chile, waiting for a rescue to Antarctica.
Ross, a South African expatriate living in Canada, had been
pretty much thrown at John and me: as I was not sure until quite
late if I'd be going Anne had organised a Plan B, which was for
John to be guided by an ANI guide, assisted by Ross, himself
a competent mountaineer. But now I was going to be there and
Anne had asked me if Ross could tag along. I was reluctant, seeing the possible addition as more complications and extra work.
I talked it over with my Jon and with John, and we agreed that
three people on a rope could be safer to cross the Antarctic
crevasses, which had a reputation of being enormous. If one of
us fell in, it would be easier for the other two climbers to pull the
unfortunate one out of the icy chasms. But I still had misgivings
about spending time at close quarters and climbing with someone I'd never met before, so meeting the man was an interesting
experience.

Ross was the type who babbled his head off until he
finally felt comfortable with his new acquaintances. A little
scattered, full of goodwill, Ross ended up being good help with
running errands for the expedition, and a never-ending source
of entertainment. A little too entertaining for John, perhaps,
who shared a room with him. The weary look in his eyes led me

to believe that if Ross shared a tent with us on the mountain, it might soon turn into a crime scene. I went back to the drawing board for my expedition logistics, and asked Anne if Aaron, the guide who was to have taken Ross and John on the climb had I not be able to come, could join our group. That would mean taking a couple of tents, and organising ourselves in two pairs of climbers. Too bad for the crevasse-crossing theory – keeping John happy was the priority in my mind.

Between sightseeing, buying food and waiting for our flight in Punta Arenas, we also ended up spending a fair amount of time sampling the cafe culture with Guy and Yukimitsu (better known as Yuki). I had met Guy a long time ago in New Zealand when I was making my first hesitant steps in the English language and the art of mountain climbing. I remembered a young man with a fresh smile and a wispy moustache, and I looked forward to getting to know him properly, now that I was equipped with climbing confidence and better English. The moustache had gone, but the smile had not changed. Guy had become an accomplished ski instructor and mountain guide, and he exuded a sense of self-contentment. He proudly showed me a picture of little Elmo, sitting in his bath with a rather serious look in his beautiful eyes.

Looking at Elmo's photograph made me wonder if I'd ever carry around pictures of my own brood. Did I want children? Did I want to go through the trauma of childbirth? Would any woman go through it, given the choice? Climbing mountains was hard work, but from most accounts it was child's play compared to giving birth and nurturing a child into a well-balanced adult. I was still a child myself, discovering myself and the world and people around me. I didn't think I had it in me to take on the enormous responsibility of children. I'd leave it to parents who could do a good job of it. But the picture of Elmo in his bath . . .

Jon had called Anne's office and left a message saying that no matter how long it took, I was to climb Vinson before heading for Mendoza and our January Aconcagua expedition. He was prepared to take it on himself to look after eleven tour members while I tried the sixth summit in my quest to climb the 'Seven Bloody Mountains'. Really, I was a lucky woman – I had a life partner who let me be myself, who understood that being free to spend time without him and to roam mountains was an integral part of my enjoyment of sharing time and life with him. Jon also needed his time without me, especially since he had developed a passion for exploring the Australian outback and living off the land. I did not share his sentiment, thinking that there would be time to discover Australia's remote corners once I was too old to climb mountains. That was all right, though – he had friends he could share his passion with, and he also loved being in the bush on his own. 'Live and let live' was something our separation in the late eighties had taught us. We tried to respect the other's wishes, and help each other realise our dreams.

It seemed my dream had come to a standstill, as I found myself condemned to wait, and wait, and wait. Yuki, a youthful-looking Japanese real estate tycoon, occupied his days by exercising on the floor of his hotel room, and studying to become a lawyer. He had decided to climb the Seven Summits, much to the disgust of his elegant wife, and was hoping to climb Vinson before joining an American expedition to Aconcagua, and Rob Hall's trip to the Everest South Col Route next April. 'You tell me what colour downsuit you wear, so we recognise each other on the summit!' said he, as I exposed my hopes to climb Chomolungma during the same period, but from the north, the Tibetan side.

Anne called at seven a.m. 'The bus will be around to pick you up in a couple of hours.' Her voice sounded tired. 'You need the patience of an angel to fly in Antarctica,' she warned. 'Sometimes I wish I had a job in a supermarket . . .' The continuous radio schedules between her office in Punta Arenas and the ANI base at Patriot Hills, the logistical nightmares and dealing with clients disgruntled at the inevitable backlog of flights due to bad weather and limited flying resources were a few of the things keeping her busy, day and night, but she still managed to make herself kind and available to everyone. I liked her, and admired her professionalism. And this time, I believed that we would make it to our destination: two nights before, we had gotten ourselves properly drunk on Guy's advice that if we didn't, we'd never get to Antarctica. And it worked, just in time to save us from cafes and sightseeing overdose.

'Well, once again, here we all are!' This time there was a view through the round windows of the Hercules. Icebergs were floating in a sea of clouds, well below the racket of our four engines. Then the clouds closed in on the view, or so I thought. In fact, although there were clouds around, the ground was emerging. Grey shadows appeared under the clouds, ripples of white and dark blue. That blur underneath us was Antarctica! Finally I had made it to the seventh continent.

We took turns in the cockpit, looking at the mountains on the horizon. 'Which one is Mount Vinson?' asked Mark, the South African pilot. 'I don't know!' Laughter. Every summer, ANI chartered the Hercules from Safair, a South African company specialising in relief flights to various places in Africa, and the crew came with the plane. They were all nice folk, happy to have a change of scene, and so used to flying in difficult conditions that they found landing on the long, bumpy, hard ice runway at Patriot Hills a piece of cake compared to touching down by night on a short airstrip in war-torn Sudan – 'You need a helicopter with brakes for that!' Their only complaint about the job was that they had a rule of not drinking for twenty-four hours prior to flying, and because of the uncertain weather conditions, they were never sure how long it would be before the next flight to Antarctica. Being a resourceful lot, they had compensated for the problem by always carrying a huge icebox full of beer on board and by the time the bus taking them home at the end of the return journey hit town, they were all under the seats!

Suddenly a siren interrupted our shouted conversation, and I was told to return to my seat and don my downsuit and mountain boots: we would be landing in half an hour. Buckled to my seat, I had to twist my head to look at the ground approaching through the window behind me. My heart beat faster. I had heard that landing was the scariest part of the climbing trip, that we would shake and rattle and bump along the tongue of hard ice that was the landing strip. But as the wheels touched the ice I was only aware of the wholesome power of the plane, and the quiet control Mark exercised over it. Maureen Somers, one of the other passengers on the plane, exchanged a few excited giggles with me. At seventy-four, she was taking her first trip to the ice. She had come to visit her son Geoff, who was managing the camp at Patriot Hills that summer. Geoff Somers had gained fame in the late eighties as member of a large team to have completed the longest traverse of Antarctica, with dogs. They spent two hundred and twenty days on the traverse. I wondered if the members of the team parted as friends or foes after such a long time in such trying conditions!

The tail of the plane opened up on an expanse of endless white. Geoff ran in to hug his mum and John and I exchanged winks. I slapped Guy on the back, 'Aren't you excited?' He looked as cold as the ice surrounding us, while I was jumping up and down, waiting for the go-ahead to disembark.

'I will be as soon as we are out.'

How can you put a time and a place on something as spontaneous as excitement? I thought. I stepped out, and sat on the ice to attach crampons to my boots. I had heard that the runway was extremely slippery, and had not believed ANI's advice that the surface was all right to move on without crampons. I was glad to have them as I ran around barrels full of supplies being lined up on the ice, and people who seemed to appear from nowhere to empty the cargo. I walked away, putting a few hundred metres between myself and the commotion. Taking pictures was a convenient excuse, but really what I wanted was a chance, however short-lived, to grasp the reality of being in Antarctica. I was not able to, as nothing I had seen before could have prepared me for the feeling of otherworldliness of this last wilderness on earth. Puppets wrapped up in bulky clothing were running around, pushing and pulling bits of equipment; skidoos slid to and fro between the huge aeroplane and a small tented settlement on the shimmering horizon to my right; the blue of ice and sky dominated the surroundings, broken by the black gravel of the Patriot Hills, losing their shapes in the distance. 'Wow!' was all I could come up with.

———

I queued for seconds, piling more roast beef dripping with sauce, chips and steamed greens onto my china plate. The big yellow mess tent was a swarm of steaming bodies, all holding a plate or picking up a wine cask. Dinner time in Antarctica. How long would we be at ANI's base for? At least until the fog lifted from the snowfield at the foot of Vinson, where Aaron was waiting, where we would start the long walk to the summit. The weather noticeboard recorded conditions at each radio schedule. A woman who introduced herself as Rachel, in charge of public relations, explained to us how everything functioned and took us on a guided tour of town. We followed her away from the pot-belly stove, into our jackets, and out into that blue other world.

There were permanent guest tents where we were welcome to stay, and after we dropped our packs in our respective new quarters, Rachel shepherded us to the toilet facilities and explained their use; there was a barrel with a funnel sticking out of it that we were supposed to use for peeing, and a couple of ice cubicles for heavier waste, also stored in barrels, although these ones were thankfully much lower. ANI removed all waste from Antarctica, flying it to the Punta Arenas dump, and we were asked not to litter the camp area – or any place for that matter – as there was very little snowfall in Antarctica, and the snow surface remained pretty much the same from year to year. ANI policies must have been God's words to its employees – the camp and snow around it were absolutely spotless. We were also told that once on the mountain, we were expected to poo in black plastic bags and carry the bags out at the end of our stay. There were designated pee areas at each camp. Being quite obsessed myself with poo policies on expeditions, I was pleased to meet kindred spirits.

The tour continued with a visit to the radio tent, the repair shop, the storeroom dedicated to smokers, and the shower tent. Then it was time for afternoon tea, and we scampered back to the mess tent and its delights. New faces had appeared, among them Norman Vaughan, an Antarctica veteran who had just returned from the Transantarctic Mountains, where he had climbed his namesake, Mount Vaughan, so baptised because Norman had been part of the dog-sled team who had made the first sighting of the mountains back in 1929. Norman was to turn eighty-nine years old the next day. I caught myself hoping that the weather would remain unsuitable for landing on Vinson at least until after his birthday party and dinner celebrations.

The tent filled up with ANI workers, lured by the appeal of chitchat. The people around our table seemed obsessed by one subject – Everest and the Seven Summits. I supposed that the place, having been created as a springboard for Vinson hopefuls, was peopled with 'summits hunters', but listening to them you could come to believe that there were only seven mountains on earth! I carefully hid my intention to climb the Seven Summits. What I had started so long ago had turned into a worldwide craze – everybody, especially non-climbers, wanting to find the new Grail in this age of financial security obsession, that elusive feeling of self-worth to be plucked only from the top of the Seven Summits. I cringed as I imagined the ranks of climbers charging uphill, the masses united in the same quest, but not necessarily for the same reasons. Many would try, and some would succeed. Most of them might never climb another mountain in their life, having achieved their goal of proving to themselves and the world that they could do it, plunging back into their high-achieving lives. I had started my quest for the same reasons. I had gained some confidence along the way, but I also knew that climbing mountains was not a tool to achieve something for me. It was a *raison d'être*, it was the force which made my heart beat, my soul soar into the sky, my being explode in unison with creation. Alternatively, maybe I was fooling myself, and just lived permanently in a state of mid-life crisis.

I left behind the conversation I did not want to be part of, and retired to the tent I was sharing with Maureen. She had nothing to prove, and talked to me about living in the Channel Islands, a much more interesting subject. A night of light went by, and a second day at Patriot Hills. Geoff asked his ma, John and me, if we'd like to visit the underground storage area. To the centre of the ice we went, down some steps into a huge freezer which became a labyrinth of storage rooms, a huge snow cave, which must have taken hundreds of hours of work. In the flicker of candlelight we saw rows of frozen turkeys, shovels, spare parts for the planes, old wooden huts, gear of all kinds and descriptions, the snow room where the Cessna which was going to take us to the Vinson Massif spent the winter. We came out thinking it was tropical on the surface, and rushed to the mess tent for another check of the weather report, and another meal.

On Norman's birthday we volunteered to blow up the balloons which would be strung along the walls. The weather was improving at Vinson's Base Camp; there was a chance that we would be able to fly tonight. I prayed for the fog to lift *after* the party. *Please, please, please.* The smells coming out of the kitchen would make it cruel to leave immediately. My prayers were answered. We sat down to an incredible meal of roasted meats, fresh vegetables and chocolate cream puffs, and champagne. I remember the closing line of Norman's speech: 'Dream big, dare to fail.' How appropriate. As a birthday cake of cream puffs and chocolate sauce was dished out, Aaron radioed the mess that the fog had lifted. The landing at Vinson Base Camp was clear, and Max and the Cessna were ready to take the first two or three climbers in. Guy had been looking anxious. I walked up to him and offered, 'Why don't you go first?'

He shrugged his shoulders. 'I don't mind.'

'Ow, come on Guy, off you go!' I knew that he was planning to go to Camp One straight after landing. I did not want to break our sleep pattern, so it only made sense for him and Yuki to go on the first shuttle. We also had to meet up with Aaron, our new climbing partner, and sort out all the gear between the four of us; that would take time and, considering the late hour, was better dealt with in the morning. That's what felt right at the time, and I stuck to it.

We went to see Guy and Yuki off at the 'departure lounge', a patch of snow beside the Cessna. 'Good luck, mate, look after yourself!' We probably would not see each other for a while. In a way, I was relieved to see them set off before we did. Guy had a job to do, and so did I, and I did not fancy too much moving as a group, as I knew that I would feel more confident and free as the master of my own ship. I waved goodbye and went back to camp to sleep the champagne off.

———

Unclimbed mountains as far as the eye could see. The midnight sun shone on the horizon, bathing the landscape in golden light. Max, a Kiwi pilot with a passion for flying over ice, showed us a small turquoise lake created by snow melting down deep runnels on a steep, dark mountain face. A thick blanket of snow and ice two kilometres deep covered everything underneath us, the thickness of it apparent as it broke off in icefalls over steep sections. I tried to imagine the mountains without their cover of snow and ice. They would be gigantic, their bases 2000 metres lower than today.

We flew over the Minnesota Glacier, a giant ice river flowing from the Antarctic Plateau across the Ellsworth Range, and I was glad that we did not have to cross it on foot. The crevasses would have housed city blocks in their depths. Soon the Vinson Massif blocked the horizon. It looked very impressive, and massive – much bigger than any of the mountains we had seen so far. The weather was perfect. Within minutes we were landing in a curvy valley of snow at the foot of a huge rock wall leading straight up to the summit of Vinson. I could see two dots approaching the shade at its foot: Guy and Yuki, on their way to the site of Camp One. Aaron, who had been at Base Camp on his own for the last ten days, was happy to get some company, and breathed a sigh of relief when I told him that tomorrow morning would be early enough to get going.

We moved at a steady pace, pulling sleds and carrying packs. Camp One was not too far in distance, but the terrain was reasonably steep, and it took us a leisurely six and a half hours to reach it. My policy had always been that there is no point in burning yourself out on the first day – we are here to last the distance. This approach also made for spectacular sightseeing, as we took the time to sit and look around at the incredible world we were in. Having Aaron on the team was a definite advantage; he knew when the sun left and returned to a camp, so we planned our movements accordingly. No-one was keen to be walking in the shade, where the temperature literally plummeted; much better to snuggle in a sleeping bag until the sun made the world a friendly place to be. As soon as we finished our dinner – fresh chicken casserole – we dived into our bags for a fitful thirteen hours' slumber. Sleeping in the brightness of twenty-four-hour daylight was a little awkward, but I soon solved the problem by pulling my woolly hat down to my chin, creating some privacy in the process as well. Flicking on my walkman and listening to the Moody Blues completed the feeling and allowed me to enjoy many a lazy hour pretending I was alone in the world.

The walk to Camp Two, between Mount Vinson and its fin-like neighbour Mount Shinn, was shorter, and the ground flatter. We had perfect, windless weather, and enjoyed magnificent views of the majestic peaks surrounding us. Epperly came

into view, a forbidding fortress of dark rock which we heard had
been ascended for the first time very recently: Eric Loretan,
Swiss climber extraordinaire, had soloed it a couple of weeks
before, then ticked off Shinn and Vinson as an afterthought, in
a fifteen-hour climbing marathon. We would be content to
climb just Mount Vinson. In ten days, as it turned out!

We left our sleds at Camp Two, as the last part of the climb
to our base for the Vinson attempt was too steep for them. At last
the ground looked more interesting climbing-wise than what we
had done so far, which was not much more than plodding. Aaron,
who had been pessimistic about the weather changing because in
his two months as a guide for ANI on Vinson he had never seen
such a long spell of windless days, pointed at the sky where high
clouds were speeding by. 'Each time I have seen that, the
weather's come in real fast,' he moaned.

Aaron carried with him three cameras, including a monster which took three-hundred-and-sixty-degree photos, and
a heavy tripod. He swore at the sky: 'I have carried this bloody
thing twice to the summit, both times in fucking awful weather.
Then I spent ten days at Base Camp in perfect conditions, and
now it is going to do it to me again!' I prayed for a break in the
weather.

The wind picked up. Shinn soon put on a cloudy hat, and
the clouds gathered momentum as we made our way up a pretty
little icefall to the Col where our camp was. At the top of the
icefall we encountered a maze of big crevasses. My steps
echoed back to me, a sure sign that I was walking on a thin layer
of snow with a void below it. Yuk. There was no sign of
a crevasse but I knew it was there, right underneath me. Aargh!
This was a big one. Ten metres, and it still sounded hollow. If
the snow gave way, both John and I could kiss the world as we
knew it goodbye. Fortunately, the snow did not give way.
I breathed a sigh of relief. It was so good being on solid ground
again, I could have kissed the snow. In the excitement of the
crevasse crossing, I had not noticed that we were getting quite

close to camp. Guy and Yuki welcomed us, big smiles on their faces. 'You did it?' we asked.

'No. We started and got as far the summit pyramid, but a white-out forced us to turn back . . . of course, half an hour after we hit camp it cleared!' I was quite happy that Guy and Yuki had not made it yet. It meant that we would have the pleasure of their company, and I looked forward to it.

Aaron's fears were confirmed; the weather changed for the worse. The clear outline of the plateau on the horizon misted over, the wind picked up, and snowdrifts encumbered our tent's vestibules. Cooking and brewing became a nightmare. By evening the sky had cleared, so we planned an early departure the next morning. John was electrified by the thought of the action ahead. 'Have another drink, John, I want you to drink heaps before we go.' Dehydration is the enemy at high altitude, because the air is so dry and so cold that it can drain a body of energy by desiccating it. Just breathing in is enough to dehydrate, and drinking six to eight litres a day is a prerequisite to saving energy. The summit was not exactly close, and I wanted John to have the best chance to reach it.

Early the next morning we set off towards it, skirting a crevasse area and steadily plodding up a steep rise to the plateau leading to Vinson's summit. A few rocky peaks were bordering its southern horizon. I asked Aaron which peak was Vinson – easier than getting the map out of the pack. He pointed at one which was not even the furthest one. *Oh, shucks.*

Ominous clouds appeared behind Vinson, and the wind blew viciously. We slipped our down gear on, blowing on fingers as they became numb handling zips. 'How are you, John?' I howled in the wind.

'Oh, I've seen worse in Scotland!' Cheeky bugger. I promised myself to give Scotland a wide berth. We could see Guy and Yuki ahead of us, disappearing towards the summit ridge, but as we neared the summit pyramid, the only part of the ascent where we would have the opportunity to do some actual climbing, the wind became even stronger, forcing us to stop and present our backs to it. I started plodding up the slope leading to the summit ridge. John was beginning to show signs of fatigue, staggering at the end of the rope. The sky was black, and things were not looking so good. Yuki and Guy were on their way down. I decided to turn back; we could try again later. We waited for them to reach us, though – we wanted to know if they had made it to the summit. 'Yep. But it must have been the shortest time I've spent on a summit,' said Guy. 'What do you reckon, Yuki, three minutes?' We reached camp in a total white-out, and dived for our respective tents.

'Merry Christmas, John!' The wind howled outside, throwing snow at our tent with the force of a full Antarctic gale. Our sleeping bags were wet from the showers of frozen condensation coating the inside of our small shelter. The ground had melted under our sleeping mats, and I had the impression of lying on a big dipper. 'I'll have to cook inside the tent, John, the vestibule is full of snow again, and anyway, it is too windy out there.'

John assumed the crumbed sausage position in a corner, while I went on with the brewing. 'Some Christmas, isn't it?'

'Yeah. You know, I have a Christmas wish, John. I want to see Mount Shinn before the end of the day!'

Someone up there was listening for a change, and by the end of the day we were able to dig our way out of the tent, to take a quick look at the mountain and queue for the toilet. No-one had been game to bare their bottom in the middle of the storm!

I had saved a packet of sliced ham for our Christmas celebration. I rolled the slices on a plate, splashed them with some mayonnaise and went from tent to tent with the platter. 'Merry Christmas, Guy and Yuki!'

'Oh, how thoughtful of you!' exclaimed Guy, and put a brew on to wash it down.

The wind blew snow in my face as I made my way to Ross and Aaron's tent. 'Merry Christmas, guys. Any luck with the radio?' ANI had equipped each camp site with a powerful radio set; and most of the time we were able to talk to Patriot Hills and give them news of our progress. The Vaughan expedition, which was waiting for our return to fly out, was becoming quite impatient, and we were told that Anne was thinking about sending the plane in. Which to me amounted to a disaster, as the next scheduled flight was not before January the fourth, well into our first Aconcagua expedition. I felt guilty at the idea of being stuck in Antarctica for another two weeks while Jon was looking after such a big group on his own. I felt like leaving, and I felt like staying and finishing what I had started. John told me that he'd like to go down with Guy and Yuki as soon as the weather improved sufficiently. He had a demanding job and felt he had been away from work for too long already. Nobody had counted on the ten days waiting in Punta Arenas!

'Are you sure, John? We can go up again, you know.'

'Well,' said John, 'Antarctica was my dream, to be part of an expedition. The summit I always saw as a bonus, really. And I am getting a bit tired of being cold and wet in this wretched tent!'

I was sure that John could climb Vinson, but he had made an executive decision and he stuck to it. I faced the wind once more to visit Guy and put John's request to him. 'I don't have a problem with that,' he said, saving me the trip down to Base Camp. Guy, Yuki and John would also be able to get Max and the Cessna to fly to Patriot Hills; Aaron was to leave the mountains as well, and that meant we'd have to fly out in two groups of three.

The next afternoon the weather cleared sufficiently to allow the descent to Base Camp. Once again, I plied John with drinks before he set off. It was sad to see them go. We hugged, waved goodbye and they disappeared towards the icefall, a tell-tale black plastic bag in tow. Guy had been the closest to a friend in the group, and John and I had developed a warm complicity in our days together. I felt very much alone as I zipped myself up in the now spacious tent, and cried my heart out. What the hell was I doing here, with people I hardly knew, trying to climb a lump that would not even have drawn one look from me had it not been the highest lump on this wretched continent?

The outburst made me feel better. I stepped outside and went for a walk along the Col to get a view of our barometer peak, 'the Blob'. It was a snowy dome on the side of the plateau leading to Vinson. If high winds and snow plume were adorning its summit, it meant that the conditions on Vinson were the same. The telltale snow plume was there. Nonetheless, the walk cheered me up. I finally absorbed the fact that I was in Antarctica, practically alone in the middle of a huge mountain range, on the loneliest continent on earth. I was here to climb its highest summit, and I would, regardless of how long it took. To think that I had thought of giving up the Seven Summits just a few moments before!

I decided there and then to work on making the remains of our team united and happy. We were not going to climb this mountain if we clashed. I trotted back to camp and went visiting. It happened to be radio time, and we listened to Guy talking from Base Camp to Patriot Hills. Max was coming to pick them up tonight, despite windy conditions. 'Don't forget to turn the radio off and put the cat outside!' chimed in Aaron.

'There ain't no pussy here!' chuckled Guy.

From Patriot Hills we learned that the Herc was ready for departure in Punta Arenas, and my only hope to catch it was if the weather was unsuitable for landing at Patriot Hills for a couple more days. I crossed my fingers and hoped for the best. My mind raced ahead with 'what ifs'. We could go up tomorrow, race back down and be at Base Camp in time to catch the Hercules . . . maybe.

The wind changed direction during the night; it was now coming from the south, which meant that our camp at the Col was sheltered, and that gave us the impression that we were sitting around wasting our time. We took a walk up the Col every hour to check on our barometer peak. In the afternoon, the wind seemed to abate slightly and we charged up the hill, full of hope. Two and a half hours later we were back in camp. Once again the wind had stopped us: it came from the south, the direction we were walking towards, and hit us full in the face, burning our skin with millions of icy pricks. John had given me a neoprene face mask which I had not tried yet, relying instead on my good old cold air mask for protection from cold air. I wished now I had worn John's mask, as it protected the whole face rather then just the mouth area. We would still have had to turn back, but at least I would not have ended up with a face looking like an overcooked lobster. Not that I cared. I had resigned from all wild hopes: we would climb Vinson when we would climb it. *Inch Allah* – May the will of God (Allah) be done.

———

The Hercules still had not left Chile as we set off for take three twenty-four hours later. The time was five p.m., and we had been up all day spying on the weather and building snow walls to stop snow building up around our tent entrances. Aaron, thinking about lugging his heavy photographic equipment up one more time in less than ideal conditions, ummed and arrhed about going. I did not share his concerns. I was going. *It's now or never . . .* echoed in my head. Ross shared my opinion and determination, and together we convinced Aaron that the wind would probably abate long enough for him to take his photo. 'We'll hold the tripod, promise!' We had started this together, and both felt that it would be wrong if Aaron stayed in camp and missed out on a possibly perfect summit. He agreed to join us for a while to feel it out.

Once again we faced a strong headwind, but this time I was wearing my neoprene face mask. And my cold air mask on top of it. And a polartec suit, a windsuit and a downsuit. I needed every bit of equipment I was wearing. This truly was the coldest place on earth! That evening, it must have been the most beautiful as well. The whole mountain range was visible, dark mount after dark mount, bathed in the most amazing light – a gorgeous golden colour, which gave the whole landscape a warmth negated by the extreme cold. I felt privileged to be where I was, fighting the unforgiving wind to reach the highest point of this amazing land that I so hated. Forgotten were my doubts on the why and the how – I was in the middle of doing what I did best and loved most, working my way uphill, against all odds, to touch the sky.

Ross was moving leisurely, looking strong and comfortable. Aaron was slowing down, thinking about turning back. Ross and I encouraged him on: 'Come on, it's definitely getting better! We can do it!' He swore, and kept going. Stopped again, complaining of cold hands. I gave him the chemical heat packs I was keeping for emergencies. If my fingers got cold, I'd just wiggle them more . . . The shade caught us in the middle of the summit pyramid, and the temperature dropped dramatically. Aaron screamed at us to go faster, that his left hand was frozen, that he needed to get to the sun fast. We sprinted to the summit ridge, puffing madly. I was now feeling the effects of altitude, having moved at a speed which was not natural for me. Ross was moving faster than me, and reached the ridge and the sun. 'No wind!' he yelled.

Arriving on the summit ridge was magical: another amazing view, and a delightful-looking rock-and-snow scramble to the summit. Ross and I discussed Aaron's hands. 'I'll put them on my stomach,' said Ross. Aaron soon appeared, to announce that his hand was much better now. *Bloody hell.* We unroped and climbed again towards the summit. That little sprint had not done me any good. I breathed quite heavily and took it slowly, while Aaron and Ross overtook me. The summit was now just moments away. I topped the summit a few minutes after the others. Ross turned back, arms outstretched. 'Well done!'

'Well done yourself! You are a strong bugger!' We hugged.

A mad photo session for my sponsors followed. It could

have been anyone kneeling beside the upside-down skipole marking the summit – with my downhood, goggles and black neoprene mask I was not able to share the frozen smile hidden behind. In fact, I can't even remember if I bothered smiling. I was thinking about the picture to take, about warming up my fingers between corporate flag-waving, and about how long it would be before I could piss off. If the summit ridge had been thoroughly enjoyable, the summit certainly was not. It was extremely windy, and terribly cold. Ross and I had to wait, crouching down in the wind, while Aaron set up his tripod and three-hundred-and-sixty-degree camera. A torrent of swear words made it obvious that the operation was not entirely successful. We made ourselves very small, and took a few more photos before scooting down out of the wind. Aaron decided to stay behind a while longer to try to warm up his camera. We left him to it, collected a few rocks and strolled down, stopping every so often to snap shots or look at the view. I noticed that the landing strip at Base Camp, 2000 metres straight below us, was covered in mist. Blast. Maybe it would clear tomorrow.

We roped up again, and powered down in a universe of yellow flickers of snow travelling horizontally past us. The landscape looked totally different from the one we had first travelled. The snow plateau had been replaced by an intricate universe of sastrugi, dyed yellow by the low rays of the sun. We had reached the summit just past midnight. Pressed on the rising wind, we were back in camp at three-thirty a.m. We fired the stove in Ross's tent, which was more comfortable than mine, and unwound with a shot of whisky and a hot drink. Ross and I had finally met, somewhere along the line. I was glad we had climbed the mountain together. And now that we had done it, I wanted out. The next radio schedule was at seven-thirty a.m. I asked Ross to make sure that Aaron made it. There was a slim chance that the Hercules had not made it to Patriot Hills yet, and I was prepared to go to Base Camp in the briefest time to have a chance to catch it.

ABOVE: *Our merry team at what was then known as Leningrad Railway Station. Leningrad, 1990.*

ABOVE: *Anne Tindall and I looking cool in the freezer at the Pyrmont Fish Market during a fund-raising stunt. Sydney, 1990.*

RIGHT: *Jon (centre), Jonathan Chester and I on the top of Elbrus … with Homer the penguin and Krondorff the dog. I got myself a stuffed friend, Sheila Koala, for my next summit. Elbrus, 1990.*

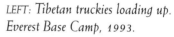

ABOVE: Chomolungma, the Goddess Mother of Earth, presented us with this magnificent first view of her slopes from Base Camp on the Rongbuk Glacier. Everest, 1993.

LEFT: Tibetan truckies loading up. Everest Base Camp, 1993.

LEFT: Norman Croucher, Jon and I shared a tent at our high point on Everest. Even without Norman's legs, it was still pretty cramped! Everest, 1993.

ABOVE: *No room for hugs and slaps on the back on top of Shishapangma's West Summit! Shishapangma, 1994.*

ABOVE: *Ross Nichols and I were elated to have summited on our third attempt to climb Vinson. We were photographed here after our marathon descent – necessary to make our connecting flight back to South America. Vinson, 1994.*

ABOVE: *After my unscheduled night out on Everest's North Ridge. Everest, 1995.*

LEFT: *From the wind and freezing shade of Vinson's face we entered a world of golden light and calm on the summit ridge. Vinson, 1994.*

TOP: *Tibetan women and children near Everest Base Camp, one of the harshest places on earth. Tibet, 1995.*

MIDDLE: *On the Pang La, dreaming of Everest's summit, which is looming on the horizon. Tibet, 1995.*

BOTTOM: *Jon and I enjoyed climbing together on Everest in '95 until the very end of the expedition, when he came down with bronchitis. Everest, 1995.*

ABOVE: *Henry Todd on the icefall giving Paul Deegan, TNT and me a lesson in ladder crossing. Everest, 1996.*

ABOVE: *Michael Joergensen on the Yellow Band. Everest, 1996.*

ABOVE: *Tina Sjögren practising ladder crossing on our first foray in the Khumbu Icefall. Everest, 1996.*

ABOVE: *Mal Duff, Tenzing Lama, Kipa Sherpa and Sharkie looking very official at the Puja ceremony at Everest Base Camp. Everest, 1997.*

RIGHT: *From the ridge to the Hillary Step I could see Illy Pauls, Yuri Contreras and Dawa coming down from the summit. I knew then I would make it up. Everest, 1997.*

ABOVE: *Sheila Koala and I having a well-earned rest on top of Everest. Nine years after I started, I had finally completed my Seven Summits quest! At last! Everest, 27 May 1997.*

ABOVE: *Jon and I bouldering in our backyard at Mount Arapiles. We lived in a tent at the foot of Arapiles for two years after we were married. Mount Arapiles, 1983.*

ABOVE: *I love Australian native trees and forests — they are the soul of this country. In the Victorian Alps, 1995.*

I retired to my tent and shivered miserably in my wet bag and clothing until eight a.m. The dampness was something I had not expected, but I just had to put up with it. Ross came over and told me that Max would pick us up from Base Camp in six hours. The poor quality of the radio communication meant that we did not know if we had missed the Herc or not. Betty, the radio operator in Patriot Hills, had been saying, 'Give me a string of Rogers if you want to be picked up in four hours . . . no? . . . in six hours.'

'Roger, Roger, Roger,' yelled Aaron into the microphone. So we packed everything, cleaned the camp and ran down towards Base Camp and the promised pick-up. Somehow we made it in six hours, trashing through deep snow accumulated by the wind, picking up the sleds at Camp Two, racing along the never-ending track to Base Camp. As we approached Camp One, the Cessna flew over us. We hoped it might land beside us, saving us another two hours of hard slog, but it was not to be. It tilted its wings to say hello, and flew down valley to wait for us at the ANI Base Camp hut. The last hour down was terrifying, with huge areas of freshly dumped snow settling under our feet with thundering noises. Finally Base Camp and the little orange bird waiting for us appeared in the distance.

Max smiled and gave me a hug: 'Congratulations! Let's go, the Herc is arriving in half an hour, and they said they'd wait for you guys.' Wow. A tight connection. We somehow piled everything into the little plane, giggling under the influence of the one can of beer Aaron had presented us with on arrival. We'd need a corkscrew to get out, though. Fast, so fast. It had been the story of this expedition, really. I chatted away with Max as we flew back to Patriot Hills, feeling like life was overtaking me. Everything had happened so fast, so suddenly. The summit, the descent, flying back to Patriot Hills, just about to fly out to Punta Arenas and to meet again with John, Guy and Yuki. I smiled and automatically reached for the gold chain and charms around my neck. My fingers found skin and nothing else.

My first communion medal of the Holy Virgin/Goddess Mother, the lapis lazuli I had rewarded myself with after climbing Shisha-pangma, my evil-looking crystal . . . all gone. Sacrificed to the mountain gods of Antarctica so I could stand on the highest summit of that heartless land. *Everything has a price*, I reflected, and looked out of the window into nothingness.

Everest –
North-side Story

'You are going,' said Ian, his rich brown eyes looking down into mine. 'Don't worry about a thing, you are going back to Everest, and we'll make sure the Big Weird Thing goes along too!' I sighed and returned to peeling potatoes. Right. Well, if Ian was sure that he could find the money for Jon and me to go back to Everest, I should relax and concentrate on getting ready for it. And right now, that meant keeping fit by going as high as possible on the slopes of Aconcagua. I was responsible for making sure that the people who had joined our Aconcagua expedition had the best possible chance to reach the summit, and it was also my responsibility to keep them well fed for dealing with the hard conditions and the deep snow we were encountering on the mountain. I gathered my potatoes, retired to the kitchen tent and chained myself to the stove once more.

I had finally caught up with the team, arriving at our Base Camp at Plaza Argentina the day after everyone else. While I was making my way from the depths of exhaustion in Punta Arenas to our Aconcagua Base Camp, Jon had had to organise supplies in Mendoza and manage the feeding and looking after of fourteen people on his own, so he had been quite happy to see the cook finally come to the rescue. Happy, too, that I had not given up, and had managed to climb Mount Vinson. Only one of the Seven Summits to go.

Ian and his wife, Min, as well as their friend Roddo O'Connor, had become my most fervent supporters, and had welcomed me with hugs and kisses. Now, though, it was back to the grindstone, and the hard work of looking after a big group of beginner climbers. People helped Jon and me by collecting water and peeling the odd carrot, but mostly it was up to us to make sure that everyone was fed and taken care of, and given the best chance to climb Aconcagua. Which did not happen that January. The weather was shocking: high winds blasted every day, and the snow was so deep that avalanches were pouring over slopes we had known to be absolutely safe and bare for as long as we could remember. But the team spirit supported by Ian and his friends made the expedition one of the most enriching I had ever taken to Aconcagua.

The weather improved for our February expedition, and allowed me to take Eli Dyer and Rob Pillans to the summit, while Jon stayed at the last camp to look after Kevin Rohrlach who, at sixty-eight years, was the expedition's veteran. Kevin had found the cold and the deep snow hard to deal with, but had done very well to get himself to 5900 metres in the conditions experienced.

I came back from the summit feeling very strong, and reasonably confident that I was physically and mentally prepared for my next attempt on Everest. Ian had managed to secure another sponsor for us, which meant that I would be climbing with Jon. We would be joining yet another Out There Trekking (OTT) expedition to the North Ridge of Everest, and this time would be given the opportunity to discover some new toilets, as we would fly from Katmandu to Lhasa and then travel by road across Tibet to the Rongbuk Glacier. This time I was not scared, and I was not feeling like Jon's understudy any more. I had earned my high altitude ribbons on Shishapangma, without him, and for once realised that although I would never be as strong as Jon, I could certainly be stronger than a lot of people around. The hard bit was to remember that at all times.

———

The plane was packed with tourists en route to Lhasa. A tourist, that's what I felt I was, as I peered out of the window and tried to see the highest mountain on earth in the monumental jumble of peaks obscuring the whole horizon. And there it was, bigger than life, taller than anything else around, black and ominous, snow flying from its summit. As I looked at Everest, I wondered how I felt about climbing it. I checked inside my heart, and was not too surprised to find that there was not an awful lot happening in there. No anticipation, no fear, no excitement. A summit to be ticked off, a mountain to be climbed not because I was in love with it, but to finish a quest I had started so long ago that it seemed to have become my entire life, the thing that people, even friends, thought of when they heard my name. 'How is it going? One to go, isn't it?' It was going to be my second attempt at Everest, and Jon's fifth. We had made it to 7600 metres in 1993, and I hoped that once past my high point on the North Ridge, excitement would replace the thoughts of hard, unrewarding work.

If nothing else, Jon and I would both enjoy catching up with the friends who were part of the huge OTT group going to the North Ridge of Everest. Eighteen western members, twelve Sherpas and three company guides would be the world we'd live in for the next two months, and I was looking forward to catching up with my dear Jon Tinker, with George Kotov and Pat Falvey ('No singing this time Pat, all right?!'), with Babu, Lama and Ang Rita, and with those not so well known: Mike Smith, who had been on Shishapangma with Jon Tinker and me; James Allen, from Melbourne, at twenty-two the baby of the expedition; Kelly Armitage, a Canadian doctor Jon and I had met on our first Aconcagua expedition; and Mick Chapman, a seasoned and very entertaining trekking guide based in Melbourne. The high number of Sherpas meant that our workload on Everest would be reduced to a minimum, and I knew from previous expeditions with OTT that our time in the mountains would be a bit of a gourmet outing as well, what with four cooks dedicated to providing us with incentive to eat, and a vast number of barrels filled to the rim with delicacies to munch on between meals.

It took us two days to fly to Lhasa as our flight kept being redirected to Chengdu, a Chinese town located thirteen hundred kilometres west of our destination. Unfavourable conditions for landing caused further delays.

On our third attempt the weather became reasonable – the plane glided smoothly above brown hills, and we finally landed on the Tibetan Plateau. But what a disappointment Lhasa was! The drive from the airport took us through industrial estates and blocks of concrete square buildings lining soulless streets. The Potala Palace loomed above the town, gathering its white walls in an offering towards the sky, with blue and yellow window curtains fluttering in the icy wind. Mick Chapman, who had married a Tibetan woman, gave us much insight into the situation. He told us that most of the tortuous and colourful streets of the old town were being demolished to make way for broad avenues and concrete boxes in an attempt to eradicate possible foyers of a resistance, which only had a chance to form in the narrow alleys and intricate Tibetan tenements of old. As a result Lhasa looked like any other communist town, except for its heart, which was still confused, crowded and beautifully Tibetan. I hoped that tourism and the lure of foreign currency would help save whatever was left of the original town.

We spent two days in Lhasa, getting used to the high altitude and doing the touristy thing for a change. Visiting the Potala was a moving experience I will never forget. It was alive with the faith of the Tibetans who had erected it, who continued worshipping the Dalai Lamas buried in its chambers. The whole building, from the paths meandering up its flanks, to its thousand and one colourful rooms, full of whispered prayers, rancid butter lamp smells, Lama photos, peaceful Buddhas, dark corners and tinkering bells, uplifted my spirits and created in me a sensation of peace and of oneness with the whole world.

———

10 April 1995, Xegar

> We saw Everest from the road today, and all I could think was, *So there is it, eh?* It looked big and difficult. I'll do what I can. Tibet is beautiful, and people in the country villages look happy. Not so in bigger towns, where misery is extremely obvious. Such a contrast too, between the Chinese who look reasonably clean (although throwing rubbish straight out of the car onto the road is a natural thing to them), and the Tibetans, grime covering their skin and tattered clothing, begging for scraps and small change. I don't like it.
>
> How do I feel about climbing 'that mountain'? I hope that I will be able to acclimatise in different places from last time, so as to expand my horizons, and I know now that once over the known ground, it will be terribly exciting. May my health and fitness be up to it! Tonight I have been drinking a fair bit of beer (do or dare?), maybe to give myself a chance to explore the hills around here before heading to BC. We'll see. If I feel good tomorrow, I'll go; if I don't, I'll stay!

There is a god for pissheads. I felt really quite fantastic the next day, and joined half the team for the last leg of our journey to Base Camp. We stopped on the Pang La for a peep at our mountain, then plunged down the other side of the pass to rejoin the valley leading to Base Camp. Our camp had been established higher upvalley than last time, and we shared its vast windy expanse with another few expeditions. Russell Brice's camp was next to us, as was Henry Todd's, and both being friends of Jon Tinker's we ended up seeing a fair bit of each other. Life on Everest was always an extraordinarily social event, a way to catch up with old friends scattered all over the world and herded by the wind of adventure in godforsaken corners of the planet . . . There had to be cheaper ways to meet! Jon and I were happy to be together, and we pitched our huge derelict Base Camp tent quite some distance from the main camp – no point in making celibate team members envious!

No-one had set foot on the mountain yet, as the wind was still blowing too much for safe climbing. A few expeditions had their camps organised at 6400 metres, at the foot of the North Col, but Jon Tinker had decided that members had to be acclimatised to that altitude before being allowed anywhere near Everest. This suited me nicely, as I would rather have gotten my high-altitude training on different horizons – the road to Advance Base Camp was not a particularly attractive one, except for the Magic Highway part of it, and if I was already used to its altitude, the torture of walking it would be shorter.

So Jon and I went for a 'good day out', as he calls them! We climbed a 6200-metre big blob above Base Camp – travelling through frozen creeks, lateral moraines and glaciers, clambering up rock gullies and plodding up endless scree slopes – Jon sauntering in front, me staggering behind. It was quite a way from camp at 5200 metres, and I did my fair share of coughing and spluttering, cleaning up my lungs from unappetising muck.

We were back in camp eight hours after we left – not bad for a first outing. The plan was to put in long days of exercise at altitude to prepare for a possibly very long summit day. All I was interested in was to give it my best shot, and for both of us to return home in one piece.

After a day of rest, we were on the road again, this time as part of a team of twelve. We all went up a side valley to camp higher than Base Camp. The access to our high camp followed the bed of a frozen creek, which at some points linked both sides of a narrow canyon, creating an amazing blue frozen water flow in shiny terraces. It was lovely to walk up the fairytale creek slowly, and to have happy talks with whoever was around.

We camped at about 5600 metres, and early in the morning Jon and I went for a twelve-hour marathon walk up a ridge to a summit at 6400 metres, down steep slopes and across a frozen lake, up the other side of the valley towards another 6400-metre summit, except that I gave up just above 6000 metres, falling asleep on my feet! Our descent to Base Camp took three hours. We arrived as darkness fell.

19 April 1995, Everest Base Camp

Pat has told young James to stick with him if he wants to climb the mountain. It is good to see that other people are starting to establish care patterns for new climbing partners. I am so lucky to be able to share with my Jon. I think it could happen this time. I felt it when we were on top of our 6400-metre summit yesterday, gazing at that huge mountain at the head of the valley, Chomolungma, looking like the goddess she is. She is truly magnificent, and as I look at her just now, golden in the sunset, she looks too far out of this world for mere mortals to even contemplate setting foot on her. I can see, though, how all-engulfing she will become once one is actually in her midst. Fortunately for me, my ties to this world down here are strong enough to bring me back, to keep me away from her powerful embrace. I shall pay my respects to her, and then tiptoe back to earth . . .

So, why am I here? It feels like the last, biggest hurdle in a race against myself, a race that has lost its meaning to me but has become important to others. I wonder if it is my fear of success that makes me look at reality with such detachment, or if maintaining aloofness is the only way I have to deal with the enormous task ahead?

I carried in my heart the trees that Jon and I had planted in our garden, my lavenders, the bicycle rides around Natimuk, Susan's massages and happy laughs, the bouldering sessions with my dear Rudy (complete with coffee, cake and hugs), Arapiles just before sunset, the cries of black cockatoos. One carries so many emotional packages when going to face the unknown. Climbing a mountain *was* a bit like a war campaign, preparing to face the 'enemy', not knowing when the danger will come, or where from. The teamwork, the strange places mountaineering takes you to, the feeling of being so alive. But not the feeling of conquest. One does not conquer nature.

I wondered whether I would have been there if Ian Darling had not found the money for Jon to come? Probably not! I would have postponed it, or forgotten about it. Why? Climbing Vinson was a bit of an anticlimax, something I had to do because I'd said I would. Chomolungma felt a bit the same. I could have been using some unconscious black magic, mind you, pretending I didn't care so it could happen.

20 April 1995, Everest Base Camp

There is one thing I am scared of, as always: I don't want anything to happen to Jon, who is only here because he wants to help me climb Everest, not because he wants to climb the mountain himself. Knowing his new passion for Australia, I am sure he would rather be paddling up Cape York or something! I love him so much. He is part of me, I am part of him, and if I fought it in the past, I don't any more. I do believe that we are all multi-faceted, though – that loving one person is not enough, because it does not allow us to express ourselves fully. So Jon has his close friends, and I have mine. I think we love each other, and respect each other, and understand that our respective freedom is there to be enjoyed, because we know that neither of us is going to run away anywhere . . .

I think of the friends I love – Rudy, James and Tess in Melbourne, who are family, really. Tess is pregnant. Does that make me an auntie? Briana, Jon's twin sister's daughter, already calls me 'Auntie Brigitte'! Children. There is an English woman here, a delightful short and pudgy and friendly girl called Alison Hargreaves, who has two children back home. She wants to climb Everest without supplementary oxygen, and without help from anyone. She is a hot-shot, has done a lot of technical solo climbs in the European Alps. I wonder how she deals with being a mother and being away from her children? Can I see myself as a mother?

Tomorrow we are having another day's rest here. Luxury. I look around me, at all the luxury junk in our super-duper mountain tent, and I think of our palace in Australia, which some people would call a dump. Happiness has nothing to do with material possessions, it is a state of mind. You have to see how some people live to realise it, and it makes me angry to hear some people back home whinge about this and that when they have it, when we have it so easy. It is obscene to cry in self-pity when one does not even have to fight for survival. I have done it, and I am ashamed of it.

A palmist in the Gangotri once told me that when I turned thirty-five years old, I was going to go downhill, give up jumping obstacles. That scared me no end. He had read other things in my palm that he had no way of knowing. But he also told me that it was possible to change your destiny by meditation and will.

———

I had to go and see Russell's doctor, Richard Price, for some drugs; I had come down with a cold. Richard had attempted Everest four times. He gave me some antibiotics and ordered me to rest for a while. There was no rush to get anywhere, so I listened to him. Most climbers in our team were at Advance Base Camp, but as none of us punters were in charge of working on the route, it made sense for me, and for Jon – who had caught my bug as well – to stay low until we felt better. It really was quite a decadent expedition, just lounging around and enjoying wine, baguettes and goat cheese with the few French members of our team, while listening to Mick Chapman's never-ending supply of Lord Redding's jokes . . .

With time we both started to feel better, and were able to look up towards Chomolungma once more. One fine morning we started on the walk to Advance Base Camp, strolling to camp in a leisurely two days, before heading up to the North

Col at first light the next day. Then we had one day's rest at Advance Base Camp, and charged back up the route for a couple of nights of good sleep at 7000 metres, and a miserable night at 7800 metres. The wind had been blowing very hard on the way to Camp Two, and I came down with another cold. *Oh well.* I had learned to be patient in the mountains, and to go with the flow. Jon had another chest infection on the go, so once again we retreated to Base Camp, and ate and rested and cuddled. We still had three and a half weeks before having to pack up and go, so it was just a question of timing it right: too early, and we might not be fully recovered, too late and we might miss our turn to attempt the summit. The weather was pretty average then, with snow covering our footsteps on the North Ridge, and most people were resting at Base Camp. Tension was starting to mount as climbers could now sniff the summit in the air, and wondered how to best organise their time and climbing partners.

I finally recovered, and started to hope again. The snow stopped falling, and a group of climbers summited: four Sherpas, including Lakpa, who had been with us in 1993, and two Japanese climbers, reached the top in two and a half hours from a very high camp below the Second Step. Wouldn't it be fantastic to get to the summit too? I imagined myself getting on the phone in Russell's camp and calling Ian Darling with the news. *God! He would be so happy!* I was certainly strong enough to contemplate the idea of summiting, and what a wonderful present that would be for someone as unselfish and supportive as Ian. Jon would be pretty relieved too, wouldn't he? We could take pictures of our summit kiss . . . I went on dreaming, a snug smile on my face.

There were about ten different teams attempting the North Ridge. Some of them had been around for longer than we had, and were now in a position to go for the summit. So when the wind stopped to offer the first window of perfect weather for a summit attempt, a vast number of people made their move. Sherpas and 'white men' alike started to summit left, right and centre. It was incredible: every man and his dog was getting to the summit. The thin fixed rope left by the Japanese Sherpas all the way to the top was the main reason for success on the route, being a certain psychological aid, as well as a physical one; despite its flimsiness, it prevented many a fall from exhausted climbers. Climbers who would have fallen to their death, bouncing down the unforgiving North Face, had there been no rope on the summit ridge. The incredibly long period of windless days high up had certainly been a deciding factor, too.

The time had come for Jon and me to get a ticket and join the crowds queuing for the summit. We steadily made our way towards Camp Three, and did not experience undue difficulties on our way, although heavy snowfall reduced visibility in the last part of the climb. We found ourselves sharing a tent at 8200 metres with George Kotov, Russian guide and friend, and Nasuh Mahruki, a young Turkish climber who hoped to be the first Turk to reach the highest point on our planet. Nasuh was acting the client, letting George look after him. George collected some snow, and Jon, who was the closest to the stove, found himself melting snow for brews all night. I mixed the drinks in cups, while Nasuh lay down and did nothing at all. Jon was quite annoyed at having to keep everyone hydrated and their bottles filled up for the long haul to the summit, but said nothing at all about it.

After George and Nasuh left, shortly after midnight, Jon and I looked at each other. There was a funny feeling in the air. I couldn't put my finger on it, but I knew something wasn't right. Maybe the lack of lustre in Jon's eyes, always so intense when he does something important that you feel his eyes are going to burn through you. I did not know. We talked about going up once our four one-litre water bottles were filled up. The snow took so long to melt into water at high altitude. 'It doesn't matter,' said Jon. 'We can still go at daybreak. It is not

that important to start during the night if we move all right.'
Yes, but . . .

I unzipped the tent door and screwed my nose up at the
high clouds fluorescent in a sliver of moonlight. I sighed. 'Your
heart is not in it,' stated Jon. I had to admit it wasn't. Here I was
at 8200 metres, getting ready to go for the summit of the highest mountain on earth – the potential apotheosis of seven years
of hard work – the weather was fine, I was stronger than I'd ever
been, and I didn't feel like it!

It was a puzzling feeling, but I could only surrender to it.
And thank God I did. 'Let's go down, Jon. I want a perfect day
when I stand on the summit, and this doesn't feel like it.'

We decided to doze until daybreak before our descent.
This involved lying down against each other without moving
a muscle, because although we had brought our sleeping mats
with us, we had left our sleeping bags at the last camp to avoid
any unnecessary exhaustion on the way: we had thought that
we would only be in the last camp for a few hours anyway, just
brewing and drinking, and had been willing to put up with the
cold. We had not planned on waiting for daylight. Any movement displaced the air, which happened to be rather chilled at
8200 metres on the side of a big mountain. Even inside a tent.
I snuggled against Jon's chest, and could hear his heavy breathing. Nothing to do with the throes of passion I am afraid, more
the fact that it was quite hard to breathe in the thin, cold air.
'I love you, Jon,' I whispered, trying not to move.

'I love you too, darling,' gasped Jon between two deep
breaths. I closed my eyes, imagining that I would feel warmer
that way.

Orange light finally touched the tent, and painted the
thousand and one blue and white mountains down below. It was
time to move. 'You are in charge,' said Jon. 'I feel a bit weak.'
When someone the size and strength of Jon Muir says that, you
start to panic. I understood why my heart wasn't into going up.
Jon needed to go down, and fast. It took us a long time to make

it to the North Col at 7000 metres. Jon was on oxygen, experiencing great difficulty in breathing. He fumbled with his safety sling at each rope attachment, and I soon realised that not only was he getting very weak, but he was also having problems seeing as his eyes were now encased in pus. We staggered to the North Col, where I put him to bed and made him some brews. Jon Tinker, who had been living at Advance Base Camp attached to the radio almost twenty-four hours a day since the summit attempts started, was quite relieved to hear that we had made it safely to the Col. Jon had been so stressed by his huge responsibility on this expedition that our closeness of Shishapangma and Cho Oyu had been but a memory.

The next morning we continued our descent to Advance Base Camp, and Kelly Armitage auscultated Jon, who was now looking more dead than alive. 'Bronchitis and conjunctivitis,' he announced. 'I would not go back up if I were you.'

I had had my priorities right, but I was still raring to give the summit a shot. I felt so strong, and more determined than ever to try and climb Everest. So many inexperienced climbers had gotten up in perfect conditions, surely the weather would hold a bit longer and give me a chance? Jon and I walked back to Base Camp and I indulged for two days at the luxuriously low altitude of 5200 metres, eating some more goat cheese and French sticks while sipping on Chinese beer. George and Nasuh, who had summited the day we turned back, arrived at Base Camp and we celebrated their success with a bottle of something stronger.

People in our team were summiting practically every day now, and Jon Tinker allowed me to try again for the summit with the last group to attempt it. I would meet up with Mike, Pat and James, and we would go for the top together. 'Remember, stick together,' said Jon Tinker, who was getting thinner by the day. 'Whatever happens, stick together. Work as a team, and look after your mates.' This had become Jon's mantra throughout the trip.

On the morning of my leaving, my Jon's orders were somewhat blunt and to the point: 'Go and climb that fucking mountain, will you?!' We hugged and I was on my way. I felt ready to conquer the world. I had never been that strong at altitude before. Having already been at 8200 metres was going to help me, I was certain of that. I cruised up to Advance Base Camp in one day and caught up with Mike, Pat and James. The next day, Pat and James (now following Pat like a shadow) went up to the North Col at 7000 metres. Mike and I were planning to skip a night at the North Col, and to climb up in one go to 7600 metres, Camp Two, so as to minimise the time spent at high altitude, a good way to stay in top shape. If one can move fast enough, of course.

I surprised myself. I climbed up to Camp One in exactly the same time as the time before, nothing to rave about, and lounged about on the North Col for a few hours. But when it came to climb the 600 vertical metres to the next camp, I took one and a half hours off my previous time and arrived nice and fresh, even though I was carrying a heavier pack this time round. It felt great. While Mike and I had established residence at the 7600-metre camp, Pat and James had climbed up to our alternative Camp Two at 7800 metres, wishing to have a shorter day to the top camp at 8200 metres the next day. We chatted on the radio, and all settled in our respective tents for the first night of our summit attempt.

The next morning, getting up from 7600 metres to 8200 metres was a breeze. Once more we left our sleeping bags behind. Mike was carrying a bottle of oxygen left at 7600 metres, because we wanted to have as much oxygen as we could at the top camp, and we knew that there was a definite shortage. Bad planning, with previous summiteers using far more than the three bottles allocated to each member, meant that every bottle counted if we wanted enough of the stuff to use high up.

I had thought to use oxygen again from 7800 to 8200 metres, like I had on our previous attempt, not knowing how many hours it would take to get there in the middle of a snow-storm, so I started with a mask on my face, carrying a bottle in my pack. After one hundred vertical metres, I had had enough of it; I had found out on the last attempt that wearing a mask was reducing my visibility and as I felt good anyway, I could not see the point in complicating my life. At the bottom of the rock band leading to the 8000-metre mark, I took the mask and regulator off and stuck them in my pack with the mostly full bottle of oxygen. On the other side of the rocks I sat to wait for Mike, who was a fair way behind. I felt quite pleased: there I was, with my reputation of being slow, going a lot faster than a 'guide' who had a reputation for being very strong at altitude. *I must be doing all right*, I thought.

After a very happy and easy climb, I arrived at Camp Three and gate-crashed James and Pat's tent for a cuppa. James was brewing, and gave me a cup of black tea. 'Sorry, there is no sugar,' he apologised.

'Did you check with the Sherpas next door?' He hadn't, and I went over to get some, and see if I could share the Sherpa tent with them.

'No room,' they said. I did not know any of the Sherpas snuggling in the tent, and I wished at the time my friends Babu and Lama had been around instead of these guys, who did not seem to give a damn.

I left my pack at Pat's tent and went looking for a home for the night. The camp, which had been established on a steep slope, consisted of six tents at different levels. Pat's and the Sherpas' tents were the lowest, then about ten vertical metres higher there were two more tents, unoccupied, belonging to Henry's group, Russell's tent, another ten metres above, and finally a big red tent twenty metres higher than Russell's. I started by checking that one out, and it looked fine to me. I took my harness off and decided to call it home.

When he arrived, Mike switched the radio on and proceeded to talk with Jon Tinker. I came back to him at the Sherpa tent, and told him the highest tent was empty. He did not like the idea of dragging himself all the way up there, and told me to use one of Henry's before returning to the radio and conferring with Jon for as long as it took me to get our packs to the tent, hack a bagful of snow from an out-of-the-way (out of pissing distance) snow slope, and start brewing. And once we were in the tent, he was in an awkward position to do any work. But he did borrow a couple of sleeping bags from Russell, who was looking after one of his clients in a tent nearby, so we lay down and snuggled in the bags, and I kept brewing, while recapitulating what still had to be done before departure: I had to fill up two water bottles for Mike, and two for myself, get my harness from the empty tent I had first checked while Mike was on the radio, find myself two full bottles of oxygen, and take their safety bolts off.

By screaming at Pat and James from our tent, we got them to turn their radio on, and Mike started chatting away with them. They told him that they were pretty much ready to go. Well, we were not. Being master brewer, I could tell we would be some time. 'Get them to check and organise some oxygen bottles, Mike.'

'Don't worry,' said Mike, 'there are plenty of them around.'

We extracted ourselves from the tent shortly after midnight, and went down to the boys' tent to pick up some oxygen. Mike had already earmarked his bottles, and I was left to find some for myself while he organised his pack. By the time I had found the key and some bottles, and picked up my harness, they had disappeared. I caught up with them as they were floundering about, looking for the start of the fixed ropes. Having started last, I ended up last in line at the start of the ropes, and we all scrambled up some pretty unpleasant ground, with uncertain old fixed ropes and loose gravel on top of sloping rock. James was right in front of me, and was so scared he could hardly focus on what I was telling him: 'James, tell me, is the blue rope or the yellow rope okay for jumaring on?' I wanted to make the most out of being last, and not clip on a bad rope if I could help it. James jittered about, looking up at Pat, who was getting away from him, and back at the ropes I was asking him to assess.

'Oooh, the blue one. Oh God, I just want to get out of here!' He scampered to catch up with Pat's heels and the questionable safety of their proximity. I shrugged and kept going at my own comfortable pace.

Two hours after leaving the camp we all stopped, one behind the other on the fixed rope. I had tried as much as possible to avoid pulling on them, as I had heard that some of them were pretty flimsy. Mike had run out of oxygen, and Pat was helping him change bottles. James talked nervously, and I chattered away with him, hoping it would help him relax. Five metres above us, Pat and Mike had completed the bottle change and started to move again. It was then that I noticed my headtorch light getting dull. 'Damn!' I exclaimed, to no one in particular. 'My headtorch is going!' No-one responded. Mike and Pat never looked down, never asked if everyone was all right before setting off again, and James was too new to high-altitude mountaineering to be relied upon. And despite being a lot more together and much better acclimatised than any of them, I did not realise at the time that if I did not shout my head off just then, I could kiss the summit goodbye. My brain was not working that well, I guess, and I had not realised that I would soon be in a potentially lethal situation. Jon Tinker had told us to stick together; that's what climbing partners did on a mountain, and why should I worry? I had spare batteries and a spare bulb, and could put it all right in minutes and be on my way again.

Back at Base Camp, my Jon tossed and turned in his sleeping bag. He turned his light on, and checked the time. Two a.m. . . . One more hour before the first radio call. His thoughts were high on the mountain. He coughed a little. There was no floor covering in the mess tent, and the dust was drying his throat. He looked at the base radio station, and wondered if Jon Tinker, at Advance Base Camp, was sleeping near the radio as well.

I swore again. My spare batteries, which I had kept in the front pocket of my downsuit, had suffered from the cold, and replacing the bulb did not make any difference to the situation – my headtorch was useless. I blew on my fingers, which had become very cold in their single glove layer while I was fumbling in the dark, stuck them under my armpits and looked up. The wind had started to pick up, and the vague line of the rope I was clipped on had disappeared into total darkness. Mike, Pat and James had vanished. I was alone in the dark, high on the North Face of Everest. *Damn, damn, damn. Bastards!* I could not believe it. They had just kept going! I had been naive in my expectations, too used to climbing with partners who know, at any given time in a climb, exactly where their partners are, and too sure I could deal with the situation on my own.

I squinted at the slope ahead. Being short-sighted, I wore contact lenses, and my night vision was not very good at all. Not that there was an awful lot to see – it was a moonless night, and the light of the stars only vaguely touched the steepness of the slope. I scrambled on rock and snow to the stance where Mike and Pat had changed bottles only minutes ago. From there, the rope went diagonally up to the right across a sloping terrasse, not quite as steep as the terrain below. I could manage that without pulling on the rope, so I slowly made my way to the end of it and found myself on a steep snow slope with no contrast to help my progress. The rope was still there, shooting up out of sight, but there was no way I was going to put my weight on it. I remembered my friend Heather McDonald, an Aconcagua guide who had been on the same route on Everest the year before, and her words echoed in my head: 'Whatever you do, don't pull on the ropes on the Yellow Band; some of them are pretty old. You never know what you'll get!' And I was on the Yellow Band, a large layer of yellow rock stripping the whole of the Everest pyramid just below the summit ridge, and I was not going to die pulling on a dicey rope. No summit was worth the risk, however remote.

Damn, I thought again. I could not go up, and I could not go down. Before the bottle change stop, we had climbed a vertical section, and I had not liked the look of the shredded rope 'protecting' it. I was definitely not going to pull on that. My nose hugging the ground, I made my way back to the tiny rockshelf and sat down, parallel with the slope, my back to the wind. It was quite windy now, and my pack, with its two bottles of oxygen, was the only protection between me and the icy gusts. I sighed and searched the horizon for signs of sunrise. I would have to wait for a while.

———

'ABC (Advance Base Camp) calling Mike, ABC calling Mike, do you copy?' Jon Tinker's disembodied voice bloomed in the cold of the summit ridge.

'Yes Jon, I copy'

'Well, how is everything going?'

'Oh, it's pretty cold and windy, but we are all doing well,' announced Mike.

Jon at Base Camp cut into the conversation: 'And how is Brigitte?'

'Brigitte?' answered Mike, 'Well I don't know, I haven't seen her for ages!'

'What do you mean?' exploded Jon.

'I don't know, I suppose she went back down.'

The cold was becoming unbearable. I had developed a routine to try and keep it at bay, and it was not easy in the cramped position I was in. I could only sit with my legs bent at the knee, resting as I was on a small rock step surrounded by steep snow. I stamped my feet for a few minutes, then swapped over to shaking my upper body. I looked at my hands – they looked like claws, even inside my double mitts. I tried wiggling my fingers, an exercise which required enormous concentration.

No, it was not working. Not enough blood circulation. I was feeling sleepy, very sleepy, and toyed with the idea of a nap to escape the cold. Only I knew too well that sleep would mean death, as the cold would creep inside and never let go again. I shook myself and thought about what I would do at first light. *Right. I will only have one bottle left by then, not enough to go to the summit and back. I'll probably be too cold anyway. So, the best thing to do is to go back to camp, and give it another go from there.* I knew that two experienced friends from Russell's team, Richard Price and Tim Rippel, a Canadian guide, were planning to come to the last camp that day. Hope soared again. It could still happen! I was not going to give up that easily!

At Base Camp, Jon was devastated. There was no news of me; he had no idea where I was, or how I was. And there was nothing he could do, nothing but wait and listen to the radio.

I could guess, more than see, a twinge of colour on that horizon I knew now by heart. The black outline of the mountains lost its sharpness, melted in light pink and yellow. It was beautiful. Every single mountain around me was miles below – Everest was a giant, a monumental mass going up forever and ever into the sky. I considered taking a picture, but thought better of it – I didn't want anything to remember this experience by! I started contemplating the idea of moving. It was not easy. I was stiffened by the cold, and movement did not come naturally for quite a while. I stumbled down, fuelled by anger and determination. I was going to try again, *yep, you wait.* Movement finally restored some life in my hands, and my grip on the ice-axe felt more assured. I did not take long coming down; I had a lot of strength and energy left in me. A lot of cold, too.

I made straight for my tent, and dived into my sleeping bag. I did not know what was happening outside of my single concern to get warm. I sobbed and shivered uncontrollably for hours, and finally resolved to let Russell know that I was back. He had been talking to Jon Tinker and had passed on the news that our Sherpas, still ensconced in their tent, had apparently seen me coming down below camp. I yelled at him from my tent, and he was able to reassure Jon at Base Camp: I was in camp, and apparently well. Russell invited me to come over for a brew, and I reluctantly left my sleeping bag to make my way to his tent and to tell my story. I was so disappointed, now that I had come down and did not need anger and hope to keep me alive. I talked with Jon on the radio, Russell talked with Jon Tinker on the radio, and a new plan started to emerge.

Richard and Tim were not coming up after all — the wind was too fierce between 7600 and 8000 metres, and they had turned back and retreated to their tents. That only left Russell as a possible climbing partner. He agreed to give it a go that night, as long as Mike, Pat and James did not need looking after. News had come that they had reached the summit, but Mike was not well; he had been losing his balance a lot, and was being looked after by Pat. James had two frostbitten fingers, having spent a very long time holding onto the aluminium ladder which the Chinese had placed on the Second Step in 1975. They were slowly making their way down, and our Sherpas had been sent with more oxygen to meet them. I checked all the tents for stray bottles of oxygen; action was helping keeping me sane and hopeful again. I found enough bottles in my travels around camp to sustain another attempt, and came back to Russell's tent with the good news. Russell had Jon Tinker on radio and he wanted to talk to me.

'Brigitte, I have changed my mind. I don't have any Sherpas left to help you if things go wrong. I want you to come down: it is too dangerous, and you are too slow to climb with Russell.' Here we go again. I was anything but slow, but Jon had etched in his memory the times I had spent walking slowly with Mike on Shishapangma and Cho Oyu, and nothing was going to make him change his mind.

What could I do? I did not have it in me to contest Jon's decision. He was my leader, he was my friend. He had taken me on board more than once without charging me full price, and therefore had been sponsoring my attempts. And now he was scared that I'd go out on a limb without back-up. Russell told me that the boys sounded like they'd need looking after, and I knew in my heart that Jon's words to him while I was hunting oxygen bottles had made him change his mind about going up. 'They'll need some brews,' he said. 'I'll go and melt some snow . . .' Heart heavy, I returned to my tent and spent the next few hours filling up water bottles, and following my climbing partners' incredibly slow descent through tears.

As darkness fell once more, they stumbled into camp, Mike to Russell's tent, Pat to the tent in front of mine, so I could pass him brews, and James, oblivious to my shouts directing him to Pat's tent, into the tent they had occupied on the way up. I unzipped my door and passed a water bottle to Pat. 'Do you want a hot brew?' I sobbed.

'No, thanks,' he said. 'I'm fucked, I'm just going to crash. Why are you upset?'

Everest –
South-side Attempt

It was not a happy expedition end. I could not wait to get away from the group, to go back home and bury myself in grief and despair. Jon was furious that the boys had not noticed my ordeal, and had 'left me behind to die'. I sent a fax to Ian, Min and Roddo when we arrived in Katmandu, describing what had happened high on the mountain and ending with these lines:

> I am pissed-off and sad at the missed opportunity, but I am also happy that I was so strong and survived the night. I want to go back and do it! (From the south this time?) I am sorry I have failed your confidence. Talk to you soon.
> Love to you, Roddo and Min,   Brigitte.

To which Ian had answered:

> Dear Brigitte,
>   Congratulations, you have set another Australian record! We all understand your frustration – we all shed a little tear – but we are all so proud of you! And yes, you will do it again!
> Lots of love,   Ian, Min and Roddo.

I was not proud of myself. For months on end I did not sleep, replaying in my mind every move, every decision of that fateful night. Wondering again and again what I could have done to save the day, to get myself to the summit. In retrospect, there was not a lot I could have done differently considering the way my brain had been working. It is very easy to have a skewed perception of reality high on a mountain. I felt like I had withdrawn, consumed by grief.

Obsession, obsession, obsession. Of course I had to go back, despite my promise to Jon before our last expedition that I would only try one more time. I didn't want to be someone who only lived to climb Everest! But how could I give up, knowing I could have done it? I was trapped; I had to finish what I had started and re-conquer my self-confidence, or die of shame and self-pity.

I had to go back. That meant finding an expedition to join, and the money to join it. I asked Russell, who was going back to the North Ridge, and he invited me at cost. But I was not sure I wanted to go back to the Tibetan side of the mountain – I had too many painful memories linked to the North Ridge Route, and I had already been there twice. I thought that a change of scene would help motivate me. Everest was a totally different mountain from Nepal; its approach would take me through lush, forested hills and strings of colourful villages, and that was something I was looking forward to after the pervasive dust of Tibet.

I had made a decision about partners, too. I knew now that I was strong enough to climb and to look after myself at extreme altitude, and I desperately wanted to prove it to myself again the next time I went to Everest, preferably by reaching the summit. Jon had always told me that he never wanted to go through the icefall again, as he had been through it fifty-eight times already, and I did not want to have him in a place he did not want to be in. I knew how dangerous the icefall was, and if Jon was scared to go back, I did not want to tempt fate. If something terrible happened to him, I could not have lived with it. I also decided that it was a great time for me to try Everest without Jon. I had proven that I could be strong without him as a climbing partner, and I realised that Jon had had enough of going back to Everest, no matter how much he wanted to help me climb it. He had already climbed the mountain in much harder conditions than those we had encountered on commercial trips, especially the last one, where Sherpas did most of the work and punters just turned up and cruised when food and camps were in place. I did not have the ready cash to book Everest ahead (at that time it cost fifty thousand US dollars just to 'rent' the route for a two-month period) for a private expedition, so the only way for me to join a trip at short notice was to book a place on a commercial expedition. I knew a lot of people in the mountain-guiding business and could get special deals reasonably easily, thanks to the attitude of most commercial climbing leaders, who drew a line between making money out of strangers and helping friends achieve their dreams.

I wrote to Rob Hall, who I knew was going to the South Side every spring, and asked him what his price would be. Rob, of Adventure Consultants, specialised in upmarket trips and offered a 'deluxe' service to people who wanted to climb Everest but did not have the experience to look after themselves on the mountain. I could look after myself all right, and I had decided that I would do without climbing partners this time. It would be just myself and my own tents and food (and *two* head-torches), so I was not fussy who I went with, as long as they had a permit and it was affordable. Rob, who had never met me before but had heard about my quest and the previous year's misadventures, wrote back saying I could come at cost. Cost with Rob was a lot cheaper than the sixty-five thousand US dollars he normally charged, but it was still a lot more than what I had in the bank.

I went to see John Clarke at HIH Winterthur Insurance. Hearing that I wanted to go back, he said, 'We are not quitters

225

either!' and presented me with a cheque for ten thousand dollars. Then Henry Todd, whom I had been in touch with because I wanted to sell his trips through our newsletter, faxed me to tell me that he was trying to get a permit for the South Col Route in spring. His quote for my participation was quite affordable, much lower than Rob's, and made the idea of my return to Everest something which could really happen.

Foxtel, approached by Ian, contributed another ten thousand dollars, and Ian and Roddo once again happily plugged the hole. I met up with Henry on Aconcagua, where he was guiding that summer. We spent time going over the prospective climb, and he wrapped me in swirls of feel-good words about the trip and his organisation, and suddenly it all became real. I was going back to Everest. I was going to walk the hills of Nepal one more time. I buried the pain of the last months, I made peace with my past, and looked forward to roaming the hills on my own and to rediscovering the self I was in their midst.

———

Björk was singing loudly in my ears as I slalomed down the slopes of Chukhhung Ri, puffs of dust punctuating my fast and numerous turns down the track back to the village of Chukhhung. My heart was pounding and I yapped every so often, letting out exalted bursts of freedom and happiness. A three-hour return trip, 2000 metres up and down, the memory of Everest upvalley, the thrill of being in the hills and of meeting new people, the total bliss of encountering again the 'me' I loved.

Joining Henry's team had been a good idea. I was surrounded by expeditioners who were prepared to look after themselves in the mountains, and there were people within the group whom I felt I could relate to. Paul Deegan and Neil Laughton were climbing partners, both from the United Kingdom, both army-heads, serious about climbing Everest and having a good time doing it. Thomas and Tina Sjögren ('TNT, the explosive couple', as I was to fondly call them later) came from Stockholm, where they owned their own business supplying restaurants with paper towel and toilet rolls, which they had started after getting tired of exploring remote corners of the planet. We spent a lot of time together, sharing stories and laughs. Tina was originally from Poland, so we had a common Slavic fire and respected and liked each other. Something made us differ though: Thomas and Tina could have spent the whole expedition tied to a fifty-metre rope because they never ever let go of each other — a practice that Henry Todd found a bit disturbing. Although getting on extremely well, he and Peta Watts, his life partner, were more used to spending time apart than together. Henry found this co-dependence difficult to understand. Their closeness did not really worry me. I was bursting with energy from being in the hills, loving every minute of my time galloping up and down, taking people at face value and paying no attention whatsoever to power struggles and insecurities endemic to large expeditions. I was determined to climb this mountain without having to depend emotionally on anyone. I felt strong, happy and free from the past, and that was that.

'It's not a matter of life and death, it's more important than that!' So summarised Paul about doodah, the dice game which took every spare moment of our time together. I was more interested in watching and laughing it off than participating, but boy, some people took it seriously. Competitiveness lurked, and who was trying to reassure who, anyway? There was that big, scary ghost at the head of the valley called Chomolungma in Tibet, Sagarmatha in Nepal and Everest in the rest of the world. Anything was acceptable to make one feel strong and competent in front of it.

That night the moon was full, and a comet was lurking above the horizon making the Sherpas in our midst uncomfortable. I saw only the overwhelming beauty of it, and donning my walkman once more, stepped into the night for a dance and totally out-of-tune song under the stars. The mountains were magic, pure essence without need for names. Gosh, mountains gave me so much energy. Every cell in me was awake, gasping for attention and satisfaction.

We had been trekking the Khumbu and going up 'little' 5000-metre-plus hills to acclimatise for our more serious climb ahead. It had felt like a holiday really – a lovely way to rediscover the Khumbu and get to know fellow climbers. Only one member of the team was missing – Michael Joergensen, who had climbed Everest last year on Henry's trip from the north, with oxygen, and wanted now to try without oxygen from the south. Michael was working for the United Nations peace-keeping force in Sarajevo, and would catch up with us at Base Camp.

Despite the hopes of developing friendships, I felt at times a little lonely. Not when I was moving – I was too con- sumed by adrenaline and bliss then – but when I had to stop, I missed having a close friend along, and I dealt with it by retir- ing to my tent and poring over photographs of Jon, our friends and our home. I also enjoyed spending time with the women on the trip. I had been so used to being the only female on moun- taineering trips that I had forgotten how wonderful it was to talk and share thoughts with soul sisters. Linda Whylie was ten years older than I was, and I hoped I would be like her when I turned forty-seven. She had come on the expedition, along with her son Jacob, to visit Pumori, where her husband had died a few years earlier. A very emotional enterprise, but one which would give her peace and understanding, and allow her to meet a new partner. Linda was an old hippie at heart, and being one myself, we got on very well. We got talking one day and she observed, 'You look like a woman on a mission.'

The deep snow stopped us from reaching the foot of Island Peak, which we had been supposed to climb as part of our accli- matisation programme. The yaks, which were carrying most of our gear, experienced immense difficulty trudging through the thick layer of snow and refused to budge once they had encountered too much of it. Henry was happy with what we had done so far anyway, and he gave us the destination Base Camp go-ahead before flying back to Katmandu, where he had to assist in the clearing of a shipment of oxygen bottles held by customs. This was Nepal, after all, and one could not expect red tape to get any shorter, or to take care of itself. We waved Henry goodbye, half expecting to receive a postcard from the Bahamas in the next few weeks, saying, 'Wish you were here'. We made our way with much excitment to the Khumbu Glacier and the foot of Everest.

I met Rob Hall at Lobuche, a smelly tourist settlement one day's walk from Everest Base Camp. We smiled and shook hands and then he had to rush off to take care of the other members of his group. Henry's and Rob's expeditions were as different as chalk and cheese: Henry was selling a trip, at minimal cost, to allow himself and like-minded experienced climbers to participate in an Everest expedition without the bother of extensive organising. The highly efficient sirdar (foreman), Kami Nuru, was in charge of organisation, and if enough people were interested in joining the trip, Henry would even make some money out of it. Rob's Adventure Consultants expedition operated at a completely different level. Tour members were not expected to be able to look after themselves on the mountain or to carry anything, and were pampered every step of the way, with Sherpas, a Base Camp doctor, Base Camp manager and western guides to take care of their every wish. The climb was definitely a money-making venture, and aimed to make every client feel like a king. Michael Groom, an Australian high-altitude climber I had met briefly with his wife in Katmandu the year before, was working as a guide for Rob.

Our yaks finally arrived, exhausted after walking in the deep mushy snow. At one point, eight Sherpas had had to lift a poor yak which had sunk into snow up to his belly! I did not feel like spending the night in the Lobuche cesspit, so I collected my sleeping bag and pillow from their yak and charged up to Gorak Shep, the last settlement on the way to Everest Base Camp. 'Ho Brigitte, namasteee!' Babu Chhiri Sherpa and his client, Thierry Renard, were coming down the track for a rest in Lobuche. I was happy to see dear Babu again, and interested to hear that Thierry, who had been with us in '93, had decided to give Everest another go, this time with the assistance of two Sherpas. He seemed a lot more relaxed than in '93, no doubt happy to be master of his own expedition, on a permit-share basis with the South African expedition. I was extremely pleased to hear that my friend Lama, whom I had climbed Shishapangma with, was working with the South Africans. Vaguely knowing western climbers on trips was one thing, but having Sherpa friends in the vicinity was a real advantage. I knew instinctively, from the good relations we had had in the past, that they were people who could be counted on.

What I had really done by leaving Lobuche for Gorak Shep was to jump from the frying pan into the fire – or from the toilet into the septic tank. Gorak Shep, a cluster of lodges at the foot of Pumori, was a totally disgusting place to consider spending any time in at all. The few of us who had kept going spent the night in a dusty, smoky tea shop, with trekkers coughing out viruses for everyone to enjoy. And it was too bad if you felt like privacy – there was only one overcrowded dormitory to cater for the enormous number of people wishing either to walk to Everest Base Camp and risk begging cuppas from expeditions, or to summit Kala Pattar, a bump on the ridge eventually leading to the top of Pumori, for an early morning peep at the summit of Everest.

The yaks caught up with us in the early morning, but I did not leave until lunch, taking time to drink, eat and socialise before heading off for the last leg of the trip. I walked the glacier on my own, having flashbacks of my last time here, seeing Veronique and Jon behind this rock, that ice blade. Base Camp was bigger than Ben-Hur; I walked through its first suburbs, and had to ask for directions to find Henry's camp. There were eleven different expeditions at the head of the Khumbu Glacier, and the local tourist office would have done well to organise an information board with a 'You are here' map. I felt great. I hardly looked at the route ahead, taking one day at a time. What I needed to do was to relax, acclimatise to the altitude (we were at 5200 metres, after all), organise my gear, read, rest, write, listen to music, film, take photos, talk with people. Anything but climb!

———

Gongs sent their messages through the crisp air. Every expedition had one, an oxygen cylinder that the cook bashed with a spoon, or an empty, soon to be bumpy pot. Every gong had a distinctive sound that expedition members learned to recognise if they wanted to get to the mess tent in time to get their share of the meal.

Then it was time to take the first trip up the icefall. This could only be described as hell. First of all one had to get up at an unspeakable hour — ten past three was the usual time for me. I had to wear my alarm watch inside my woolly hat, in front, to make sure I heard the alarm I did not want to hear. Keeping my watch here also enabled convenient time-checking every hour or so during the night, because of course I did not sleep, too anxious I wouldn't hear the alarm. When the alarm sounded I turned my headtorch on for long enough to locate and light my candles. Then I lit the stove, because I always wanted to drink at least two litres before starting on the day's exertions. Back to closed eyes while I defrosted my contact lenses on my belly, opening an eye occasionally to check on the stove. Yep, the water was boiling. First coffee down the throat, unknot every single stomach knot that every single thought of getting anywhere near the mountain seemed to create, get the contact lenses in — easier said than done in the dark — drink another two coffees, swallow vitamin tablets, pick up last night's packed backpack from outside the tent, stumble to the kitchen for a light breakfast and another two cups of tea to top up the liquid intake. More often than not, have one cup of tea too many, and puke the lot before heading off to the dreaded icefall.

A number of people were making their way to the bottom of the icefall behind me. American accents. I recognised one of them. 'Hello, how are you, Charlotte?'

'Brigitte, good to see you!' I'd met Charlotte Fox in Lhasa last year, and on Aconcagua, where she had helped with the Breast Cancer American Women Expedition.

'You're working here?'

'Nah, not this time. I'm with Scott Fisher.' I plodded up slowly but very steadily, while most of Scott's people overtook me, moving quite rapidly.

The icefall was like an icy blue castle of frozen cards. Any move from any of its players – gravity, cold, heat – could upset and rearrange it dramatically. We walked in crampons across aluminium ladders, one, two, three or even four two-metre sections tied together by string, holding tightly onto the safety rope, balancing across seemingly bottomless chasms. We hurried under unstable ice towers, pulled ourselves over steep walls, hopped on top of an ocean of broken ice islets, and hoped, prayed, begged that the sky might not fall on our heads. I am amazed it has not been turned into a video game yet.

The icefall was not a pleasant place to be. I went up, and up and up, hardly stopping, keeping a pace I could maintain for hours on end, trying really to get the hell out of there as fast as I could. I overtook the American group, jumared up to the top of another wall. A man, blond ponytail, dark glasses, athletic body resting languidly on the snow, smiled at me. 'You've done that before, haven't you?'

'Yep, I have.' I smiled at him. I learned later that he was Scott Fisher, the leader of another five-star expedition.

I was on a mission, and kept moving. I went and touched Camp One, and dumped my load. Then it was time to run the gauntlet again, down the icefall, underneath the 'mouse trap', a serac with a Tower of Pisa penchant. We had to duck-walk our way under its broad belly, and run or crawl, depending on whether we were going up or down negotiating ladders. There were often people going up who were inevitably slower – or people running down – so everything always took longer than anticipated. But what I am talking about? I went through the ice-fall that year four times up and four times down. Sherpas were going up two or three days in a row, broken by a day of rest. That added up to a hell of a lot more traverses across the icefall than my eight times. I remembered Jon's personal best – fifty-eight times over three expeditions. No wonder he did not want to come back! I'd only done it once, and I never ever wanted to do it again!

'Hello, my darling!' I whispered into the phone, aware of eyes leaving whatever fascinating words they were reading to burn holes in my back. I was in Mal Duff's mess tent, giving Jon an overdue call on the Danish team's satellite phone. At ten US dollars per minute it was definitely extravagant, but very much needed. The expensive words we exchanged replenished my motivation tank, while making my tenderness for Jon overflow. Aaahhh, how I loved that man . . .

'Go for it, but be careful. I love you,' he had said. Good advice, that I planned to put into practise the next day. It was time to move to Camp Two, and as I had decided to take my own tent, stove, extra food, still camera, tape recorder and Hi-8 video camera, and was carrying it all myself, it would be a bit of a test for me. Part of the gear was already at Camp One, where we would spend the night before plodding up the Western Cwm to Camp Two. The Cwm is a valley of snow, bordered by a horse-shoe of mighty peaks: Everest on the left, Lhotse ahead, and slender Nuptse on the right. Camp Two was at the foot of Ever-est's West Face, on a side tongue of strewn rocks spat by the glacier as it moved forward towards the joys of tumbling in the icefall. A very convenient spot for a camp, as it was always 'warmer' to pitch one's tent on rocks than directly on the ice. It made for interesting night wiggling, though, as one tried to organise one's body around the sharp corners underneath.

The icefall was engulfed in mist, and I did not lose any time admiring the ephemeral look that the atmosphere reinforced. I walked past Rob, who was waiting for a client. Smiles and greetings in little cold clouds of breath. I turned around, a thought crossing my mind. 'When is your baby coming?'

Love in his eyes, in his smile. 'In July.'

'That's great! See you later!' The icefall was not a good place to stop and socialise.

Ian Goodall, Cathy O'Dow and Bruce Herrod, from the South African expedition, were sitting at the bottom of a small gully having a bite to eat before getting stuck into the steep wall ahead. I reeled as I noticed some very new-looking ice blocks all around them. The blocks had obviously fallen recently from high above, and the gully was a place I definitely would not choose to stop for a chat.

At Camp One I was happy to share a tent with Henry, Paul and Neil, and noticed that Paul seemed to find brewing a natural thing to do. Good! That meant I would not be the only one working if I happened to be moving up with these two. Henry had started to cough badly, and it did not look like he'd be climbing in the same timeframe as me and 'my boys' as Tina came to call them. I did enjoy their ebullience, especially Paul's. He was a born entertainer, with a heart of gold. Nothing was ever too much for him. Neil gave me the impression of having come from a male-dominated background, and of taking female attention and devotion for granted. He also seemed to be one of those who sat on their bums at camps, carefully ignoring the work to be done. I don't know what they thought of me, maybe that I was a bossy bitch. Both, being at least ten years younger than me, kept asking me questions on how to make love last. I laughed and told them that one day they would understand.

There was competition in the air as we made our way up

the Cwm towards Camp Two. Neil was charging uphill, seemingly oblivious to the altitude, and to the heat which was now plaguing everyone in the Cwm. I was glad to be wearing a broad-brimmed hat, but still had to stick snowballs underneath it to keep my brain from boiling.

The Valley of Silence was another name for the Cwm, and I pondered on its suitability as the route took me very close to the Nuptse Face and its numerous rock falls. The first time I heard the noise, my reaction was to look around for a nose-diving plane. Of course it was only a rock, taking on speed and screech as it catapulted down the mountain on its way to a snowy grave. I walked quite fast until I was away from the war zone. As I approached the site of Camp Two, I started to feel familiar with my surroundings. I had seen Jon's slides of their attempt up the West Shoulder in 1984, and recognised the shapes ahead, the snow and the rocks that they must have seen too. I thought about Craig, and Fred, and sent them my love, and asked them to look after me, please.

Scott overtook me, moving at a rapid and steady pace, on his way to sorting out business at Camp Two. He smiled greetings to me, and kept going. I remember thinking his bum looked nice on top of his long legs, wondering what his eyes looked like. I would never find out. My hips were sore when I finally dumped my pack at the entrance of what looked like our mess tent. 'Shit! That was heavy!'

'Mmm, about seventeen kilos, I reckon,' Michael said.

Michael Joergensen was a handsome guy, slightly shorter than me and about twice as fast. I'd been sniggering at him, Paul and Neil as they engrossed themselves in army talk back at Base Camp, but now that I was getting to know Michael better I quite enjoyed his company, and started longing for the happiness of shared mountaineering pleasure. His English was a little extravagant, but it was a hell of a lot better than my Danish. With him was the expedition junior, Mark Pzetzer, a sixteen-year-old American who hoped to become the youngest person to climb the highest mountain on earth. 'Hi!' he had said when I had asked him to introduce himself to my camera. 'I am sixteen years old, and I owe the bank thirty thousand dollars!'

———

23 April 1996, Everest Base Camp

> The diarrhoea is back, and silly me, I don't have the drug I should have to get rid of it. Blast! Literally. Base Camp is so filthy, though, with people shitting everywhere, and I mean *everywhere*, and the only water available must be melted from the ice surrounding us. Even boiled, I would say it is not safe. Water boils below one hundred degrees Celsius at this altitude, so what do you expect? I don't have problems on the mountain, but each time I come down, it hits me again. Boring, and debilitating. In a couple of days I am going up once more, to stay at Camp Three this time. Oh dear, the icefall game again.

The icefall must have had digestive problems, just like me; regular rumbles had agitated it during the night. Pumori had also been chucking ice like mad, presumably a consequence of hard partying between clouds and summit. I readied myself, took my usual bit of stone bench in the kitchen, drank hot water. Outside, the wind picked up. The icefall was hiding behind a heavy fog curtain, and it was now snowing lightly. It would not take much to convince me to go back to bed. TNT told me they had decided to go tomorrow instead of today, and that did it – I filmed until the cold froze my fingers, and retired to the cosiness of my sleeping bag.

Next door, Paul and Neil, who only ever got up twenty minutes before leaving, allowing for one miserable cup of tea, were arguing about what to do. They went, and so did Rob's group. One less bunch of people to overtake tomorrow. I settled for a guiltless sleep-in. Later on in the day I visited Rob's camp and asked Helen Wilton, his Base Camp manager, to send a fax to Jon for me. I missed him, and hoped I'd get an answer from him before tomorrow's departure. The inaction of the last few days had weighed on my morale, and the lack of a climbing partner was starting to wear me down. I did have a partner of sorts on this trip – my hand puppet Sheila Koala, who was hoping to become the first koala, male or female, to climb Mount Everest. But unfortunately she did not talk an awful lot.

What was Camp Two to Three like? Well, steep and icy, and my brand-new, lightweight, heavily priced crampons fell into bits a hundred metres up the fixed ropes, and I had to come up with an emergency solution halfway up a blue ice pitch. There was only one rope fixed on the face, secured by ice screws every so often. A lot of people went up and down it, and 'Get off my rope!' was the first thing that came to mind when encountering heavy traffic coming in the other direction. Then one got used to the steepness, and the overtaking.

Camp Three was an island of brightly coloured tents, built on ghosts and shredded old tents set in the ice of the Lhotse Face seracs. The Sherpas did return day trips, carrying loads from Camp Two to the South Col, and never stayed at Camp Three if they could avoid it. Us poor sea levellers struggled from Two to Three and called it a day, lying down in a tent with altitude lassitude and terrible headaches. What a laugh! Sherpas tell me that I am strong, though; it's all relative.

I made a mistake for my first time higher than Camp Two: because of space and time pressures, I had agreed to stay on my first trip to 7300 metres. *Ouch!* Should have known better. My body did not like that at all – it is used to going high, and staying high, but only on the second trip to a new altitude. TNT spent the night with me up there, arriving nine and a half hours after leaving Camp Two! Tina was so happy to have made it to there. There followed some resentment from the previous occupants of Camp Three, as the Camp Two cook carried TNT's sleeping gear to Camp Three under orders from our sirdar and after TNT had asked him for help in advance. But there always seems to be resentment somewhere on expeditions such as these; an outlet for inner tension, I think.

1 May 1996, Everest Base Camp

By touching the pictures I bring to life the smell of the grass, the cries of galahs in the evening skies, the peacefulness of a day at home. I just returned from Camp Three, 7300 metres, to Base and needed to make myself strong again, so I skipped dinner, poured myself an Irish whisky and went through my photos, through every single detail of them, to remind myself why I am here, and also that there is a real world waiting for me, with real people I love, and people who love me. I do enjoy pushing myself, getting higher on the mountain, but day after day I recognise the futility of it all as the Sherpas are the ones building the foundations of our possible glory.

So far and yet so far. Base to Camp Two in seven hours, Camp Two to Camp Three in five hours forty minutes, Camp Three to Base Camp in five hours fifty minutes, including a one-hour breakfast stop at Camp Three. Not too bad, considering the heavy packs. I felt happy with my performance.

Tonight, I am escaping in alcohol, music and candlelight. Will I ever be free? There are so many dangers on the way to freedom. I pray every day for the icefall to be clement to all of us. Yesterday, a member of Mal Duff's team got clobbered by something falling in it and ended up in a snow-filled crevasse with a twisted ankle and two broken ribs. It could have been worse. I am getting better at balancing my ladder crossings, learning from watching Sherpas dancing their way across them with heavy loads. I can't say I enjoy it – it still requires a huge amount of concentration for me not to break apart and sit down and howl – but I am definitely getting into the swing of it! I just run through the icefall, always out of breath, always thinking, *Shit, if this goes, I am gone.* Some people call it beautiful. I call it plain scary, and ugly, in a fascinating way. One hopes to see it crashing, but not from within. It has changed a lot in the few days since my last going up some sections of it are unrecognisable, and the mind tries to make them familiar to quieten that accelerating heartbeat.

Avalanches have become more regular, showers of rock from the Everest West Face hit the side moraine, snow explosions from Nuptse and deep settling noises in the ice at Camp Three make it pretty unsettling up there. What if the whole mountainside decides to go for a ride down valley? Do you say, 'Hey, I don't have a ticket. Let me out!'?

I feel confident I can do it, given the right weather and the goddess's willingness. Could I deal with getting up that mountain? I must remember that success for me is going to be relief and happiness for Jon and a lot of dear friends who believe in me. I am detached from the issue right now, but I can't wait to go back up. *Jon.* The name I call when I need to gather strength. And Min, Ian, Roddo, who believe so much I can't believe it, and love regardless, and I feel so full of everything tonight I am going to burst, and thanks to Sally Potter's music and words I reach for the sky, and maybe I will be free soon?

As long as I was prepared to stand in the queue. Since most expeditions were now at Base Camp, resting and regrouping before the final assault, a few leaders decided to get together to organise movements on the upper slopes. Rob, who had guided Everest successfully a number of times, was seen as the natural chairman for the meeting. I think he loved directing the orchestration as well, and took it to heart to do his best. Due to the high number of people on the mountain, and to the cost of equipping it with fixed ropes, the work had been divided between all, and every group had been responsible for part of it. Not everyone did what they were supposed to do, though, and this of course led to friction and nasty exchanges. The leader of the South Africans, for example, did not take kindly to being told what to do. Other groups disagreed with the idea of organising teams on a fixed schedule, with, surprise, surprise, Rob's and Scott's groups going before the bulk of the expeditions; they decided that they would summit on 10 May, a date which had been auspicious for Rob in the past, and asked all the others to follow one day behind, to 'avoid traffic jams high on the mountain.' There were rumours of deep snow, which a couple of renegade groups had encountered on their (failed) summit bids in the last few days. So of course it made sense to someone like Henry, who was an old mate of both Rob and Scott, to comply with their wishes. Their teams of Sherpas were much bigger than ours, and would trench a route to the summit for all to enjoy afterwards. In theory. I was a bit reluctant to have to follow orders and the two most expensive trips on the mountain, but I certainly did not feel like going for the summit with forty-odd people, most of whom would probably be very slow, and hard to overtake.

The few days between coming down and going back up were a mixture of socialising, waiting and playing the ostrich. In our team, the group to follow Rob and Scott was to consist of Paul and Neil, Mark, Michael, Ray Door, Graeme Ratcliffe and me. Henry, still plagued by a chest infection, was to direct operations from Camp Two, and TNT, feeling sick and a little run down, would follow suit later. Because Rob, once again, had decided to leave the mountains on 17 May, we were supposed to do the same. Which did not allow for weather problems or a second go at the summit. I should have looked then at the options of jumping onto another team if needed, but I was extremely reluctant to do so, as begging was not my style. That was also the reason I did not visit other teams more. Rob had told me that I was welcome any time, and I had made friends with some of the South Africans and Americans as well, but as our team was renowned for its primitive fare, I did not want to be seen as bludging. I would have liked to spend more time with Henry, but unfortunately he did not like hanging around his own punters much, and preferred instead the company of friends on other teams. He raved about the coffee on Scott's trip, and enjoyed Sandy Pittman-Hill's vintage port and socialite stories. Sandy was one of Scott's clients, a New York socialite hoping to climb the Seven Summits. Everest was the last mountain on her list.

Michael and I were getting on very well, and I found myself hoping more and more that we'd end up climbing together. Being ten years younger than me, he took to calling me the 'tough old bird'. I took it as a compliment! There was no suggestion of teaming up, though. In fact, at the time, it felt like every climber was for him or herself within the frame of the group. I managed to call Jon one last time before going up. Talking with him gave me a renewed faith in my ability to summit, and I started to jump up and down with excitement again. Summit fever was definitely in the air.

On 6 May, Scott's and Rob's expeditions went up, en route to their summit attempt. I read a whole book that day, trying to keep panic at bay. This climbing Everest business was so hard . . . never knowing if the two months spent on the mountain would hold the summit reward, or if I would die in the attempt, or if I would miserably run out of steam . . .

From Camp Two, I could see that the wind hadn't abated high up, so I went to Rob's camp to see if his team was going higher than Camp Three today. It was twenty to nine in the morning. 'Yes, we are going up,' was Rob's firmly affirmative answer. 'We are leaving now.'

'Okay. Take care up there . . .'

'Of course. *You* take care.'

It was to be the last time I talked to him. The team had already left, and sighing, despite a strong feeling that I should stay put in camp, I prepared to follow.

Last chat to Henry, sick in bed, nursing a radio which only worked on his team's frequency. My pack was heavier than I expected it to be, but I seemed to be moving well anyway. The ropes on the bergschrund were in a pitiful state. I jumared up the vertical pitch with my heart thumping and an urge to wet my pants. There were chunks of blue ice everywhere at the bottom of the face. I caught up with Michael, who had been filming, and Ray, still coughing. No way was I sharing a tent

241

with him at Camp Two. Michael shot off, and I followed with Ray at a more sedate pace. A few minutes later, a group of Sherpas came down, supporting someone who looked like he had altitude sickness. Wobbles, stops, staggers. *Shit, I forgot the Adalat at Camp Two.* 'Ray, do you have any drugs? That guy looks like he could do with some.' Ray took his pack off, and dug some Adalat and Dexamethasone out. The little sick man was not a Sherpa, but a Taiwanese who did not speak English, so the Sherpas did not know what was wrong with him except that he had slid head-first into a crevasse last night while squatting outside his tent with only his inner boots on. I held his hand, told him to take it easy and other soothing things. He did not understand, but it did not matter. Before setting off again he grabbed my hand and whispered, 'Thank you' before they resumed stumbling down. I learned the next evening, after arriving at Camp Four on the South Col, that he died at the bottom of the fixed ropes, presumably of internal bleeding. It hurt.

Back at Camp Three, the Sherpas had erected a third tent. Up at the Yellow Band, the commercial groups were moving slowly towards Camp Four. 'What are we doing here?' The wind had picked up high on the mountain, and snow was falling heavily at our altitude.

'I don't know,' said Michael. 'We should have stayed down. Maybe we'll hang around – the weather could change.'

The next morning we heard on the radio that the other groups, Rob's, Scott's and the unscheduled Taiwanese, had left the Col and were on their way to the summit. It was already eleven a.m. before we decided to start, and we would not get to the Col before six p.m. for sure. Would that give us enough time to rest before a midnight start?

We started, anyway; Michael without supplementary oxygen, the rest of us carrying bottles weighing seven kilos on top of the gear we would need up there. Michael and I moved together. I filmed him on the Yellow Band, and took pictures. I noticed the huge snow plume covering the upper reaches of Everest. Ang

Tshering pointed at some dots close to the summit. *Shit! They were still going for it, in this weather?* Even down where we were, the wind had picked up, the snow came in flurries and bands of clouds reduced the visibility to a few metres at times. It must have been about two-thirty p.m., past the one p.m. sacrosanct turning-back time for Rob, and they were still going up? Up a snow bowl towards the Geneva Spur and the long traverse to the South Col.

Up the black rock ridge of the Geneva Spur, the fixed rope stops, although strands of old string show the way to the Col. By the time I got to the two tents the Sherpas were setting in whipping wind, I was shivering out of control. Lakpa pushed me inside the second Himalayan Hotel. The other one was already full of Sherpas, Mark and Neil. I was so cold that I couldn't decide what to do first. The karrimat was on the ground, so I could sit on something that was not freezing. My hands didn't work properly, they were too cold. *Silly coot, you should have stopped and put your downsuit on.* I scattered my gear around, finally getting my downsuit out, and managed to squeeze into it. I warmed my hands on my belly, howling softly to myself as the circulation painfully re-established itself.

Little did I know that higher up, the people coming down from the summit were having a total epic. The weather had cleared as I arrived in camp, and later I had seen headtorches coming down the last slope to the Col. I had been too engrossed in my own misery to care. Besides, those teams were led by experienced guides and had a hell of a lot more Sherpa help than we did. They'd be all right, dead tired, but what do you expect if you go for the summit in that kind of weather? Neil moved into my tent, and so did Michael and Graeme when they finally arrived. Communicating was not easy as we were all tired and the wind was buffeting the tent walls, creating a hell of a racket. Ray did not appear, so Lakpa went down in the windstorm to look for him, but came back minutes later as the wind was too strong.

Maybe Neil knew how serious the situation was out there; maybe he had not realised. Henry had decided to appoint him in charge because, being an army-minded fellow, he would have been able to make decisions and sort out the mess. Our main worry was Ray, but no one was going to look for him. There was no need to – there was a rope showing the way, and if things got tough, going down was very simple. It involved turning around and following the rope back to Camp Three. Which he apparently did, after his pack fell off while he was getting his downsuit out of it. Paul, who had turned back earlier, had the surprise of Ray stumbling into his tent at Camp Two the next morning.

At two a.m. I woke up. My oxygen had run out. I shivered miserably until morning. At five a.m. Neil was on the radio, cursing it. The batteries were running low, there were no spares around. I used the bits of wire I carried with me to fix my crampons if needed, and rigged my headtorch battery to it. Henry sent Neil out to do a head count. He came back saying we needed to brew for the survivors. Five people had apparently fallen from the South Summit. There was nothing we could do for them. We brewed. 'Shall we bring it to them?' I asked.

Neil shrugged, 'They'll come and get it.' I didn't think about questioning that. 'We are all re-hydrating nicely,' he told Henry.

We learned on the way down that everyone at Rob's camp had been listening to all radio schedules and felt horrified by his answer, as their people were totally exhausted after being out for most of the night thinking they would die.

It was total chaos. Henry, smelling a dead rat, had offered help the day before, telling Rob's base that his Sherpas could 'crawl a bit higher' and help those coming down. He had been told to stand by. 'Too many Indians and not enough chiefs,' we'd been told on our return. My feeling was that they thought they could deal with the situation, and that getting help from a shoestring expedition was a definite no-no. Everyone had faith in their leader's capabilities, and calling us to the rescue would have been unprofessional and unnecessary. Totally unaware of the situation outside, we announced our will to hang around another day if needed, to give the summit a shot.

Graeme went down, feeling ill. Mark and the Sherpas followed. Most of the other groups had trailed by. We heard that Todd Burleson and Peter Athans, guiding another group one day behind, were on their way up to help; Rob was still up there, and so were Scott and the Taiwanese leader, Makalu Gau. I got out to collect ice. One of Rob's client's was up and about, and so was Bruce from the South African team. 'Can we do anything to help?' I asked. Bruce smiled.

'Well, there are two people as good as dead near the Khanshung Face, but no, we'll let you know if we need you.' I did not even register the words. *As good as dead.* Dead. Same thing. I reported to my tent. We all huddled up, buffeted by the wind.

Scott and Rob still needed help. I felt much better, and went out again. Todd and Peter had arrived. They stood with a few others, looking towards the summit. Eager to help, I approached them. Peter I knew – he was with Jon on Everest in '87 – and we had met before on the lower slopes. 'What can we do? Shall we go up?'

Peter smiled. 'Sherpas are on their way. It's okay.'

It was not okay. Anatoli Boukreev, whom I had first met on Elbrus, and who had been working for Scott, walked into our tent. He told us snippets of the night's epic, how he had rescued some people who were waiting to die in a white-out last night two hundred metres from the tent. *What white-out? No-one ever came to ask us for help last night!* Michael and I took turns at the stove to make Anatoli brews. He wanted to go back up and try to rescue Scott.

I went out again when I heard that Michael Groom was in camp. I felt I could go and ask if he needed anything, as I knew him. He looked scary – totally spaced-out, and his ears were grey. I gave him a hug. John Taske, a Queensland doctor, shared his tent. 'Can I do anything?'

'No, I think we're all right now.'

He told me how Andy Harris, another guide in his group, had left his down-jacket on the South Summit, and must have gone down the wrong gully and died.

'You mean, he fell down from the South Col?' Someone had told me the story of him walking through the camp, and wandering to the top of the Lhotse Wall.

'Yes, yes, I mean . . .' More chaos. The mind definitely does not work very well at altitude. Try drinking two bottles of red wine one after the other at sea level, and making conscious, life-and-death decisions just after you finish gulping the last glass. It is about as easy as using your brain at 8000 metres and above.

Night was falling. The wind's speed had increased so much that the tent's walls were flattened on our faces as we lay in our sleeping bags. Michael and I realised that if we didn't sit up and hold the tent, it would be destroyed and we'd die. 'Neil! Wake up! We have to hold the tent up!'

'Mmm . . . surely, it can wait until morning?' And with that Neil stuck his feet up a little on the tent wall.

'Damn! The strings holding it must have broken,' I swore.

No movement. I got up and out, and strung the tent back. It was so cold out there, so hard to attach the strings with mitts on. I finally succeeded and dived back in. Michael and I proceeded to hold the tent up again. Neil continued to sleep, fitfully.

We heard from Base Camp that the wind had been blowing at over one hundred miles per hour. Rob had just spent his second night out on the South Summit, his last words transmitted to his pregnant wife in New Zealand. Anatoli came back earlier on, devastated. Scott, who had been left behind by the two Sherpas who had gone up the first slopes and had rescued Makalu Gau, had been too far gone, his body twisted by the cold, his eyes sunken in their orbs. Anatoli had said goodbye to Scott and come down, his heart heavy.

Anatoli was going down, and so were we. The night was so scary, with the roar of the jet stream just above our heads, sounding like a train roaring by. *God, if it comes down a little lower, we are dead meat,* I thought. I got Neil to untangle some strings so we could tie the tent down before we descended. I caught up with Peter and Todd, who had had the surprise last night of Beck Weathers stumbling into their tent looking like the living dead after two nights spent out in the storm. Todd asked me to pay off the belay rope holding Beck. I did, and walked down with him along the fixed rope. *My God!* His face looked like a potato which had spent too much time in the open fire – black, swollen. One of his arms was frozen to the elbow. He was extremely cheerful and in control, all things considered. I enjoyed doing my bit, and was prepared to come down all the way to Camp Two at his side if needed. At the next anchor, Peter told me they'd be all right, that the anchors could take only so much weight. I didn't understand. Ed Viesturs, another Himalayan hot-shot, was coming up to help them. Was he lighter than me?

Back in Base Camp, Michael and I talked with Henry, trying to understand. We found out that at the end of that first night Beck Weathers and Yasuko Namba were still alive, although very far gone. None of us had registered the fact at the time. 'As good as dead,' Bruce had said. Had someone given us straight orders to go and get them, via the radio, we would have – they were only two hundred metres from camp. No one had, thinking we were up there knowing what was happening. Still, no one had come to us and asked for help, and Neil's explanations had been misleading at the best. We would have to live with it now.

I went to Rob's camp to offer my sympathy and hug Guy Cotter, who had come over from an expedition he was leading on Pumori to help with trying to convince Rob to make a move down on his own. The Sherpas also sent to his rescue had not been able to get to him in the storm, and Rob had been too far gone to follow advice from Base Camp to try and come down on his own. Guy looked more dead than alive. Rob was an old friend of his, as Andy had been, and he had been powerless to do anything to save them. Our reunion could not be a happy one, despite the intense time we had shared in Antarctica.

On 14 May we all gathered at Scott's camp and had a memorial for those who had died. It was a very emotional occasion, with people standing next to the puja rock cairn and talking about the dear ones they had known. Helen, who had been Rob's Base Camp manager, her voice quavering over the Sherpas' prayers, voiced her feelings for the departed with what she said was an anonymous poem, and sent shivers down the spines of all present:

> 'Do not stand at my grave and weep, I'm not there, I do not sleep. I am a thousand winds that blow, I am the diamond glint on the snow . . .'

Anatoli walked to the cairn too. ' Sorry Scott, I was too late . . .' Many people followed, talking with tears in their voices, until we all gathered in Scott's mess tent for a serious piss-up, sharing fond memories. Anatoli got his guitar out, and had us howling at the moon with heart-breaking Russian songs.

People drifted out of Base Camp after that, but the few who were still keen to go back up stayed, and listened intently to the weather forecast, now bought from a British company, to plan their moves high up. Henry had told us that soon we'd have to pack up and go, as he had to be in Alaska on 1 June. He gave us two days' rest at Base Camp before a last attempt.

The weather was still terrible, but if we wanted to go back up, it was now or never. I wanted to go back up. I'd asked Michael if he wanted to team up, but as he had a Lhotse permit and had already climbed Everest, he fancied trying the lower mountain with Anatoli, who wanted to climb it in a day. Everyone was out of the game but Paul and Neil, who had thought that if they came back to Base Camp they'd never go up again. They were hanging around at Camp Two. Graeme was keen to go back up too, and convinced Henry to lend us the Sherpa support we needed for the ascent. Henry agreed reluctantly, but his Sherpas were not so motivated any more: 'The gods are angry,' they said, and when their wives came up to Base Camp in the aftermath of the tragedy they were even less keen to try for the summit. They would clean up Camp Four, but did not want to go any higher.

The good news was that I had talked to Jon again, and he was on his way to meet me in Katmandu. Hopefully I'd have something to celebrate then, besides our reunion.

22 May 1996, Everest Base Camp

I came down from the mountain yesterday for the last time. Eerie feeling that I might have left my chance to climb the mountain behind at Camp Three. But the wind has been howling non-stop, wearing me down. David Breashears, who is filming a multi-million-dollar Imax movie, is now getting a five-hundred-dollar-a-day forecast from the United Kingdom, but it does not show any consequent improvement for the next few days, which are the only ones left for us on the mountain.

Neil and I are the only climbers left on our team willing to go for it. So no Sherpa support, and Henry continually on the radio reminding us that the weather is terrible, that everyone at Base Camp is waiting for us, that the Sherpas want to go home. All facts that are lost on us in our determination to give it our best shot. I got to Camp Three in four hours and ten minutes, by far my best time. I feel strong. On the way up, I met Michael and Anatoli on their way down from Lhotse. Anatoli got up, Michael did not.

The wind was still a problem though – it just didn't ease. On the way up, I chilled my chest. My lungs feel cold and my breathing was restricted halfway through the night. A huge snow plume covers the South Col in the morning. Going up would be ridiculous. Wait and see until tomorrow morning. Regular vicious gusts shake the tent all through the second night. My decision to turn back was born that night, when I suddenly realised that I could not handle the idea of fighting a single further wind gust.

Back at Camp Two, I went visiting, and was invited for lunch by Thierry and Deshion. A strange feeling of peace and satisfaction has descended upon me. I know I have done my best, that I was strong until the end; the weather beat me. At least I did not let summit fever lead me to loss of toes, fingers or life. I can always come back . . . if that does not jeopardise my marital bliss! All I can think of now is reunion with Jon and tandoori chicken. Preferably together, with gin and tonic to loosen up our tongues! I love him and I miss him. Not long now . . .

On 23 May, the yaks were in to take our expedition down. It was then that we heard the news that Thierry was on the summit, and that the Imax expedition was on its way there as well. I fumed, cursing Henry for having made us rush up so he could meet his Alaskan commitments, and myself, for not having begged a place with one of the expeditions staying on. *Not much I could do about it now . . .*

I walked down the valley with Michael. I had come down from the ice of hell, and re-entered paradise in the hills of the Sherpa country. I was alive. I had done my best under the circumstances. I had not summited, but I was content, strangely content. This expedition had given me a chance to meet wonderful people, and after the harshness of the last month I was aware of the fact that I was alive, so intensely alive. Smelling that flower. Feasting on the colours of a peacock's feather, as the flying rainbow glided above the depths of the valley. Looking forward to the next beer stop on our pub crawl from Pangboche to Syangboche Airport, to the words and smiles and laughs exchanged between us, who had come back from Everest not only alive, but also friends for life.

Everest –
Flight to Freedom

Kurt Cobain's stretching whines were in time with the swings of my skipoles and my cadenced steps. I danced up the hill above Namche City, elated to be free again. Free of the worries of how to get there, Ian had sorted it all out again; free of ten days in Katmandu, ten days full of uncertainties, ailments and pseudo cures. Now it was just me and the hills, and that big mountain on the horizon . . . Nirvana?

The urge to return to Everest had been inside me from the time I descended from Camp Three in 1996. As soon as I had been reunited with Jon in Katmandu at the end of the ill-fated Everest season, I whispered to him, in the middle of our first embrace, 'You know I'm going back, don't you?'

He looked at me. 'I understand, Brigitte, but don't you want to give it a rest for a while?' I couldn't. I knew I had to go back as soon as possible. To wait an extra year would only add another twelve months of uncertainty and misery to an obsession already nine years long.

Foxtel and HIH Winterthur Insurance were behind me as soon as I reported to them upon my return to Australia, and Roddo O'Connor found another supporter for me – Deloitte Touche Tohmatsu. With Ian, Min and Roddo generously presenting me with the extra funds needed to join another Everest expedition, and with my determination fuelled by their love and support, I had no choice but to follow my destiny and my intuition.

The serpentine track was as busy as Melbourne's Tullamarine Freeway at peak hour. Trekkers, future climbers, Sherpas and loaded yaks followed each other at a sedate pace suited to the altitude. I was far too excited to slow down to their rhythm, and let the music carry me. A sharp corner in the track, two slow, plodding yaks in front of me. I accelerated, ran onto the uphill shoulder, jumped in front of them and skipped along towards my mountain. Oh, it was so fantastic to feel good again! My health had been less than satisfactory since I'd left Australia, following a short and hectic three weeks at home after coming back from the usual exhausting summer Aconcagua spell. I must have been mentally and physically tired, because as soon as I relaxed into life in Asia I found myself plagued with an eye infection — followed by a nasty cold and vicious hay fever — thanks to too many days' exposure to Katmandu's dirty atmosphere. Then the weather had been bad, and our departure for the mountains delayed, day after day. Trips to the airport, stand-bys, trips back to the hotel as the cloud cover descended and made flying to the mountains impossible.

Finally, on 3 April, the sky cleared, and we took off for Luckla. Most people on the expedition had a few days' advance on me, and were either already at Base Camp, or on their way there. Only Mal Duff, Everest leader, and Andy Clarke, whom Mal had promoted to Lhotse leader, were left behind with me. It was a little funny to be on a trip with people I did not know, but I had decided to give Mal's trip a go, for a change I guess. My friend Henry was also leading an expedition to Everest and Lhotse, and I had met up with him, his partner Peta Watts and daughter Matti back in the capital. Michael Joergensen was there also, to help Henry on his Lhotse trip, and I had no doubt I'd be spending a lot of my time at Base Camp drinking coffee in their kitchen tent. In fact, it looked like life at Everest Base Camp would involve a lot of visiting and socialising: Thomas and Tina Sjögren had come again, having bought part of a permit to have their own small Swedish expedition; Guy Cotter, who had taken over Adventure Consultants, was leading this year's expedition to Everest, as was Jon Tinker for Out There Trekking (OTT); and Anatoli Boukreev had been hired to coach a team of Indonesians to the summit.

Mal had stayed behind to sort out more red tape, so Andy and I, as well as Michael and his parents, whom he had convinced to try the trek to Everest Base Camp, started on the walk from Luckla towards Base Camp. Andy, better known as Sharkie, was a young British climber, a bit of a hot-shot at Scottish ice-climbing, and friendly in a puppy-dog way. I was quite content to be walking up with him, and I looked forward to a stress-free few days to Base Camp. We talked a lot, strolled, raced up hills, ate potatoes, and drank *chang* in tea shops. Well, he did not in Deboche, and I should not have. The morning after, I woke up feeling very rotten and announced I would have to stay behind. Andy, who had not been very high before, was keen to get to our next scheduled stop, Pheriche, for a couple of days acclimatising at a more suitable altitude. He wished me well and went on his way.

The sky had clouded over every afternoon since the start of our walk, and today was no exception. Snow fell heavily, covering the rhododendron forest and giving the landscape a peaceful Christmas atmosphere. The yaks' bells sounded softly past the lodge, muffled by the whiteness. I looked through my window, hoping tomorrow would see me in better shape. That night I had a dream, rather weird, but one which made me feel I had finally laid ghosts to rest.

7 April 1997, Dream in Deboche
> The streets of Melbourne were lined with people cheering and aiming rotten tomatoes at the little old horse pulling my rickety

cart. Floats, vaguely defined in my outer vision, were slowly moving alongside mine. 'It's great, isn't it?' said one of the people sitting on my stomach.

'Mmm . . .' I replied, trusting my head up to look around. 'I guess, but I think it's not fair on the horse!'

A tall, shiny wall of giant coaches caught my attention on the other side of our modest cart. Here were the private-school boys, all blond, all white-tombstone smiles, proudly displaying the Melbourne Cup trophy for all to see. I recognised the one in front, in the position of honour. 'James, it's James!' I happily yelled. 'James!' He had climbed Everest, achieved recognition among his peers. He stood, tall and proud, and did not hear me. My cart was below the plimsoll line of his carriage, and as I was lying down, held down by hemp ropes and the sitting people, it was not easy for me to make myself heard. I did not mind, though, I was proud of him, and I was happy to be on my way to climb Everest, no matter how I got there.

I was woken up by my alarm watch. Still in a daze of bizarre contentment from my dream, I stumbled down the stairs to order my first coffee. I did not hate James any more. I was sure of it now. It made me lighter for the task ahead, relieved that I did not have to carry negative influences of any sorts.

I was still a little wobbly as I started towards Pheriche, gasping for breath as I followed a caravan of yaks skidding on the icy path through the forest. Worried. Gosh, would I be up to it?

8 April 1997, Pheriche

It was hard to leave Ang Kamchi and Deboche, but hey, a girl's gotta do what a girl's gotta do. Had a terrible time for the first two hours, short of breath, and someone put rocks in my pack, I swear! Felt much better after lunch at Pasang's place, blasted through to Pheriche (4243 metres). Still a horrible place. I hope my head allows me to go on to Lobuche (4930 metres) tomorrow.

Just to put all the chances on my side, I went for a two-hour walk up the hill above Pheriche, and that should have taken me high enough to help my acclimatisation (I stopped at more or less around 5000 metres, I think). If nothing else, it will help me sleep tonight! Apparently Henry went through to Pangboche yesterday, on his way to Base Camp today. Good luck to him! Michael and his folks are somewhere ahead I think, and Simon Yates, our mate Joe Simpson's friend, and, like Michael, working on Henry's Lhotse trip, is supposedly one day behind. It will be interesting to meet 'the man who cut the rope' known to me by Joe Simpson's *Touching the Void* and Simon Yates's *Against the Wall*. The cloud descended again, sprinkling a little snow on me as I came down the hill. I felt great.

Not so great the day after, though, which made me decide on another night in my slum. The next morning, I went hunting for better 'fooding', as they call it here, and bumped, unexpectedly, into Simon Yates. He told me that Michael and his parents were in the lodge next door. Michael's parents were on their way down, and plans were made for the departure next morning to delightful Lobuche. Simon and I talked all the way to Base Camp, the walk a breeze. I stopped at Henry's camp, feeling like I should stay. Michael was already there, and Henry, Peta, Pasang, Kami, Pemba, and now Simon. Instead, I had to go on and find myself a life with people I did not know, or hardly, at Mal's camp.

The white mess tent was the centre of a village of smaller tents, just below a five-star Japanese camp. I went in for a cuppa, saw lots of people I had vaguely met in Katmandu, lots of other people I had not met yet, and wondered where I was going to set up camp. Space was important to me, buffer zones. I did not fancy hearing people do whatever it is people do in their tents. The only flat spot available within reasonable distance from the mess tent, without being too close to the centre of town, happened to be between the two toilets. But it had a lovely view onto a sunken lake, and I decided that I would rather listen to farts and coughs than to conversations between tent mates, so there I settled, erecting my spacious, derelict tent and covering its dying outer fly with a bright blue tarpaulin held down by a collection of strings and stones. That decision earned me the nickname of Bag Lady, living in the slum behind the latrines.

Our camp was, as usual these days, at the foot of the only mountain on earth, surrounded by vast tented suburbs. OTT's camp was near us. The Malayans had a huge national team spreading their identical red conical tents on acres of moraine. The Indonesians had arrived early and employed Anatoli to drag them to the summit. Peter Athans and Dave Breashears were there also, making a film on physiology at altitude. Guy had a New Zealand chef, a Base Camp doctor and manager, and chicken and fresh food flown in quite often. A Russian expedition – at the lower end of the comfort scale – was planning to traverse Lhotse and Lhotse Shar, and to descend on the other side of the mountain. They became our barometer. When the Russians were down in camp, it meant the weather was *really* bad up high. Our own camp, sandwiched between others, was not exactly high in comforts either. The main fare was reasonable, provided by Sherpas used to catering for the western world, believing the more fried the food was, the better, but we sorely lacked appetising goodies to get stuck into between greasy meals. Thank God I had my private supplies. And so did Mal, as we were to find out later.

There were thirteen members in our team: six for Everest, seven for Lhotse, and a Base Camp manager, Mike Burns, with a delightful Scottish accent and hippie habits, who Mal employed to organise camp and supplies on the mountain in exchange for as much beer as he could drink. I don't know if it was such a good deal for Mal.

The Everest team consisted of Mal, veteran Himalayan

climber, myself, and three young Mexican climbers, Luis Corona, Carlos Guevara and Andres Delgado. Andres was accompanied by his girlfriend Vivian Bravo, who was in charge of communicating with the homeland via regular Internet reports. She spoke French as well as English and Spanish, and we'd often get stuck into international conversations on books and movies. Then there was Mike Trueman from Hong Kong, who had been with Mal the previous year. Having served with the Gurkhas, he spoke fluent Nepali, which enabled us to get hot chips more often at meal times.

Lhotse would be assaulted by Andy, who was there to work in exchange for a free trip, and could still not understand why he had been given the title of leader given his limited experience at high altitude. In fact, he turned out to have a ceiling to his acclimatisation capabilities: each time he tried to go higher than Camp Two, vomiting forced him to go back down. Ivan Loredo, Mexican and dark of temperament, could down three full plates faster than his shadow, and would still go to the kitchen and claim food from Sherpas' bowls to fill in the holes. Ari Piela, from Finland, looked like an albino elephant seal wearing prescription swimming goggles, and a red bandanna over his bleached locks. He had a wicked sense of humour. Gary Guller had lost an arm in a climbing accident, and aimed to conquer the icefall, a challenge certainly big enough.

Then there was a British couple, Mark McDermott and Alison Wright. They had spent their last five years working as a computer programmer and a civil engineer in Muscat respectively, and were both ultra-marathon runners. Finally, we were graced by the presence of Alan Hinkes, English mountaineering idol on a quest to climb the fourteen peaks higher than 8000 metres. Lhotse would be his ninth. He fancied himself a bit, and at times had the dirty, giggly mind of a ten-year-old. He made me laugh. Sometimes.

Base Camp was a freezer of monstrous proportions. Last

year I had been running around wearing my Treksta sport sandals, but this time I was mighty glad I had brought along a pair of seventies vintage moon boots that Jon had scavenged from our local dump. Unfortunately, they did not tolerate the cold; the outer plastic cracked into numerous pieces as soon as I trotted over from my abode to the mess tent. But with some TLC, Leucoplast and liberal amounts of Kwik Grip glue, they lasted the distance, and enhanced my bag lady image. So did the recycled rum bottle which Thomas had filled with some of his cough medicine to help me overcome one of the numerous upper respiratory tract infections that bothered me during the trip. I stuck it in a brown paper bag, in my dirty duvet pocket, and took every opportunity to swig it at meal times . . . You can be anyone you want to be in the mountains!

We had the usual debauched puja, throwing handfuls of *tsampa* at each other and downing numerous cups of creamy *chang* before setting foot on the mountain. Andy, Mark, Alison, Mal and I made our way towards Camp One for a stay there, and to catch up in acclimatisation with those who had been at Base Camp for longer than we had. The icefall was the usual horror story, seemingly easier than last year, but throwing us with abject surprises higher up. There were far fewer big ladders than last time, the route meandering a lot, but some areas were hair-raising – popcorn fields of ice shifting on a regular though unknown basis, bottomless chasms skirted by unstable and broken ice fields, tottering towers which we had to surmount on too-high flimsy ladder arrangements.

The last ice tower was crowned with garlands of prayer flags, which meant that the icefall 'doctors', Ang Nima and Pasang, had little faith in its stability. The ropes over the top of the tower led to a narrow band of snow where Camp One was, an uncertain haven in a sea of towering seracs. Heart-stopping clamours of the glacier moving under our tents made me swear that I would spend one night, and one night only, at the site of Camp One.

This year, as I had sworn it would be the last time I ever, ever went to Everest, saw me putting all chances on my side. I hired the services of a Sherpa — whomever was available at the time — to help me carry my personal gear up. I was on a mission, filming the ascent for Channel Seven, and did what every self-respecting filmmaker did in conditions such as these: reduced my load to afford myself the luxury of decent footage. It worked well, allowing me to film in the icefall, something I hadn't dared to do the previous year, burdened as I was at all times by heavy packs.

16 April 1997, Everest Base Camp

Back at Base Camp. Jon Tinker, whom I haven't seen yet, walks into our mess tent. My heart beats faster. Jon is happy to see me, though, hugs me, invites me over for dinner that night. Talks a little fast maybe. Love and hate story. I have in my mind the happy times of our Shishapangma year, and the heartbreaking memories of Everest '95. I agree to go over. The OTT mess tent is the same as the one we had in Tibet in '93 and '95, and the little drawings and graffiti I made in '93 are still on its walls, looking incongruous in different company. The tent is full of an Icelandic expedition — tall, blond, tough-looking guys thirteen to the dozen crowding the limited space. Jon has stocked the expedition well; we feast on wine and Dorje's haute cuisine, while enjoying the luxury of a gas heater.

———

After a couple of days' rest at Base Camp, I was ready for the next leg, which I hoped would be a hop to Camp Two and a trip up to Camp Three. The less I saw of the icefall, the better. It turned out that Simon, Kami and one of their kitchen boys, Pumpkin Head (so baptised because the altitude seemed to have expanding effects on his face), were going up the same day. We all met in the icefall, and made our way to Camp One together. Simon and I were getting along well, and it was a pleasure to spend time with Kami, Henry's sirdar, again. Babu was on Everest too, having been promoted to sirdar rank by Jon Tinker. It was great to have him around one more time. I could not understand people who treated Sherpas as just workers at best, and servants at worst. Despite the difficulties in communication, I'd always felt a communion with them, at least those who climbed not only because Everest and other Himalayan peaks were good earners, but also because they thrived on pushing themselves high in the mountains, and took their roles in a responsible way. Babu was a friend.

Kami, Simon, Pumpkin Head and I pushed on to Camp Two under an increasingly grey sky. Snow and wind joined the dance, and kept us company until we reached Henry's camp, which was about half an hour's walk closer than Mal's camp. It became a compulsory stopover on my way to our camp, and it was wonderful to duck into the mess tent and spend time with my friends. 'How is my Australian flower?' Michael would greet me. A definite improvement on his usual name for me, the 'tough old bird'!

It was a little hard for me to leave Henry's camp behind, and to keep going up the slope to the camp site which had been Rob's last year. OTT had taken over the space, with two big mess and kitchen tents offering untold comforts to their participants.

Our people were hiding from the sun in their tents. I found another reasonably isolated spot to set my tent up. I did not expect any help to make the platform and erect my tent, which was just as well as I did not get any. This was a strange expedition. There was no team spirit whatsoever – no one ever thought of meeting up and discussing strategies. It was all every man, or woman, for themselves, although we all got on pretty well. Teamwork was never part of the equation, not even theoretically.

My plan from here was one day's rest, then one swift visit to Camp Three before I went down to Base Camp for a rest. Ho hum. The next day, I woke up with a head like a balloon.

Nothing to do with altitude sickness, oh no, but something which stopped me from going higher all the same.

21 April 1997, Camp Two, Everest

> If you think that being sick at sea level is not much fun, you should try it at 6400 metres. My throat hurts, my sinuses feel like they are ready to explode, my chest disgorges yukki green stuff. I should go down this afternoon, but I've never been energetic in the afternoon, and the idea of getting dressed and putting on my boots to go to the kitchen, fifty metres away from here, is more than I can take right now. I need to go down, though, to see a doctor and to get better, because this dream prison will be my end if I don't escape from it. Hurt pride kills.

Hard work doesn't, and I found myself on the road to Base Camp again. Mal was already there, having descended the day before. We enjoyed a happy evening, although a cold one, as usual. Mal retired early, and as he got up to leave I noticed the pockets under his eyes.

'Gee Mal, you look tired.'

He raised his eyebrows at me: 'Me? I feel great!'

———

I tossed and turned in my sleeping bag. I looked at my watch; it was way past breakfast time. Bloody Nima must have forgotten my morning bed coffee again. Living in the outer suburbs of camp did have its downsides at times. I sighed, and equipped myself for a trip to the mess tent with an empty cup. All was very quiet outside – the only noise was the sound of prayer flags whipping in the furious wind. I noticed a gathering in the middle of the main tent, and thought of taking my camera and video. I made tracks for the mess tent, though, thinking it would be more suitable to enquire there first. Wobbling up in my moon boots, disintegrating once again, I reached Kipa's tent. Kipa was Mal's sirdar, in charge of overseeing the climbing Sherpa team.

He was a tall, solid man, with the face of a thug, and that of a happy schoolboy when he smiled.

Kipa was standing near his tent, frowning and motionless. 'What's up?' I asked. Kipa's stare was dark.

'Mal,' he said in his deep voice, '. . . dead, in his tent.'

'What?!'

Mike Burns was a little more explicit. 'The cookboy went to his tent with morning tea, you know, and he could not raise Mal,' his rrr's rolling behind his blond Braveheart beard, 'so I went to shake him, and I opened the door and the zip broke, and he was there, his eyes open. There was a book still in his hand, and vomit everywhere . . .'

We stood in silence. A rather distraught-looking Nepali, wearing the garb of liaison officer – wool balaclava, oversized down-jacket, thermos slung around one shoulder, camera around the other – walked into Zebra Ice Station, as our Base Camp was now called, and introduced himself as our newly arrived liaison officer. Talk about timing. Henry and Peta were following him, looking devastated. Mal was an old friend of theirs, and as well as coping with the shock of his death within days of his forty-fourth birthday, they had now to find a friend back home to go and knock on the door of his wife, Liz Duff, with the news. Henry used our satellite phone sponsored by the Mexican Government to call various Scottish friends to ask them to do the sorry task.

The day came and went in a daze, with people dropping in and out offering their sympathy, with us team members looking incredulously at each other. I felt cheated. I had only just warmed up to Mal, having spent time with him at Camp One, and now it was too late to be friends. I was concerned, too, immediately after the feeling of loss hit me. Obsessions die hard – the spell of Everest was on me, was on us all, and there were questions in our eyes. What would happen to the expedition? *No, we can't give up, we won't pack up and go!* I looked at Andres, the one Everest member I felt close to; we shared the same intensity. Andres was twenty-seven years old, had been on the North Ridge of Everest the previous year, and had failed to reach the summit without oxygen. He was intent on climbing Everest this year, with or without supplementary oxygen.

Later in the day Henry returned, having spoken to Liz on OTT's Icelandic phone. She and Mal's mother wanted his body back. A helicopter had been organised to pick up the body, which would wait in the German Embassy freezer in Katmandu while Liz made her way there to take her husband home for burial. It was all so sad. *Poor Liz*, we all thought, our hearts going out to her, our stomachs cramping at the idea of leaving behind our own loved ones should something terrible happen to us while under the mountain's spell.

Mal's tent had been fenced off by the liaison officers with a yellow tape marking the 'scene of the crime'. I wandered by, feeling guilty as I took a few shots of it. I went back to my own tent and grabbed my sun hat. There were two pretty roses on it. On impulse, I tore them off the hat and took them to Mal's tent, pinning them to the door.

The next morning I was woken up by a roar in the sky, a helicopter arriving. No-one had thought of waking me up, so I could only say goodbye from the big boulder beside my tent. Peta told me later that my flowers had gone to Katmandu with Mal, on the shroud his tent had become. The usual crowd started to gather in our mess tent for breakfast and to share our grief. We washed down the fried eggs with whisky, then when that ran out, we moved on to Nepalese rum, vodka from the Indonesians, tequila from my cellar, white wine from the Canadians, more whisky from Guy, beer and whatever else we could lay our hands on.

Twelve hours later, we were still at it. Exactly the kind of wake Mal would have wanted, we were all certain of. It did wonders for our team spirit, too. No matter how unfortunate Mal's death had been, the one positive consequence of it was the determination of everyone, Sherpas and western members alike, to keep going.

——

After a couple of days eliminating the poison from our blood and reorganising our life without Mal, it was time to go back up. Anatoli had summited on 26 April at three p.m., whipping his Indonesians to the top and back again. We were all way behind them in our climbing schedule, having arrived at Base Camp a good month after they had. For me, it was time to go and check out Camp Three. My sinus infection had been cleared by the drugs Dave Fearnley, Guy's doctor and old climbing friend, had given me. Was it my third or fourth course of antibiotics? Ridiculous!

I was now feeling great, and determined to make the most of my spell of good health. After a day's rest I hit the Lhotse Wall, and made my way to Camp Three and beyond – the higher the better. I went to the start of the ascending traverse to the Yellow Band before declaring myself happy with my effort and zooming down to Camp Two. Tomorrow I'd go up to Camp Three and stay. Which I did, spending an entertaining day and evening in the company of Ari, the wacky Finn. I felt so full of energy that I spent all afternoon digging a decent toilet, a huge pit that I thought people could use instead of dropping their pants all around the tent. All to no avail, as the wind blew like mad during the night and filled my hole. People resumed the habit of pooing in their own backyard.

Back at Base Camp, climbers were starting to feel like giving the summit a go. The weather did not look favourable, though, and as I had just put in a serious bit of exercising at high altitude, there was no way I could have gone up in a hurry. Despite the fact that Guy's team, as well as Dave's and Jon's, were all gearing up for a summit attempt, I decided that what I needed now was a few days 'holidaying' at a lower altitude. Michael did not want to leave Base Camp, and it was with Simon that I made my way to Dingboche, where he knew a good lodge to stay, run by Kami's sister-in-law. I found myself losing sight of Simon on the way down, a definite sign that I needed a rest, with lots of good food and hours spent sleeping the altitude exhaustion off. Just living in the shadow of Everest was draining, let alone facing traps on its flanks.

After too short a break, anxious about missing any window of calm weather up high, we walked back to Base Camp in driving snow. I was concerned about my shortness of breath. *Here we go again, another chest infection.* Yuri Contreras, an Everest member on Henry's team who was Mexican, slightly mad, and a doctor, listened to my lungs. He announced they were free of infection. It was just another upper respiratory tract problem. 'Ere, take zis,' he said, presenting me with yet another course of antibiotics. 'Better be safe zan sorry.'

While I had been enjoying rest, recuperation and potato pancakes in Dingboche, a few impatient teams had ascended on summit attempts. Guy's and Dave's teams, it seemed, had been worried about crowds high on the mountain, and had wanted to be ahead of potential trouble. They had joined forces with Guy Cotter, Dave Breashears, Peter Athans, Ed Viesturs and Veikka Gustaffson – all Everest summiteers and high-altitude guides – accompanying Tashi Tenzing and Dave Carter, two of Guy's clients. OTT was on the run too, the Icelanders bent on conquest. Unfortunately for them, the mountain was not in a mood to be conquered – they all had to turn back and wait some more.

I felt overcome by the stalling, inside and outside me. I had not been communicating with Jon much this time, because really, there was nothing that positive to report: *I have been sick again, the weather is still bad high up. Waiting . . .*

8 May 1997, Everest Base Camp

> I walk the icy streets of our town. When I look up, above the white towers and walls, the wind whips my face, picks up my hair, and I have to spit it out, opening my mouth to breathe

easier. My heart is heavy, heavy with the wait, the wind above, the longing below. We are prisoners of the gale, of our hopes, of our fears, of our obsessions, of our need for freedom and intensity. Funnily enough, visitors come and go, but not us. We can't leave. The only way out of here is up, over the top, into the black sky. There are several tribes living in the town with no name, planning their own battles against the common enemy, the wind. We visit each other and exchange plans, news, concerns, hope, warmth. But we all know that we face the enemy, each of us, alone.

In our team, Andres had more or less the same idea as I had: to rest at Base Camp while the weather forecast – which most expeditions were now getting from the United Kingdom every day – was not promising, and move up to Camp Two when the last two days of the seemingly accurate five-day forecast predicted low-speed wind at 9000 metres. Luis and Carlos were more interested in being closer to the higher reaches of Everest to do their waiting, preferring Camp Two to Base Camp for their stand-by. Mike Trueman, who had assumed a sort of interim leadership with everyone's blessing, had ideas which I found disturbing.

9 May 1997, Everest Base Camp
The forecast is bad for the next five days. I had not thought about discussing strategies with Mike, who has been up at Camp Two for the last few days, but suddenly I decided to go and sit with him and Mike Burns in the kitchen tent. I learned that Mike had decided, or organised or whatever, with Guy that our team would follow one day behind his, to ensure a good track and ropes to the summit. It made me very irate, and I had to tell him, in a rather vivacious manner I'm afraid – being an impulsive person, with Slavic blood to boot – that I totally disagreed with his idea and that I would go when it felt right, rather than repeat last year's mistakes and miss out on the summit because the weather decided to sour, or because other people who went first

needed rescuing, thus destroying the chances of those following to reach the summit.

He saw my point of view, and we agreed to play it by ear. Sounds like I'll have the freedom to make my own decisions, which is what I want. It looks like three Sherpas, Dorje, Kipa and Tenzing Lama, will be helping hopeful summiteers above 8000 metres. Gompu was going to be part of the team too, but a nasty eye infection has forced him to go to Katmandu for medical treatment. I have a feeling that it is going to happen soon now, and I am going to concentrate on feeling healthy and fit again. Our little conversation has been the trigger to motivation, something I needed to get everything together. It is going to happen this time. And I have to hang around to be sure to be there when it does . . .

That night, I was told that Mal was being buried in Scotland, and that Henry had organised a get-together at the puja place to share memories of his life. It was two days later that I emailed Jon from Michael's tent about it, and about the situation at Base Camp and further above . . .

12 May 1997, Email to Jon from Everest Base Camp

Hello my love,

The old waiting game is on again, and it is not easy. The weather forecast is again for five days of high winds at altitude. Boring, boring, boring. The day before yesterday, Mal was buried in Scotland – to the sound of six thunderbolts – and of course, everybody got together to honour his memory. Not surprisingly, it ended up in a monster drinking session. Between gross Kiwi jokes, Guy informed me of the creation of Everest Anonymous, right under the puja place, with us looking at the fast-moving, contorted clouds above the Lhotse Face. Everest Anonymous. To be a member, you have to have been on the mountain four times, summiting or not, and support includes phone calls from Everest

Anonymous if you think of going back. The members endeavour to talk you out of it! I wonder if it will work for Peter Athans and Dave Breashears! One thousand dollars is payable to each member if you succumb and come back!

Well, you can imagine what we all did yesterday: moan and lie down, swear we would never ever do it again, and avoid using the brain, which would not answer calls anyway. Feel better today. In fact, went for a great run around Base Camp, with music blasting, but waiting, waiting, waiting . . . the price to pay, isn't it? I find it hard to keep up the old motivation at times. Doubts plague me – what if the wind does not die, what if I get sick again, what if . . .

What if I ran out of patience and down to Katmandu and home? *No, no, no, banish the thought.*

———

The highlight of our days, in the long period of waiting, was the weather report that Mike Burns collected in the early afternoon from Guy's camp. I made a copy of it and smuggled it to Henry's camp to pore over the unchanging figures. The mood was switched to escaping boredom there, with Michael singing 'Always Look on the Bright Side of Life' in a voice which must have had something to do with the sudden increase of stormy weather in the area.

Talking with Jon on our camp's phone, which Andres had decided would be free for everyone's use (too bad for the Mexican Government footing the bill!) gave my motivation a needed boost: 'Hang in there,' said Jon. 'Stay till the end. There is always a window of calm weather before the monsoon hits.'

17 May 1997, Everest Base Camp
Another bad forecast. Blimey, the monotonous bad weather is getting a bit boring. Except I am not really bored. See, I am not sick any more, and I am enjoying myself. Getting on well with

the team now, and doing a fair bit of visiting. Our food supplies are dwindling to not much, so we all go for cups of tea at other camps and beg for unwanted goodies. Mike found two huge coolboxes full of delicacies in Mal's tent, but they did not last long, especially after some greedy bugger raided them soon after they were moved to the store tent. I have been working on a newsletter in my vast spare time, a take-off of the *Big Issue*.

Ari has been dealing with the time that stands still in a very Ari way. All afternoon he is seen sitting still at the entrance of his diminutive tent, wrapped in his sleeping bag, holding a skipole above an icy puddle. Yak fishing. 'Can you do it again tomorrow so I can film it?' Ari looked at me down his tiny trumpet nose.

'No. Fishing finished. Now I write novel in Urdu.'

At night-time, Vivian, Alison and I donned our finery and went out for dinner, past a barrage of envious sniggers from our male companions. We had been invited by Guy Cotter to enjoy an evening meal at his camp. Tashi had been cooking, one of his favourite pastimes, and one at which he excelled. Chicken curry à la Tashi, chips, vegies, beer and other mouth-watering delights were all on the evening's menu. We salivated when we smelt the fresh chicken dish. 'Chicken, always chicken, this is getting so boring,' sighed Tashi. *Oh God, bore me to death!* The team's Sherpas, who had been on the mountain, were coming down, and the guys went out to welcome them. Alison and I looked at each other, and dived into the chicken pot.

I had asked Guy what his plans were, but he had been pretty vague. Next thing I knew, his team and Dave's team were both on their way back up, with Andres closely following. OTT was already at Camp Two. The forecast hadn't shown enough improvement, I thought, and I decided to sit tight at Base Camp for a while longer; there were still thirteen days until our permit expired and we were due to leave the mountain, and I knew that I could not cope with that amount of time at 6400 metres and above. Henry had made the same decision, which allowed me to plan going up with his partner, Peta, a couple of days later. I was getting terribly tense, excited, restless.

20 May 1997, Everest Base Camp

Going up tomorrow, despite the lack of change in weather conditions. The cyclone which hit Bangladesh yesterday has created havoc in weather predictions. OTT's first group (Nick Kekus, Chris Brown, others and Babu) tried for the summit today, and had to turn back after one hour and forty minutes (snow, possibly wind?). I am scared like before an exam, scared to fail again, scared to return home empty.

—

Peta and I looked at each other, breathing heavily. 'Shit, this is going to be hard.' We had spent too long doing nothing or not much at Base Camp. We walked steadily up the icefall, steadily but quite slowly. Last time up. At least we were going up. In my group, we had started with six climbers for Everest, and now there were only two of us left determined to attempt the summit – Andres, already at Camp Two, and myself. Mike had had to leave for Hong Kong, and Luis and Carlos had exhausted themselves hanging around at Camp Two in bad weather, and were packing to leave Base Camp. We had a farewell party for them, which I left early to be in shape for the climb ahead. I know my limits.

When I arrived at Camp Two I heard that Babu, two other Sherpas, the Icelanders and Nick Kekus were on their way to the summit and that Guy's and Dave's groups, as well as our own Andres, were spending the coming night at Camp Three. The great migration to the sky had started, a flight to freedom that only bad weather could stop.

21 May 1997, Camp Two, Everest

Thomas and Tina came up yesterday, and I joined them for some delicious fare and another radio forecast. The wind speed at

270

9000 metres is, starting with 22 May and finishing on 27 May: 40 knots, 35, 35–40, 30–40, 18–25, 25–20. We look at each other, hope in our eyes. The 26th is 18 to 25 knots. That means that if we have two days here, and go to Camp Three on 24 May, then Camp Four on 25 May, we'll be in position for the best weather prediction so far. Henry has made the trek from his camp for the radio sched. He wants the best conditions for the summit, wants to go in two days too. I have terrible pre-period pains right now, and hope they'll be more manageable soon. At the moment, it looks like Peta, Henry, Doctor Yuri and Illy Pauls from Latvia will go for the summit on the same day as me – a comforting thought as we will be the last climbers on Everest.

At Jon Tinker's camp we can see the OTT group on the traverse to the Hillary Step, way, way up on top of the West Face. A rope appears to be flying in the wind. Little dots move slowly. Going up or down? We look at the fast-moving clouds. It must be very cold and windy up there – just as well they are all as tough as nails. Chris Brown – good old Farmer Brown – arrives from the South Col, looking worn-out. I hug him, and congratulate him on his effort. Chris had been on Everest with us in '93. 'I have never been so scared in my life,' his voice trembled. 'You could not see a thing, snow flying in the light of the headtorch, and the wind . . . oh, it was so cold. I almost fell in a crevasse a couple of times. Too much. Too tired to try again today. I had to come down.'

OTT's first group has made it to the top, that's confirmed. Radio communications are difficult. Another OTT team is scheduled to leave for the summit tomorrow night. Is Jon Tinker with them? I send positive thoughts up to them.

I met Alan, Alison, Mark, Andy and Ivan at Camp Two, preparing to go for Lhotse. My dear friends Michael and Simon had already left, planning to stay at Lhotse Camp Four, then fix the ropes to the top. I crossed my fingers for them, and wished again they had been my partners on Everest. Big

Dorje, chain-smoking, and Kipa decided to join me on my summit attempt. Dorje was the strongest Sherpa on the team, and Kipa had climbed the South-west Face of Everest, so I could have done worse! How I would have loved a climbing partner to discuss things with, though! The Sherpas could not be relied on to make the best decision. They wanted to go the following day, 23 May. I insisted on going on 24 May. The Sherpas had been pushing for 'going up tomorrow' since early May, keen to get home. I also longed to be home, but not before I got the right conditions to go for the summit. I knew that I was far from the strongest I had ever been at altitude – too many illnesses, too many antibiotic courses. I had just finished my sixth course of antibiotics, to cure a recurrent sinus problem! And as graffiti in OTT's mess tent reminded me, 'Never ever think that you are from Planet Sherpa!'

I took one of the radios back to my tent to listen on OTT frequency. Their first group was back at the South Col after summiting – a twenty-hour return trip in less than ideal conditions. Where was Jon? To pass the time, I filmed Sheila Koala announcing her intention to be the first koala to climb Everest. She wanted to publicise the need to look after Australia's wilderness with her bold ascent of the highest mountain on earth. Good on her. Night approached, and I tossed and turned till morning.

On 22 May, almost thirty climbers were scheduled to attempt climbing to the summit. I was glad I was not up there, never having liked crowds. I could see a line of dots leaving Camp Three, stretching past the Yellow Band, going into the swirling cloud above. It reminded me of last year. There were members from OTT, Adventure Consultants, Nova (the film team), the Malaysian team, the Canadian team, as well as Andres and Tenzing Lama. We rested, we looked up, we ate. TNT gave me some tinned ham, which I shared with the rest of our team. Our supplies at Camp Two were quite low. Just as well I had brought my own tucker with me.

Late the following morning I recorded my thoughts on my tape recorder – partly as a record of the moment, partly to reassure myself, clarify my decisions.

23 May 1997, Tape Recording, Camp Two, Everest

Andres and Tenzing reached the summit this morning at nine-thirty, along with vast crowds, which is great news. By about ten o'clock fifteen people had summited, so that means that there is probably a nice track going up the lower part of the mountain (being the summit pyramid from the South Col). I am suffering from those little butterflies in the stomach, and a bit of envy at those that have already summited and don't have to go up any more, and can come down and celebrate.

I am confident that I will do well, and that our group – seven of us – mostly Henry's team, Thomas and Tina and myself, will get there too. That's if the weather is with us, of course, which we can never be sure of. If it's not, what will I do? What does it take?! We've been careful, following the weather forecast, and maybe maybe maybe we will be helped there with the right conditions. Mind you, the forecast for today was for reasonably high winds up there and from what we've heard, it has been very quiet – and not a breath of wind – so what can you believe?

I am packing up all my gear to go up to Camp Three tomorrow, wondering what to take, what not to take, and generally having a nice quiet time, trying not to get too stressed about things, trying to keep my energy for the climb ahead, for going to the summit, because I feel that it's not just me – so many people are up there with me, so many people. I'm going to need their energy. It's been such a long time waiting at Base Camp that it's quite hard being motivated now, but I guess as I get into it tomorrow I should be all right. And pray to God that the weather is fine on summit day, 26 May.

I tuned in on OTT's frequency again and caught a whisper from Jon Tinker. He was at the bottom of the fixed ropes with another climber, asking for some Sherpas to come and carry their packs. I ran to OTT's camp to tell them. A couple of hours later, Jon appeared on the rocky moraine above Camp Two. I went up to him. *My God!* He moved so slowly, and looked like a shadow of his former self when I had last seen him at Base Camp. I hugged his bony frame. 'Well done!'

'Oh, I did not get up,' he croaked. 'I was feeling ill, I had to turn back.'

'Well done anyway!' I was glad to see him again. Glad that he was alive, if not completely there. Glad that I could get a hug from someone I loved before I went up.

I had a last powwow with Henry and Peta. Michael had climbed Lhotse without oxygen that day, but Simon had had to turn back. I hoped he was all right. Alan Hinkes had summited too. Peta and I organised our departure time.

———

It was too hot without a sun hat. I dumped my pack and returned to camp to grab my black hat. On the way back, I met someone coming down. 'Hey, Brigitte!' Everyone looked the same in their mountain garb.

'Who's that?' I asked.

'It's Tashi!' I hugged him, and he laughed.

'Well done! How was it?'

'Oh, it was the best day of my life!' I wondered if it would be the best day of my life soon.

Higher up, I met Guy Cotter, Veikka Gustaffson and Peter Athans. Hugs and chats to everyone. Information gathering. 'There is a nice hard track to the summit,' smiled Peter. 'Good luck!' They had left Camp Four on the South Col at ten p.m., after having told the other teams that they'd leave at midnight, to get a clear run. They got it, summiting before the fifty-odd hopefuls on their tail. Peter also told me that the wind was blowing fiercely before the sun rose. So the forecast had not been wrong, after all.

Dave Carter was there too, on oxygen. He had suffered

some kind of pulmonary problem on the way down. Andres was next – more hugs, more talks. He had reached 8400 metres before plugging into supplementary oxygen. Thoughtfully, Andres had left his overboots and sleeping bag on the Col for me. Without his overboots, he said, it would have been too cold. Onwards with the task. Peta was carrying a huge pack; for some reason Henry had told everyone to bring their gear down last time they were at Camp Three. I had left most of my gear up there, and enjoyed an easier, much easier climb than their team.

At the foot of the Lhotse Face, Peta and I stopped for a break and a bite. Michael was getting off the fixed ropes, moving slowly, so slowly. One step at the time. And it was downhill. Peta walked to him and hugged his emaciated body, while I filmed. 'I have never been so tired in my life.' Another hug from a friend who was not quite there.

The climb to Camp Three was sprinkled with more encounters, exhausted summiters, Sherpas who had gone up to get gear down from the Col, and to help with the rescue of Hugo, one of OTT's members who had been benighted high on the mountain and was feared to have frostbitten feet. The Canadians brought him down. Everyone was coming down, while we were going up. It felt strange, like arriving somewhere too late for the party, with the guests leaving, all saying what a fantastic party it had been.

Camp Three was crowded. Mark and Alison were in one tent; in another Peta was waiting for Henry, who was apparently having problems on the way. Yuri and Illy were squeezed in to yet another tent; Pemba, Ivan and I shared the big one. Simon was descending from Lhotse, looking completely shattered. We offered him the vacant spot in our tent, and fed him goodies and brews. One of his toes was slightly frostbitten. He had spent two nights at Camp Four without oxygen, missing out on attempting the summit because of a violent attack of indigestion.

In the morning, the wind woke us up. Ivan, looking gloomy as usual, announced that he was going down. So were

Pemba, Alison and Mark. And Simon, of course, was intent on not missing the party scheduled that night at the OTT camp. 'Well,' he said as he stepped out, 'I'll see you when I see you!' That was it. I was alone in the big tent. I had radio contact with Henry, ten metres below. It was too cold, too windy to go up that day. More waiting. Feeling rotten. My period was due any day now. I filmed myself and broke down, blubbering teary words at the camera. Waiting, more waiting. Would I ever see the top of that bloody mountain? I hid in my sleeping bag, and cried myself to sleep.

————

26 May 1997, Camp Three, Everest

> The sky is clear, there is no wind. Kipa and Dorje are coming up today, Kipa with a bottle of oxygen for me. There should have been some here, but there isn't, so I will start later than I would have chosen. Thank God, the PMT crisis has passed. I feel great.

Snow was falling lightly, but the temperature was quite pleasant. Summer and the monsoon were on their way. Up and up I went, arriving at the Col with Henry's Pemba and Ang Tshering, who was wearing the Fairydown jacket I had given to his little brother the previous year. There was no wind. So different from my last attempt, the previous year. Mindu, who was supposed to have carried a load to the Col and gone down, was still there. He had decided to stay, to brew for Kipa, Dorje and me. He did not have a sleeping bag, though, so I gave him my jacket and spare odds. I organised my bed by the back door, so I could empty the cup I peed in without having to pass it to a giggling Sherpa. When Kipa and Dorje arrived, we all plugged in spare oxygen bottles for a few hours' rest. We planned to leave at ten. I took my contact lenses off and tried to sleep. I couldn't, of course, but I managed to rest nonetheless. At nine, I risked an eye outside. *Shit!* It was snowing so much I couldn't see a thing through the showers of white flakes hitting the tent. My heart sank. *Not again!* No, I didn't want to have to go back there, I didn't want to spend another year trying to raise money, living on stand-by. I wanted to get on with my life, Seven Summits completed or not!

The snow finally stopped falling. The tent erupted in activity, frantic preparations. The headtorch shone in my eyes as I put my contact lenses in with trembling fingers. I put my over-boots on, and nestled water bottles full of warm water inside my downsuit to stop them from freezing as they cooled down. It was a quarter to one in the morning. The crunch of the snow. Darkness. Where were Henry, Peta? Some people were already moving towards the black shadow of the mountain. I felt something warm between my legs. Of course. Started bleeding. It had to happen then. There wasn't anything I could do — it was certainly not the time to squat and stick a tampon in.

Dorje and Kipa were moving fast, intent on catching up with the first group — which soon stopped. Powwow in the dark, on the steep snow slope. *Which way should we go?* Yuri and Illy were there with Dawa. No Henry, no Peta. No TNT, either. No one I knew well. But there was no time to regret it. We were all moving up again, following in each other's steps in the deep snow. Hadn't Peter said something about a hard track to the summit? Never take anything for granted in the mountains!

I couldn't move as fast as Yuri and his group, who were now slightly ahead of us. A traverse across a wind slab took us close to the ascending ramp leading to the Balcony, a small shoulder on the ridge we'd follow towards the summit. I hate wind slabs. They sound hollow, and have a tendency to detach themselves from the mountain to go for rides down valley with whomever happens to be on them. At the Balcony, at about 8400 metres, we stopped. Drink, quick snack, quick shots with the camera. Dawn had crept in on us, and through the viewfinder I caught glimpses of the South Col, already so far below, and of the beautiful lines of Makalu, and of the climbers ahead.

A change of oxygen bottle was orchestrated by Kipa and Dorje, who just mucked around in my pack and screwed on another bottle without my help. It looked like they wanted to get me there fast. As fast as possible, anyway. A long, long rounded snow slope led to a steep snow-and-rock section with bits of rotting fixed ropes which would provide only moral protection. The steps collapsed, and the going was hard in the crumbling snow. I started coughing. It hurt. My lungs were not used to direct cold air intake, as I usually wore a material mouth mask to warm up the air I breathed, and the oxygen mask, the one that my Jon wore to the summit in '88, had a hole in it that allowed cold air to plunge straight into my lungs. By the second day of using the mask I had developed a painful and debilitating cough.

———

I couldn't believe it – around the bald snow mound on top of the steep section was the South Summit. I could see the narrow and exposed ridge to the Hillary Step. Finally I was part of the picture I had so often looked at in books, the picture that so obsessed me that I had made a painting of it all those years ago, when I had first thought of being on Everest. Kipa changed my oxygen bottle, and we were off again. Hardly any time to eat, to drink, to film. But they knew best; they knew we had to go fast, to have time to descend in daylight. A good rope spanned most of the ridge, and for that I was thankful. Clouds wafted over the top of the Kangshung face to my right where the icewall fell in one swoop to the glacier 3000 metres below. The view was clear on the other side, with steep rock and walls of ice tumbling all the way to Camp Two, more than 2000 metres away.

The Hillary Step, a fifteen-metre-high vertical rock barrier, was woven into a web of old ropes, the witnesses (and often the cause) of many struggles and deaths. *Someone should cut them all off – they are too dangerous.* Two days prior to our arrival, a Sherpa working for Todd Burleson pulled on one rope and fell with it all the way down the South-west Face. I grabbed as many as I could and pulled, my jumar clipped onto a reasonable-looking rope. Puffing, pulling, panting, straddling the top. Filming some more.

I was obsessed by filming, by getting to the top and giving my message to Australia. I knew I was going to get there now. Yuri and his friends were coming down. 'Not far to the summit,' they said. And there it was. Dorje was already there; Kipa had stayed with me, walking beside me. Conscientious to the end.

The ridge had broadened, and although one fall there would still mean death, it felt safe. 'Look Kipa, I am fine, go for it!'

He looked at me, and smiled his schoolboy sunny smile. 'Thank you!' And the bastard ran — ran! — to the summit. I followed, not quite so rapidly. I reached the bottom of the small rise which was the last obstacle on the way to the top of the highest mountain on earth. I giggled, took my mask off, my pack off. I grabbed Sheila out of my pack and made the last steps with her. It was round about ten-thirty. I threw my arms around Kipa and Dorje, in a bit of a daze. *Wow*. Kipa passed me the radio. 'It's Henry,' he said. Henry was talking, congratulating me, crying. I don't remember what I said to him, but I am glad he was the one I talked to from the summit. I love Henry.

I was on a mission now. Had to film, had to talk, had to take summit shots. But first, I wanted to have a look on the other side. I sat on the summit, beside the little pyramid of offerings left by previous summiters, and looked out at the snow slope and the North Ridge I hadn't climbed in '95. No footsteps — what a pity, it was such a perfect day. Russell Brice was on the other side, and so was Richard Price. I hoped they would make it. Then it was back to work. I set the camera on my knees so I could talk into the microphone on top of it. There was no wind, so my message was recorded without interference.

27 May 1997, *Tape Recording from Everest*
    'Well, I've done it . . . and I feel only relief, really. No more up!' Cough, cough. 'No more up. But a long way down.' Breathe, breathe. 'And I have to thank Kipa and Dorje, without whom I wouldn't be here. They looked after me so well. And I also want to thank, gasp, my husband Jon, and my friends Ian and

Min Darling, and Roddo, and Anne Tindall, and all the others, and I'm totally buggered!' Giggles.

I was relieved. Not happy, not elated, just relieved. I was finally free of my obsession, but I didn't know that yet. I filmed my two Australian flags, the official one and the Koori one, and delivered my message to Australians.

27 May 1997, Message to all Australians from Everest Summit
'This is a beautiful planet, and we should look after it. And we should look after Australia. Because there is only one Australia, and we belong to it. It is our soul. If we destroy it, we won't have a future! So stuff short-term profit – think about the future, think about the wilderness. Rainforests are not to be turned into woodchips, National Parks are not for mining . . . they're our future. Leave my country alone, I love it.'

I made an offering to the mountain – a picture of Jon and me, with 'My sister!' written on the back of it, along with a piece of driftwood from our favourite beach, Discovery Bay. A world away from where I was.

Then it was time to bugger off. I was allowed to. Mask and pack went back on. Not a glance backwards. It was time to get on with the task of staying alive.

At the Hillary Step, I caught my left crampon in one of the ropes, and sat, foot up, in a French cancan parody. *Sigh*. I was going to have to exert myself. 'Don't move, I'll do it.' Kipa was behind me. I kept still. I thought of Bruce, of the previous year's South African team, who had summited as we were waiting for the chopper in Syangboche, drinking beer and laughing. He was too late. He had last talked on the radio from the summit at six p.m., must have run out of oxygen and become entangled in the web of the Step, too exhausted to do anything about it. That's where he had been found a few days earlier. Peter Athans had cut the rope and given Bruce's body a more decent flying burial, down the mountain; better that than being prey to summit paparazzi.

Across the ridge-walk in the sky, I was not exactly skipping. Vague, light-headed. Getting tired. I coughed again. Oh, this was so painful . . .

The slope up to the South Summit was torture. I couldn't breathe. I had plenty of oxygen, but needed some food. We stopped, while I painstakingly chewed on my last Mars Bar to keep going. It was getting harder and harder. I found it difficult to keep my balance. My neck started hurting – the camera had been dangling on it for too long, and so had my ice-axe, as the safety sling was too short to go under my arm. I walked down, slower and slower. Below the steep bit, I could see a figure sitting in the snow, head nodding off. It took forever to get to where the climber was sitting, and by then, he had moved on to the Balcony. Things were getting worse. My balance was definitely going. 'Kipa, please, I need a rope, otherwise I am going to fall and die.' This was not the place, nor the time, to be proud. I wanted to live.

Kipa found a roll of abandoned fixed rope and gave me an end. They were going to belay me down. I would then sit, looking and being helpless, while they would downclimb to me and do it all again.

At the Balcony we found Yuri, collapsed in the snow, on the windless side of the ridge. He had run out of oxygen, and needed help badly. He couldn't feel his right hand any more. My friends dragged him along, and lower down he managed to walk on his own. Pemba came up to meet us. I sipped and promptly regurgitated the tea he gave me. 'Pemba, can you take my mask off, please, the bottle is empty.' Pemba looked at me, frowning.

'Oxygen working, it is on three'.

I hadn't noticed. Couldn't breathe or move my neck – it hurt too much. But, finally, we were on the flatter snowfield leading to the blue ice plunge to the South Col. Dorje walked with me, holding onto the rope which slithered along, loose. An umbilical cord.

The tent was not too far. *Gasp, rest, pant, stagger.* I collapsed in front of it, feeling utterly exhausted. Managed to fumble my way in. I was so cold now. I shivered and could not take my harness, my boots off. I called to Mindu. In a flash he was running around the tent. He dived in, and had my gear off. I wiggled slow-motion into my sleeping bag, and eased my darling oxygen bottle in beside me. I drank what Mindu passed over. Kipa and Dorje were excited. They chatted and had a mate across for a brew. I took my contact lenses off. The tent filled up with human steam and breath. I coughed and coughed, hard mucus suffocating me, and sank into unconsciousness.

———

It was only after my exhausting descent to Camp Three that I woke up to the reality of my new freedom. I felt a calm, deep peace inside. I took my time tidying up before walking out and clipping onto the rope which would now only go down. Thank God I was feeling better. Relief, as I slowly descended the rope to Camp Two, Base Camp and the world beyond. I was going to leave this place. Venture into the outside world again.

Melancholy. I would never see again the blue ice slopes of the Lhotse Face, the blond rock of the Yellow Band. My eyes would forget the curves and shadows of the Western Cwm, my heart would not beat faster at the idea of being engulfed by the icefall hell any more.

Just before reaching Camp Two, I sat on the ice of Everest, I sat still and fed my memory pictures of my surroundings. So much space, outside, and now inside. I felt infinite, an integral part of the world around me. So extraordinarily perfect. Harmony. At that particular moment I loved myself, and life, and the whole planet. That is what it's all about.

Epilogue –
New Horizons

12 July 1997, Natimuk

The aftermath. I am still in limbo, lost between a world that was mine, that was me, and the world I must repossess if I want to come back to my everyday reality. A husband, a home, a life in this country that claimed me as a child of its soul – these are the things that ground me, form the backbone of my existence of flights to freedom.

People often ask me if I have come back to reality after all the media and public attention I received following the finale of my Seven Summits quest. They should ask me if I have come back from Everest yet. Even now, the energy that I lived with in the mountains hasn't completely allowed my soul to rejoin my body, except at times of joy of being reunited with Jon, with my family, my Australian friends, my home and garden.

I am planting wallflowers this year. They bloom in winter, and will remind me of the eternal spring I left behind when I was torn from Base Camp and my familiar surroundings by an unwelcome and noisy helicopter. Had I not felt overwhelmed and caught up in the media hype and, more importantly, had Jon not been about to depart for a long journey in the Australian deserts,

I would have stayed, and walked out with my friend Henry, with Peta, with Kami and Kipa and Dorje, and those few left behind, most having already left Base Camp.

I did not have a chance to say goodbye properly, we missed out on happy triumphant farewells, my dear universal soldier Michael, Simon, Braveheart Mike. No jaunts through the night streets of Thamel, exploding in noise, colour and crowds, losing ourselves in tall tales and laughter. No proper wake to the end of us being scared, enthralled, bored, sick, hopeful, tired, happy together.

When I drive to Melbourne from my little Natimuk, I am always amazed at the amount of energy radiated by its mass and humanity. Base Camp was like that – an extraordinary energy throbbed with every pulse of that city with no name. An energy born from the hearts of those sharing a same goal, working to make their dream a reality.

Where does one go to after Everest? When I first returned from climbing the highest mountain on earth, instead of a sense of success I was overwhelmed by a sense of loss. That world of conscious and unconscious communion with the souls of my fellow climbers was gone and might not happen again, because where else would I find such a gathering of friends, together at the same place, at the same time? I knew that future mountaineering expeditions of my life might revert to groups of two or three members, and hoped that sharing with a couple of dear friends would be as rewarding as the freedom that comes from being part of a larger group of independent companions.

Where did I put the number for Everest Anonymous?

———

The moon now shines over my life. It's been one year since I climbed 'that mountain', and what do I have? Freedom. The freedom to be, the freedom to choose. I still have the passion and the curiosity – both essential to life – but I have temporarily lost the focus, the vision I had during the nine years of the Seven Summits quest. Its absence allows me to notice all those other worlds around me begging to be explored — gardening, welding, painting, the back roads of Australia, the Murray River, the Flinders Ranges — so many things, so many places, so many people. I walk in a forest of possibilities, touching one, avoiding the other.

Reflecting on my life, my decisions, my achievements, and writing down my experiences has given me a new perspective. I know where I stand today, and what is important to me. My freedom, my husband, my family, my friends, my country's forests, the mountains of the world. I live in the present, and it is such a luxurious feeling, a hot bath of the soul. Life is a place where there is no time to lose, no reason to be bored. Did I have to get through nine years of obsession to discover such an obvious truth?

If you are not trying to climb a mountain in your life, you will never know what you can do, who you can be. It was at high school, in Belgium, that I first heard the words that are etched forever in my mind — *we must live our dreams, not dream our life.* I have lived by them all those years since, and they have served me well, inspiring me to work hard and to make things happen. But another phrase has made its way into my subconscious, now that I have made my dream of nine years a reality: *the place is here, and the time is now.* I revel in that truth, which came as a reward, earned the hard way. I still want to make the dreams which surface in my curious heart a reality, but while enjoying life as I know it. That is my aim — to live every moment — and one I now know I can tackle. If I can do that, anyone can. It's just a question of trying, and of learning, always.

Glossary

abseil: to descend by means of a rope attached to a harness, under control of a friction device.

aid-climbing: to climb up rock or ice using equipment such as ropes or pegs placed by the climber, to support their body weight.

belay: an attachment or point of attachment to the rock or ice for security purposes; also, to secure the active or moving rope of one's colleague, usually around one's own body, so as to lock it in the event of a fall.

bergschrund: the crevasse formed by a change of angle in a snow slope.

bivouac: to spend a night on the mountain without the usual protection of a tent and sleeping bag. Can be planned that way, or forced on the climber by circumstances.

buttress: a projection from a mountainside.

caldera: a large crater created by the explosion or collapse of the cone of a volcano.

chimney: a vertical fissure in a rock face, wider than a crack but narrower than a gully, and large enough for a climber to get into.

col: a saddle or dip in a ridge, usually between two mountains; the lowest point between two summits or peaks, e.g. the South Col is the lowest point between Everest and Lhotse.

corner: where the rock forms two walls meeting at an angle, and asperities on both can be used by the climber for the ascent.

couloir: a snow or ice gully on a big mountain.

crampon: a steel frame with downward-pointing spikes about fifty mm long, which fits closely to the sole of the climbing boot, with two forward-pointing lobster claws or points.

crevasse: a fissure or deep cleft in the ice of a glacier, sometimes covered with a thin snow bridge.

Glossary

descender: a metal device used to support the climber when making a controlled slide down a rope.

free climbing: climbing ice or rock without the use of artificial aids, using only the rock and the body (usually hands and feet, but in desperate cases, hips, thighs, knees, chins – anything goes!). Ropes and other equipment are used only to catch a climber if s/he falls.

Gamow bag: portable pressure chamber.

harness: webbing 'seat' worn by climbers around the waist and thighs to attach themselves to a rope.

ice-axe: a tool for cutting and scraping footholds in ice and snow.

icefall: a section of extremely tortured ice, with huge crevasses and seracs, formed where a glacier flows over a steep step in its bed.

ice-screw: a steel peg threaded for easy retrieval and better grip while in the ice.

jetstream: high altitude winds circling the planet, and sometimes interfering with climbers' plans on very high mountains, as they are viciously strong and cold.

jumar: a metal clamp which will slide up a rope but not down it.

lead: to climb first up the mountain or the cliff, without the safety of the rope from above.

moraine: the long line of stones and debris thrust out from a glacier as a consequence of its continuous erosion process on the underlying ground.

normal route: the easiest way up a mountain, which might not be easy at all!

overhang: where a cliff or mountain is steeper than ninety degrees vertical.

pitch: the stretch of a rockface between two consecutive rope belays.

piton: a steel blade with an eye in its head, in various sizes and shapes, which is hammered into a crack either for security or as an aid to belaying.

prayer flag: long strip or square piece of colourful cloth printed with Buddhist prayers, whose messages are believed to travel to the gods as the wind blows them.

puja: ceremony held by the Sherpas at the start of a climbing expedition, to ask the gods for protection. Involves prayers, offering of food and drink and the display of prayer flags.

scree: rock detritus, ranging from small stones to fairly large boulders, lying loosely on a slope having fallen from crags above.

serac: an ice cliff or a tower of ice as occurs in an icefall.

sling: a loop of rope or nylon tape with a variety of uses, including as an anchor or belaying point.

snow bridge: a bridge of snow across a crevasse, often concealing the crevasse and sometimes strong enough to take the climber's weight, sometimes not.

snow stake: long metal stake used as a belay in firm snow.

static rope: a rope that does not stretch when under load.

summit fever: a state of excitement that occurs as a climber gets close to a summit. It usually creates a boost of energy, and sometimes causes tunnel vision centred on reaching the summit regardless of outside factors such as weather conditions and the capability of the climber to come down safely from the summit.

terrace: a flat area on a slope.

traverse: a series of sideways moves; or a horizontal section of climbing; or the crossing of a mountain or series of mountains by ascending one side and descending the other.

white-out: a snow condition of extremely poor visibility, when it is
impossible to distinguish between the ground and the horizon.
wind slab: a snow layer formed by the wind on lee slopes, and
detached from the main body of the slope. Making steps
through it going up, down or across can be the equivalent of
creating a dotted line which then separates from the slope, and
avalanches with whoever happens to be on it.

Index

Index

292